The Complete
Light Kitchen

ROSE REISMAN

The Complete
Light Kitchen

whitecap

Edited by Elaine Jones
Proofread by Joan Tetrault
Design by Diane Yee | Enthusiastic Elephant Illustration + Design

Printed in Canada

Library and Archives Canada Cataloguing in Publication

Reisman, Rose,
      The complete light kitchen / Rose Reisman.

Includes index.
ISBN 978-1-55285-902-5
ISBN 1-55285-902-9

      1. Cookery. 2. Low-fat diet--Recipes. I. Title.

RM237.7.R448 2007   641.5'638   C2007-901700-2

The publisher acknowledges the financial support of the
Government of Canada through the Book Publishing Industry
Development Program (BPIDP) and the province of British
Columbia through the Book Publishing Tax Credit.

Dedication

My passion and love for what I do come directly from my incredible family. Their support is paramount!

To Sam, my number one supporter. No other words than to say you're the best! I will love you forever!

To Natalie, my University of Michigan graduate who is now traveling and exploring the world. Please come home!

To David, my "buddy" who is attending McGill and watches the food shows in his spare time and inspires me with his ideas.

To Laura, who has completed her first year at Mount Holyoke and is discovering the world away from home and doing a great job of it.

To Adam, my 15-year-old "baby" who has exceeded all of my expectations.

And to my "furry" household of German shepherds and "Ragdoll" cats who give me some quiet in my days.

Table of Contents

Acknowledgments

Thanks to:

Robert McCullough, a wonderful publisher and a great friend. It's good to be "home."

Elaine Jones, a great editor who kept me on my toes the whole time.

Taryn Boyd for keeping the book on schedule.

Suzanne and Mark at The Canadian Breast Cancer Foundation for endorsing the book.

Maureen Greenstein for doing my makeup.

Lorella Zanetti, a wonderful photographer who not only takes exceptional food shots, but somehow always makes me look younger! My thanks also go to her colleagues.

Photographers Mark Shapiro, Brian MacDonald, and Per Kristiansen.

Roxanna Roberts for the intense and flawless work on the nutritional analysis.

David Mintz and Stewart Webb for bringing many of these recipes to life for our catering clients.

Peter Higley, the inspiring president of the Pickle Barrel restaurants, who has introduced many of these recipes to his nine locations with great success.

Stokely Wilson, the head chef of the Pickle Barrel, for his incredible execution of these recipes.

Lily, Dang, and Mila, the assistants in my home whom I like to call my sous chefs.

Thevaki, my office assistant who helps me with all the day-to-day details.

Parmjit, my publicist, who manages my entire media campaign.

"Happy Howie," my agent who is always looking out for me. I'm his "little bar of soap."

Kathy and Susan, my best buddies, for just being there.

Dear Rose,

On behalf of the Canadian Breast Cancer Foundation, I would like to take this opportunity to extend our sincere thanks for your ongoing interest in the Foundation—especially this year, on the 15th anniversary of your support!

Breast cancer is not a disease that discriminates between lifestyle or age, and it can touch family, friends and colleagues. The funds raised through the sale of this cookbook will help to fund vital research and promote public awareness programs that can save lives. We greatly value your efforts to educate Canadians with your approach to overall health and wellness—being proactive about breast health and making healthy lifestyle choices may help reduce the risk of breast cancer.

Over the years of your involvement with the Foundation there have been, and continue to be, significant advances due to research that have impacted early diagnosis, better treatment regimes and the overall quality of life of those living with breast cancer. The 5-year survival rate for those having been treated for the illness is now greater than 82% in Canada. Research and education programs funded by the Foundation are making a difference! Together with other caring people like you, we can continue to fund the most promising breast cancer research conducted by some of the world's leading scientists.

Our thanks for your continued contribution,
Canadian Breast Cancer Foundation

Introduction

My first cookbook came out in 1988, and since then I've had over 16 books published. I don't know where the time has gone.

When I began writing, my books contained all high-fat recipes (incredibly delicious, though not particularly healthy!). But then a chance visit to my physician revealed that my cholesterol was sky-high. With family genetics of obesity, heart disease and type 2 diabetes, I had to make some changes if I wanted to live a long and healthy life. That set in motion years of research into the components of food and the creation of recipes that taste delicious and have a positive impact on health. With my own health under control, I have been and will continue to be devoted to improving the health of others—most importantly our children, the next generation.

Over the years my career has expanded from writing cookbooks to being an owner of Rose Reisman's Art of Eating Well Catering, which specializes in providing healthy cuisine for corporate and other markets in Toronto. After operating for just under three years, over 275 companies now use our catering services. That, along with continuing sales of my books, is proof that a healthy approach to food is definitely a priority for people today!

Why This Book Is a Must

Statistics tell us that North Americans are suffering from an epidemic of obesity, heart and stroke disease and type 2 diabetes. Cancer, osteoporosis and immune system problems are on the rise.

Our children are also suffering from the results of poor diet. Obesity rates have doubled over the past 10 years. Today's youngsters are suffering from high blood pressure and high cholesterol and are at risk of getting type 2 diabetes at an early age. The onset of these diseases will shorten their life span.

The main reason I've been writing cookbooks focused around healthy eating is to lessen the risk of these problems. We all know there is no exact formula for preventing disease but it would certainly be nice to increase our odds. Eating better lessens the risk of these major diseases by lowering cholesterol and blood pressure and fortifying the immune system.

By now most of us are aware of the benefits of a healthy diet and we're searching for fabulous-tasting recipes that don't contribute to these problems. Gone are the days when we served our families and friends huge quantities of food laden with fat and calories, showing no respect for our health.

This book is the answer to those concerns. It is chock-full of recipes that will take you from everyday cooking to elegant entertaining. Light cooking was never so easy—and it never tasted so good!

I'm always flattered when people tell me how much they love my recipes from one cookbook or another. I realized, too, that I often find myself flipping through various books when preparing favorites for family and friends. But there are two major problems: I'm always forgetting which book they're in and there's not room on my countertop for all these books!

My solution was to select over 200 recipes that are tried-and-true favorites from my past cookbooks. Then I improved on their flavor and cut back on the preparation and cooking time so you can have an incredible meal every night of the week! I also added over 50 new recipes, most of which can be made in under 30 minutes. There are informative tips, along with preparation and cooking times, make-ahead suggestions and a nutritional analysis for each recipe. Whether you're just beginning to create food that's lighter in fat and calories or whether you're looking for a single practical cookbook that will take you through every day of the week—including entertaining—this book will make it as easy as possible to achieve your goal of healthy eating.

You hold the key to healthy eating in your hand. Now let's look at some basics of how to implement it.

Food and the Family

Never underestimate the influence you have on your children, particularly during their formative early years. The time you spend cooking at home allows you to teach your family healthy eating habits and introduce new foods. Unquestionably, parents and older siblings are primary role models for children, but eating as a family has been displaced over the years. Our lives are busier and often both parents work outside the home. But there are many good reasons to sit down and eat a meal together.

Family bonding

The normal day for most people is hectic and busy, often leaving no time for family members to bond. In my family, having dinner together every night is almost impossible because we all have different schedules. Therefore, I plan at least two dinners a week at which we all sit together, even if it's only for 30 minutes. At the kitchen table or in the dining room, we talk about anything and everything—our day, the world, politics, religion—you'd be amazed where the conversation can go. No matter where our lively discussions lead us, they can happen only when we are all at the table "breaking bread" together.

Health

If you are a smart shopper, food made at home is healthier for you than restaurant food. It contains fewer preservatives, and most restaurants use an abundance of fat and salt to make their foods taste better. Good home cooking means better quality ingredients and healthy seasonings to make the food taste delicious.

More than 60 percent of Canada's population is overweight, and it's disturbing to note that there is an epidemic of teenage obesity and an increase in type 2 diabetes among the younger generation. Our poor diet has been implicated in 4 of the 10 leading causes of death of adult North Americans—heart disease, stroke, cancer, diabetes and complications as a result. This should be enough to get you and your family motivated to lead a healthier lifestyle, including cooking nutritious food at home.

Financial cost

Each time you eat out, either at a fast-food restaurant or a full-service establishment, keep your bill. At the end of the month, calculate what you have spent. You'll be shocked. No matter where you do it, eating out is expensive. Even a meal at a fast-food restaurant can cost a family of four more than $35. The same dinner would cost about $10 if you made it at home.

Understanding Your Relationship with Food

Why are we so preoccupied with what we eat? The answer could be that most of us have a love/hate relationship with food.

Food means different things to different people. For many, a meal is a pleasurable activity, bringing together family, friends and co-workers. Gathering around the table is central to many celebrations and can represent fun, pleasure, romance, comfort and prosperity.

But for others, food is a great challenge. For those struggling with their weight, sharing food with others can be an activity to dread. They worry about what to eat or how to avoid the nachos or crème brûlée. Eating out is especially difficult if you're trying to adhere to the latest fad diet that limits foods from specific food groups.

We all need food to nourish our body and keep us healthy. Few of us make this important association when we sit down for a meal.

What Works for Me . . . Might Work for You

The answer to finding your balance with food is personal and individual. I wasn't able to change my lifestyle until I understood what was preventing me from maintaining a healthy eating and exercising regimen. It was only when I clarified my own needs and the demands of my lifestyle that I was able to work toward my goal. Here are some of the considerations that work for me.

- **I know what I like.** That means any food and exercise program must fit into my specific lifestyle. What's good for someone else may not be appropriate for me, so I've customized my plan. This also means I've taken responsibility for my life. I can't blame others if I'm not living a healthy lifestyle.

- **I try to be organized every day.** This means I preplan my shopping list to avoid running out of healthy ingredients in my kitchen. If I'm on the go, I either brown-bag my food or ensure that I have healthy food choices at the places I'm visiting.

- **Changing the habits of a lifetime is difficult,** particularly when it comes to a basic issue like food. Before healthy eating became a way of life, I frequently reminded myself why I was making these changes.

- **I never get to a point where I'm famished.** If I did, I'd eat more—and probably poorer-quality foods. I eat every two or three hours, but always in a healthy way.

- **Portion control is a key factor.** People eat more than the ideal amount when they're not eating enough food or nutritious food throughout the day.

- **I always pay attention to the most up-to-date food guides**, making sure I try to combine the 4 food groups at each main meal and at least 2 of the food groups in my snacks.

- **I never think of food in terms of "good" or "bad."** Every food is acceptable, within moderation. I include chocolate in my diet a few times a week. By eating everything—occasionally, and in small quantities—I never feel deprived.

- **I'm aware of the good and bad fats in my diet**—unlike food, there definitely are bad fats! But I don't eliminate fat: it's an important element in the diet if it's the right kind and eaten in moderation.

- **I remind myself every day that maintaining an ideal weight and exercising really has no beginning or end.** When you begin, do what I did and start slowly, without looking for immediate changes. The important thing is to keep it up. You'll begin to feel better and have more energy and self-esteem and a better body image. You'll even feel more emotionally balanced.

- **If I do eat poorly, I never feel as if I've gone "off the wagon"**—if I did, I'd probably continue to binge. Instead, I tell myself that for the rest of the day I'll try to stay on a balanced diet.

- **I never forget to move during the day.** Exercise has become an integrated part of my day. Consistency is more important than intensity.

- **Most of the time, I avoid weighing myself.** So many factors can tip the scale in the wrong direction. For example, a high-sodium meal, the menstrual cycle or airplane travel can all cause water retention and thus increase your weight. For these reasons, do as I do and don't weigh yourself more than once a week or once a month. I judge my weight by other indicators, such as how I feel or how my clothes fit. (Fitted clothes with buttons and zippers will always reveal how I'm really doing.)

The Key to Healthy Eating—the Four Food Groups

You've been hearing about the four food groups since primary school. But so few of us really understand the importance of this essential guide.

The first step in eating well is to educate ourselves about the basic food groups: fruits and vegetables, grains, dairy products, and meat and alternatives. Up-to-date food guides include information on how good nutrition can prevent disease. They also factor in legumes, whole grains, seeds and nuts, fish and even plant oils, such as olive oil, as part of a healthy diet. Current food guides also differentiate between which kinds of foods within the food groups are better for you, such as leaner meats and fish, fruits and vegetables with the greatest nutrient benefits, and whole and low-glycemic grains such as barley,

The Glycemic Index

The glycemic index (GI) ranks carbohydrate foods based on their immediate effect on blood glucose levels. Carbohydrates that break down quickly during digestion have a high glycemic index. Low-glycemic foods are those that take longer to digest, raising blood sugar slowly and keeping you feeling full longer. Lowering blood glucose levels is a major means of minimizing the complications associated with type 2 diabetes.

Low-glycemic foods include high-fiber fruits and vegetables, bran cereals, legumes and beans.

quinoa and brown rice. Low-fat dairy products and vegetarian diets are also emphasized, along with exercising regularly.

Here are some general guidelines for teens and adults.

Fruits and vegetables

Eat 7 to 10 servings daily. One serving might be a medium apple or banana, a cup of green salad or ½ cup of juice. Choose at least one dark green and one orange vegetable daily. Enjoy vegetables steamed, baked or stir-fried instead of deep-fried.

Grains

Eat 6 to 8 servings daily. One serving might be a slice of toast, ¾ cup of cereal, half a small bagel or 1 cup of pasta or rice. At least half of your grain products should be wholegrain. Choose those lower in fat, sugar and salt.

Dairy and alternatives

Have 2 to 4 servings daily. One serving might be 2 slices of packaged cheese, ¾ cup of yogurt, 1 cup low-fat milk or 1 cup soy beverage. Choose skim, 1% or 2% milk products and consume fortified soy beverages if you do not drink milk.

Meat and alternatives

Eat 2 to 3 servings daily. One serving might be 3 ounces lean meat, fish or chicken, ½ cup beans, 2 tablespoons of peanut butter or ¾ cup of tofu. Eat at least 2 servings of fish each week. Select lean meat and alternatives. Trim visible fat from meat and remove skin from poultry. Roast, bake or poach, rather than fry.

A good rule of thumb when planning your meals is to include something from at least three and preferably four of the major food groups in each main meal and at least two food groups in each snack.

To determine the number of servings you should consume, talk to your doctor or nutritionist. Factors include your weight, your metabolic rate and your activity level.

Combining two or three of the food groups in each meal keeps you satisfied much longer so you avoid non-nutritional snacking. For example, breakfast might consist of yogurt, fruit and whole grain toast. Lunch could be a salad with protein and a side roll. That's how easy it is.

If you use fruits, vegetables and complex grains as the foundation of your diet, adding lean protein, dairy and fat last, you'll be amazed at how good you feel and how much easier it is to attain a healthy body weight. The perfectly balanced plate consists of 50 percent non-starchy vegetables, 25 percent protein, and 25 percent grain or starchy vegetables. Use this image whenever you're planning a meal.

The Building Blocks of Nutrition

Our daily diet is composed of carbohydrates, proteins and fats.

Carbohydrates

When eating carbohydrates, your body's main energy source, the key is to choose complex carbohydrates rather than simple carbohydrates. Simple carbohydrates are the ones found in non-nutritional sugar and white-flour products, such as cakes, doughnuts and cookies—what I call empty calorie foods. Complex carbohydrates, found in fruits, vegetables, grains, legumes and dairy products, keep your blood sugar stable by releasing glucose into the blood slowly, helping you feel full longer. They make up a healthy low-fat diet and can reduce the risk of heart disease, stroke, diabetes and some types of cancers.

The jewel found in carbohydrates is fiber. Fiber has been shown to lower cholesterol, lessen the risk of heart disease, prevent bowel problems, reduce the risk of colon cancer, help control type 2 diabetes and help in weight loss.

There are two types of fiber: soluble and insoluble. Soluble fiber is found in oats, barley, vegetables, fruit, brown rice and oat bran, among other foods. This type of fiber decreases blood cholesterol, thereby possibly decreasing the risk of heart disease. Insoluble fiber is found in foods such as wheat and corn bran, and in fruits and vegetables as well. This type of fiber helps promote regularity, which can decrease the risk of colon cancer. Eating foods with fiber will make you feel full longer and more satisfied. Foods that contain soluble fiber have a low glycemic index (see page 16).

Protein

Your body needs protein to build and maintain muscle tissue and for cell repairs. It maintains strong bones, produces enzymes to help digest your food and allows your brain to see, hear, and think. Protein also boosts your metabolism and fills your stomach so you won't feel hungry. The key to fitting protein into your diet is to include a variety of sources of lean protein such as lean beef and pork, chicken or turkey breast, fish and tofu.

Allow yourself 3 to 5 ounces of protein at your lunch and dinner meals depending on your activity level. Snacks should include protein in the form of yogurt, a small amount of nuts, or milk or soy beverage. But be aware that if you consume too much protein that is not lean, you're increasing your amounts of saturated fat, cholesterol and calories. Meat, even lean meat, contains saturated fat and cholesterol, which can cause heart disease and stroke. The excess fat in meat can also lead to obesity and certain kinds of cancer, among other diseases. So eat the higher fat and saturated protein in moderation, alternating it with other forms of protein such as fish, beans and soy products, which contain no saturated fat.

Cholesterol

Fats

We are a fat-phobic society, yet certain fats are necessary for good health. These fats play an important role in hormone production, red blood formation, joint lubrication and proper insulin function. Eating the right fats in moderation will not cause you to gain excess fat. Too many people are obsessed with taking all the fat out of their diet, which is unhealthy. A healthy diet should consist of a daily intake of between 25 and 30 percent fat. However, the typical North American diet, which consists of 40 percent or more fat, exceeds that considerably.

Fat has 9 calories per gram—more than protein or carbohydrates, which have only 4 calories per gram. And fat doesn't fill you up the same way that protein and carbs do, which means you're hungry soon after you've eaten fatty foods. It's also important to be aware that low fat does not mean no fat. Low- or no-fat products can still be loaded with calories. And a calorie is a calorie. Aim to keep your fat intake to less than 30 percent of your total daily calories and your saturated fat intake to less than 10 percent.

Saturated fat is found in animal products—meat, chicken and dairy products. These fats in excess can clog your arteries and lead to heart disease and stroke. Trans fat is also a fat to watch out for. This type of fat is produced when unsaturated fat is hydrogenated, a manufacturing process that changes a liquid fat into a solid; processing liquid vegetable oil into margarine is an example.

So stick to the healthier monounsaturated and polyunsaturated fats. Monounsaturated fats such as canola, olive, and peanut oil are the healthiest. These fats reduce blood cholesterol by increasing the good type of blood cholesterol (HDL).

Transforming to the "Light" Kitchen

We all realize the importance of eating nutritious foods, but with the realities of life, this isn't an easy task. We often fall short of our goals and end up at the fast-food establishments, not making the healthiest choices.

Now—not tomorrow—is the time to make the change to a healthy "light" kitchen. Learning how to lessen the fat in your cooking takes some knowledge of essential ingredients, cooking terms, methods of cooking, cookware and techniques for lowering fat. Armed with this information, you can make any recipe healthier.

The first step is to do some meal planning. It can be as simple or as detailed as you like.

Keys to Successful Food Planning

Here are some strategies that will help you stick to your healthy eating plan.

Choose foods you enjoy

This is the most important thing you can do. Don't force yourself to eat foods you don't like just because they're good for you. Just make sure that the foods you choose aren't calorie- or fat-filled. Experiment with foods you haven't enjoyed in the past. I was amazed when I changed from loving white rice to being a brown rice fanatic!

Some of the available soy products are delicious, and they make good replacements for the saturated fat proteins, such as beef and chicken. Experiment with new, healthier alternatives.

Don't skip meals

Even if at first it's like medicine, it's very important to eat breakfast and a good lunch. We often make healthy food choices but don't eat on a regular enough basis, and this leads to portion sizes that are just too big. Your body thrives when it has a steady supply of nutritious fuel and will ultimately burn calories more efficiently.

Plan for healthy snacks

One rule I abide by is to eat enough at meals to reduce the urge to snack on what are most commonly non-nutritional items. A common mistake is to skip meals or eat too little, then snack whenever there's food. And let's be honest: usually these snacks aren't healthy choices.

Nonetheless, healthy, planned snacking can ward off hunger between meals. This is often called grazing and it seems to be a healthy way to eat for many people. I stick to my rule of eating every 3 hours. This has been my route to permanent weight loss, and it has made a world of difference. Once you get into this habit, you won't be able to skip these meals. Keep the snacks to fruits, vegetables, yogurt and small amounts of cheese or nuts. These foods have all the nutritional benefits and will raise your blood sugar slowly so you'll feel full longer. I call this "power snacking." You'll then notice that when eating your main meals you won't have extra-large portions, since you won't be starving.

Don't omit any food group

Many food plans or fad diets omit an entire food group, often carbohydrates. This approach never works for maintaining permanent weight loss and can be unhealthy in the long term. By restricting your diet you become deprived and ultimately you'll resort to bingeing on poor nutritional foods. You need the nutrients from each food group to maintain good health.

Meal Planning 101

I'm a big believer that planning the way you eat is essential to success, and this means getting organized. Many of us lead highly structured lives, fitting in work, family, friendships and social activities, but we tend to lack that structure in our daily eating routines. Planning your meals allows you to shop for the ingredients in advance, having them on hand for when you're ready to cook—you'll be ready to make a healthy and delicious dinner as soon as you walk in the door after work. If your focus is losing weight, it makes even more sense to take the time to plan your meals well in advance and have your kitchen stocked with the groceries you'll need. Planning allows you to factor in the calories of each day's meal plan. If you don't leave yourself enough time to prepare and eat a healthy breakfast or pack a nutritious lunch, it won't be long before you're back at a fast-food outlet grabbing a doughnut and coffee for a mid-morning snack or a burger and milkshake at noon. Brown-bagging your lunch gives you control over what you eat.

Choose the foods you enjoy when planning your meals. Don't deprive yourself of any one food. Eat everything you enjoy in moderation—be sure to read the food label so you know the serving size. And don't force yourself to eat foods you don't like just because they're healthy.

Plan meals weekly, daily or whatever best suits your schedule. Remember to keep your meals well balanced with a combination of food from all the food groups. Then make a list of the groceries you'll need for your meal plan.

Here are some steps you can take to become more organized about food.

Plan your grocery shopping and meal preparation, whether you do these tasks daily, semi-weekly or weekly. The greatest problem in daily meal preparation is thinking about it too late—on the drive home, for instance. If your kitchen is not well stocked, you can forget about making a healthy meal once you park your car in the driveway. Decide in advance when and how to plan your meals and when best to shop for the week. The weekend is truly the best time to plan your next week's meals. Decide what your family enjoys and actually select the meals for the next few days or the week.

If you know a couple of busy weeks are ahead, consider making extra meals on the weekend and freezing them.

Make a list of the groceries you'll need for the week. Post your shopping list where you can easily add to it. List the ingredients you'll need to buy for the recipes you plan to make. Always keep basic ingredients on hand. A good tip is to buy more than you think you'll need. You can always use the extra in the following days. Buy foods that you can refrigerate or freeze so you have an ample supply in store. Be aware of expiry dates.

Order in your groceries if you don't have time to shop. One of the greatest discoveries for me has been home-delivery grocery shopping. I order in large quantities because of the size of my family and the amount of entertaining we do. But for the average person, getting a small quantity of all the products you use on a regular basis saves you time and money. Another benefit of home delivery: your back doesn't hurt from carrying around those groceries and household items week after week! Although I like to buy my own produce and dairy products, grocery-delivery companies will also select these items for you if you don't have the time. I often order larger quantities of meats and fish from distributors at better prices and quality than the average supermarket provides. If you cook daily, it's always wise to have fish or meat in the freezer. If you have a family of four or more, consider putting an extra fridge and freezer in the basement or laundry room. You'll be shocked at how quickly you'll fill it.

Today's high-tech supermarkets—aisle by aisle

I actually find it exhilarating to shop in today's modern supermarkets. They're highly organized, making shopping easier, and they often display the items beautifully. And they offer so many choices with respect to healthier eating. Most have fresh meat, fish, cheese, bakery, organic and take-out departments, including spices and ingredients for many ethnic dishes, so you never have to go to a specialty market.

If you do need to whip up a meal on the spur of the moment, one of the best ways to ensure you're able to prepare a healthy and delicious one is to keep your pantry stocked with the various dry, refrigerated and frozen goods you need to augment and flavor your fresh grocery items.

These are some of the things I always have on hand.

Fresh produce

During the past decade, enormous research has been done on diets rich in fruits and vegetables and how they may be responsible for lowering the risk of various cancers, high blood pressure, cholesterol levels, intestinal disorders such as constipation and diverticulosis, osteoporosis and macular degeneration, which can cause blindness. Fruits and vegetables supply the majority of vitamins and minerals we need to live a healthy life. They supply antioxidants; vitamins A, C, and K; and beta carotene, folate, and potassium. Phytochemicals, health-promoting compounds found in plants that help protect them, also protect our bodies against disease when we eat these foods.

Always have a good selection of vegetables on hand. They're great, not just for salads, stir-fries and side dishes, but also for snacks. Keep a selection of vegetables cut into snack-size servings to avoid munching on less healthy food. Common vegetables

Frozen Fruits and Vegetables

Frozen fruits and vegetables usually contain as many or more nutrients than their fresh supermarket counterparts because they are flash-frozen immediately after being picked. Fresh produce often takes several days—sometimes even as long as two weeks—to arrive at the supermarket, meaning the time between picking and eating is much longer. The longer that time delay, the greater the loss of nutrients from the produce. Keep a selection of packaged frozen fruits without sugar in the freezer for baking purposes, such as strawberries, raspberries, blueberries and peaches. Unless the recipe recommends using fruit when it is still frozen, always defrost and drain frozen fruits before using them to get rid of excess water.

to have on hand are asparagus, broccoli, cauliflower, carrots, celery, cucumbers, green beans, green onions, lettuce, mushrooms, onions, bell peppers, potatoes, sweet potatoes and tomatoes.

Washing produce with soap isn't necessary. If you want to remove dirt or wax more thoroughly, buy a fruit and vegetable wash, which works very well. For convenience, you can buy greens that have been pre-washed and dried.

The produce department is also where you'll find fresh herbs. Staples to keep on hand include Italian parsley, basil, dill, cilantro and chives.

Storage

Each fruit and vegetable has different storage requirements, but most should be stored in the crisper compartment of the refrigerator and used within 5 to 7 days. Hard fruits like apples will keep for a month. Mushrooms are best used within two days and soft fruits, such as berries, spoil quickly, within a couple of days. Store bananas at room temperature.

Don't wash vegetables before storing them. If you're storing items in a plastic bag, make some holes so they can "breathe." Vegetables such as onions, potatoes, garlic, ginger, squash, sweet potatoes and beets don't need to be refrigerated until cut. I keep my tomatoes on the counter to ripen and refrigerate them only when ripe.

Egg and dairy products

All dairy products are labeled with a milk fat (MF) or butter fat (BF) percentage. Naturally, the lower the number, the lower the fat content. What can be confusing is that 2 percent milk may contain only 2 percent fat by weight, but 35 percent of its total calories may come from fat. About 23 percent of the total calories in 1 percent milk are from fat.

A diet low in fat should always minimize full-fat dairy products of any kind, such as cream cheese, whipping cream, cheese and sour cream. Many low-fat alternatives are available today. Other milk products you should include in your shopping basket for low-fat cooking are buttermilk and 2 percent evaporated milk.

Avoid non-dairy creamers or fake whipped toppings. They are made from hydrogenated vegetable fat, which is a form of saturated fat.

Always look for the expiration date when you buy these products so they'll stay fresh longer once you get them home.

Dairy

Milk is important for supplying calcium and vitamin D. It's available with milk fat ranging from 1 to 3 percent and in skim and non-fat versions. For cooking, I use 1 or 2 percent.

More nutritious than milk, yogurt contains more calcium, approximately 350 milligrams per cup (compared with 315 milligrams for 1 percent milk). Fruit yogurts contain less yogurt and more sugar than plain yogurt, making them less nutritious. Low-fat yogurts can be loaded with sugar, so read the labels. The artificially sweetened ones are lower in calories but have chemical sweeteners. Your best bet is to buy low-fat plain yogurt and add your own fresh or dried fruit.

Sour cream is great for sauces, dips and toppings. The usual fat content is 14 percent MF, but you can now find sour cream with 0 to 5 percent MF; it's creamy and delicious—perfect for baking and cooking purposes.

Use butter in small amounts as it is a saturated fat. I only use unsalted butter.

Cheese is a staple for adding flavor and variety to meals, but it's generally high in fat. Check the package for MF or BF content. Regular whole-fat cheeses can have anywhere from 24 to 35 percent MF. When buying hard or natural cheeses, such as mozzarella, Swiss and cheddar, select those lower in MF. The best-tasting low-fat cheeses will have anywhere from 10 to 15 percent MF, and they are also great to cook with. The taste and texture of cheeses with less than 5 percent MF is usually inferior, and they aren't good for cooking.

Many low-fat soft and unripened cheeses are available. For example, there is cottage cheese that can be from 0.5 to 2 percent MF and ricotta cheese with as little as 5 percent MF. The fat content of most cream cheeses has been reduced to approximately 25 percent MF from the original 35 percent.

Very hard cheeses I keep on hand include Parmesan, Romano and Asiago. Hard cheeses include cheddar, Swiss and Gruyère. Soft cheeses include brick, havarti, brie, mozzarella, blue and Camembert. Unripened cheeses include cottage, cream, goat, feta, pot and fresh ricotta.

Storage

Keep butter in the refrigerator for up to 2 weeks and freeze for up to nine months.

Hard cheeses keep the longest if unopened. Once opened, watch for mold within 2 weeks. Buy hard cheeses in large blocks to freeze and grate for cooking. Unripened cheeses have the shortest shelf life; read the expiry date.

Milk Chart

Comparative figures for fat and calories in a 1-cup serving.

Milk	Calories	Fat (grams)	Calcium (milligrams)
Homogenized	150	8	200
2% MF	125	5	315
1% MF	105	2	315
Skim	90	1	315

Cold Cuts and Cured Meats

In the deli section of your supermarket, you'll find smoked meat and fish and deli meats, such as hot dogs, corned beef and salami. These packaged cold cuts and cured meats are loaded with fat and sodium and often contain both nitrites and nitrates, which have been linked to cancer. Many are made from skin and high-cholesterol organ meats. Brands advertise "80% fat free," but that is fat by weight—such a product gets 77 percent of its calories from fat and has as much sodium in one serving as your entire daily requirement! Look for cold cuts that have 1 gram of fat or less per serving. Avoid those containing nitrates, color, additives and those labeled "smoked" or "cured."

Cold cuts can be kept for up to five days in the refrigerator and in the freezer for up to two months.

Eggs

Eggs are a good source of protein, iron and vitamin A, but they do contain saturated fat and cholesterol. All the cholesterol is found in the yolk, which can have more than 200 milligrams of cholesterol with 5 grams of fat. Since the RDI for cholesterol is only 320 milligrams, many people restrict their weekly intake of eggs.

Egg whites are cholesterol free, and one egg white has only 15 calories. The recipes in this book are all made with large eggs. Substitute two egg whites for each whole egg in a recipe, or use an egg substitute, available in cartons. Some egg substitutes available in stores today are made from 80 percent egg whites and 20 percent egg yolks. They taste great, have good color and cut out much of the fat, calories and cholesterol of whole eggs. Read the label to ensure that the egg substitute doesn't contain additives like food coloring.

To be safe, buy AA- or A-graded eggs from refrigerated cases only. Check the quality of the eggs before you buy them. Never buy cracked or leaking eggs, and if a carton does contain a cracked egg, discard it; it can be contaminated with bacteria such as salmonella, which can cause food poisoning.

Omega-3 eggs, containing polyunsaturated fat, are produced by feeding laying hens a special diet containing 10 to 20 percent ground flaxseed, which is high in Omega-3 fatty acids. These eggs help lower the bad (LDL) cholesterol in your blood. Three to four eggs supply the same amount of Omega-3 fatty acids as a 3-ounce serving of salmon, but eggs do contain cholesterol and fat.

Storage

Keep eggs in the original carton. Use within three to five weeks. Leftover egg whites or yolks can be kept for up to five days. Do not leave eggs for longer than two hours at room temperature. Hard-cooked eggs can be stored—in the shell—for a maximum of 10 days in the refrigerator. You can freeze raw whole eggs (not in their shell), egg whites or just the yolks. To freeze whole eggs, beat them and place in a container with a tight lid. If you are freezing only the yolks, beat them and add ¼ teaspoon of salt or 1½ teaspoons of sugar for every four egg yolks.

Fresh meat, poultry, and fish

Protein is essential in our diets. It helps maintain blood pressure and water balance, and it's needed to transport most substances, such as insulin, in and out of the body's cells.

Remember to remove the skin and trim the fat from all forms of protein—this will lessen the amount of saturated fat by as much as half.

A good alternative to meat, poultry and fish is soy—the only vegetable-based complete protein. (See page 27.)

Meat

Classifications of meat—AAA, AA and A or sometimes prime, choice, select, good or standard—describe its tenderness, juiciness and flavor. The classification is based on the amount of fat marbling. AAA and prime meat has the most fat and is considered by many to be the tastiest, but it's not the healthiest for you.

During the past 20 years, meat consumption in North America has dropped 28 percent, mostly due to the press about saturated fat and cholesterol leading to heart disease and other diseases. But today, meat is leaner than it's ever been. Certain lean cuts of meat can be as low in fat and cholesterol as chicken or fish.

When meat is described as lean, it should contain no more than 10 percent fat when raw, and this means it can be tougher. Tenderize these cuts by marinating them in vinegar, wine, lemon juice, buttermilk or yogurt for several hours, keep oil to a minimum. Flank steak becomes tender after just two hours of marinating.

When calculating how much meat to buy, allow about ¼ to ⅓ pound per serving of boneless meat. If the meat has some bone, then a serving is approximately ⅓ to ½ pound per person. When buying meat that has many bony sections, such as ribs, shanks or shoulder cuts, allow ¾ to 1 pound per person.

When buying beef, select lean cuts such as sirloin, inside round, rump roast, sirloin tip, strip loin, flank, blade, tenderloin, chuck steaks or roasts. The fattiest cuts are rib roasts, brisket, regular or medium ground beef and short ribs.

Ground beef is the third-largest source of saturated fat for the average person (after cheese and milk). Ground beef may be labeled 80 percent lean, but that refers to the percentage of fat by weight—20 percent— which contributes 70 percent of the total calories. Ground turkey, chicken or veal are healthy alternatives to ground beef.

Veal—meat from calves 1 to 4 months old—is a very delicate, lean meat. Milk-fed veal, the most delicate, comes from calves that have been fed on milk exclusively. Veal has less fat than boneless, skinless chicken breasts. Veal roasts, veal cutlets, veal loin roasts and veal chops are among the leanest cuts.

Lamb is between 5 months and 1 year old. New Zealand and Australian lambs are smaller than American lambs. All varieties are tender, but Australian is leaner.

Pork is 31 percent leaner than it was 10 years ago because of changes in breeding and feeding practices in the pork industry. The tenderloin, centre loin chop, lean ham, and loin and rib end roasts are the healthiest choices. The most fatty cuts are ribs, loin, blade and shoulder.

Hot Dogs

Whether made from beef, chicken, veal or pork, hot dogs are still one of the highest-fat meat choices. Even those labeled "lean" or "lite" are still loaded with fat, containing 9 to 12 grams of fat each, compared with 13 to 18 grams of fat for regular hot dogs. Hot dogs made with chicken or veal aren't necessarily lower in fat, since the manufacturers use the darker meat and often the chicken skin. Don't be fooled by the health claims on the labels.

Poultry

Poultry of all kinds is the leanest source of animal protein, provided you remove the skin before eating the meat. It has one-third the fat and calories of red meat. The white meat has less fat and fewer calories than the dark: 3 ounces of white meat has 140 calories and 3 grams of fat, whereas the same amount of dark meat has 178 calories and 9 grams of fat. Turkey breast contains only 5 percent fat calories, even less than chicken at 8 percent fat calories.

Fish and shellfish

One of the healthiest forms of protein is fish. It is low in sodium and contains less saturated fat than red meat or chicken. A 4-ounce serving of white fish has 146 calories, 2 grams of fat, and 54 milligrams of cholesterol; the same size serving of beef has 250 calories, 10 grams of fat and 102 milligrams of cholesterol.

Eat fish at least twice weekly to reap its benefits as a heart-healthy food. It contains Omega-3 fatty acids, which can help lower blood cholesterol, triglyceride levels and the risk of heart disease.

Lean fish include cod, halibut, snapper, sole, mussels, squid and shellfish. Omega-3 fatty acids are found in fattier fish, such as salmon, trout, mackerel, albacore tuna, sea bass and sardines.

Shellfish include shrimp, clams, mussels, lobster, crab and scallops. Shellfish can contain higher amounts of cholesterol and more sodium than other fish, but they are still more nutritious than meat or poultry because the fat is unsaturated.

A popular fish product called surimi is more commonly known as imitation crab. It's perfect for anyone with a shellfish allergy, or who is kosher, since it's usually made from a mix of white fish, including Alaskan pollock, a deep-sea white fish.

Storage

Keep raw meat in the coldest part of the refrigerator for up to two or three days. Poultry keeps only one to two days, and fish or seafood for two days. Refrigerate cooked meat for up to four days or, if wrapped properly, freeze for up to four months. Have protein available in your freezer for weekday meals; learn how to defrost it

Tips for Buying Fish

- *Fish should be shiny and not have a fishy odor.*

- *The eyes should bulge and look clear. Cloudy eyes indicate the fish is not fresh.*

- *Avoid supermarket pre-wrapped fish; it's not always the freshest choice.*

- *When buying frozen fish, be sure it's clear of freezer burn and is vacuum-packed.*

- *If buying a whole fish, ask the fishmonger to "butterfly" it, removing the backbone and larger bones while keeping the whole fish intact. Fish prepared this way is great for stuffing and baking.*

- *If the fish feels slimy or has a slight odor when you get it home, rinse with cold water for a couple of minutes.*

- *Buy pieces of fish that are similar in size and weight so their cooking times will be the same.*

- *For ultimate freshness, cook fresh fish the day you buy it.*

properly in the microwave oven or thaw it slowly in the refrigerator. If possible, buy it vacuum-packed to prevent deterioration and freezer burn. Your supermarket, butcher or wholesaler should provide this service. I package meat, poultry or fish in 1-pound quantities.

Canned foods

Compared with fresh food, canned food has fewer nutrients, often contains salt and other additives, which are included to preserve the food, and is inferior in texture and taste. But it's not always possible to have fresh food, and having certain canned foods on hand makes cooking easier, more efficient and less expensive. Always read the nutritional labels and look for products that, per serving, contain less than 15 grams of fat, less than 400 calories, and less than 800 milligrams of sodium.

Here are some basic canned goods I always have on hand in my pantry.

Corn kernels: purchase the peaches and cream variety in the 12 oz can.

Evaporated milk: buy 2 percent; invaluable for making creamy sauces.

Fruit: buy fruit packed in its own juice, including mandarin oranges.

Legumes: buy a wide variety, especially chickpeas, white and red kidney beans, black beans and soybeans.

Light coconut milk: be sure to buy the light type; never use regular coconut milk, which is high in saturated fat.

Olives: buy those packed in water.

Roasted bell peppers: always buy roasted peppers packed in water, not oil.

Soup: buy vegetable- and stock-based soups but avoid those that are cream based or contain excess sodium.

Tomato-based sauces: have a variety of sauces on hand that contain ripe tomatoes.

Tomato paste: use in small quantities and freeze remainder in freezer containers.

Soy: A Meat Alternative

Soy is the only plant-based food that is a complete protein and therefore it's considered to be one of the healthiest foods available. A variety of soy products are available in stores today that are as delicious as they are versatile. These include fresh soybeans (edamame); dried or canned soybeans; dried roasted soybeans; and soymilk, cheese, yogurt and sour cream. For meat lovers who don't want to eat meat, it even comes in the form of soy burgers, hot dogs and salami. You can find most soy products in the dairy case and vegetable sections of the supermarket.

Tofu, or soybean curd, is made from curdled soybean milk and is a main source of protein in Asian countries. A ⅓-cup serving of tofu would equal the protein in a 3-ounce serving of meat, fish or chicken and contain no saturated fat, no cholesterol and fewer calories. Tofu comes in a variety of textures—firm, medium or soft. Firm tofu makes a good substitute for meat or chicken and is great in stir-fries or casseroles. This kind of tofu is the highest in protein, calcium and fat.

Tempeh is a chunky, fermented soybean cake containing rice or other grains. It can be marinated, grilled or used in soups or casseroles.

Ground soy has the texture of cooked ground beef. Use it in dishes like chili and spaghetti sauce.

Tomatoes: buy both whole and crushed tomatoes.

Tuna: buy tuna packed in water (not oil).

Storage

Canned foods can be kept for up to 5 years in the pantry. Once open, refrigerate and use within 5 days or freeze for up to 3 months in airtight containers.

Dried goods

These include the dried goods and staples you need to complete your everyday cooking and baking.

Baking ingredients

Flour: keep white flour unopened for up to 1 year and for up to 8 months once opened; store whole wheat flour for 1 month and up to 8 months if refrigerated.

Sugar: store white, brown and icing sugars, and sugar substitutes, in the pantry indefinitely. To keep brown sugar soft, place a piece of bread in the bag or container and replace every couple of weeks. If brown sugar becomes hard, microwave it for 30 seconds to soften.

Baking powder and baking soda: keep unopened for up to 8 months, and between 3 and 6 months once opened.

Chocolate: keep cocoa, semi-sweet and white chocolate chips, and chocolate chunks at room temperature for up to 1 year. Freeze for up to 2 years.

Cookie crumbs: keep graham crumbs, chocolate and vanilla wafers in the pantry unopened for up to 1 year, opened up to 6 months.

Cornstarch: keep in the pantry up to 18 months.

Extracts: have vanilla and almond extracts on hand; be sure to buy pure extracts, not artificially flavoured ones.

Herbs and spices

Learning how to use herbs and spices is one of the best things you can do to reduce the amount of salt you use. Wean yourself off salt by experimenting with different herbs and spices in your cooking.

Fresh herbs are always a wonderful taste experience, but remember to add them only at the end of the cooking or as a garnish. If you add them during the cooking process, fresh herbs lose most of their flavor and texture. For a more intense flavor, use dried herbs in cooking.

Dried herbs and spices I always have on hand are basil, bay leaves, caraway seeds, cinnamon, cumin, curry, dill, oregano, paprika, chili powder, poppy seeds, sea salt, black pepper, cayenne pepper, rosemary, thyme, sesame seeds and tarragon. When shopping for dried herbs, buy small amounts that you'll use in a short time. Store them in a cool, dry place and replace them every couple of months. Smell for freshness. You can also freeze dried herbs for up to one year, which preserves the flavor.

Miscellaneous items

Nuts and dried fruits: I like to keep pecans, cashews, almonds, pine nuts, peanuts and macadamias on hand. Dried fruits include apricots, dates, pitted prunes, raisins and dried cranberries. Package them in freezer bags and freeze for up to 6 months.

Sun-dried tomatoes: Avoid sun-dried tomatoes packed in oil, which contain extra calories and fat. I pack them in freezer bags and freeze for up to 6 months.

Bouillon cubes or powder/stocks: Read the label and purchase low-sodium varieties that do not include MSG. Vegetable, beef and chicken stocks with no additives are available.

Coffee: Unopened packaged coffee will keep for up to two years; use coffee within a month once the package has been opened and keep tightly covered. Freeze coffee to lengthen its shelf life.

Grains and cereals

Grain products include bread, crackers, cereals, rice, pasta and other grains such as barley, kasha, millet, quinoa and oats.

Freezer Dos and Don'ts

Package foods properly before freezing them to preserve quality and freshness. We've all seen freezer burn and ice crystals on our frozen food. Here are four ways to avoid that.

Packaging must be moisture- and vapor-proof. Squeeze the air out of bags before sealing them. Seal the edges of containers with freezer tape.

Store wrapped foods in extra-heavy foil, freezer plastic or polyethylene-lined paper.

Label all containers and bags with the name of the food and the date.

To freeze hot foods, cool to room temperature, then divide into usable portions and freeze with enough space around the containers to permit cold air to circulate around them. This will freeze them faster and prevent raising the temperature in the freezer, thus affecting other foods.

Guidelines for storing frozen foods:

Beef and pork roasts and steaks	*6 months to 1 year*
Ground beef	*3 to 4 months*
Lamb	*6 to 9 months*
Chicken parts	*9 months*
Whole chicken or turkey	*1 year*
Fish: fattier fish	*3 months*
Fish: leaner fish	*3 to 6 months*
Shrimp in shell	*6 to 12 months*
Shrimp peeled	*3 to 4 months*
Fruit juice concentrates	*1 year*
Ice cream, frozen yogurt, etc.	*2 months*
Cooked meat dishes	*2 to 3 months*
Vegetables and fruits	*8 months to 1 year*

When buying grains, select wholegrain products, which are a source of fiber, vitamins, minerals and phytochemicals; they're also a low-glycemic food (see page 16). Always look for the label "whole wheat," which means that 100 percent whole wheat flour has been used. Be careful of the word "wheat" used alone on a product, as this often refers to a combination of whole wheat and white flour.

To determine whether you're obtaining enough fiber in grain products, read the nutritional information. Each slice of bread should contain at least 2 grams of fiber. Per serving, cereals should contain at least 4 grams of fiber, less than 8 grams of sugar and 2 grams of fat or less.

Keep these basic breads and grains on hand.

Wholegrain sliced bread: buy extra loaves and freeze.

Flavored tortillas, pitas and sandwich buns: buy whole wheat products; freeze extras.

Cold cereals: buy those containing extra fiber, dried fruits and little sugar. Keep low-fat granola and Grape Nuts cereal on hand for baking.

Hot cereals: buy the quick-cook (not instant) oatmeal.

Rice: keep brown, white and wild rice on hand.

Pasta: have a variety of shapes and sizes: lasagna noodles, macaroni, manicotti, etc.

Grains: buy grains such as barley, quinoa, millet and wheat berry in bulk and freeze.

Storage

Bread products: Freeze for up to 4 months.

Pasta and rice: Unopened, these can be kept in the pantry for up to two years; once opened, use them within one year. Other grains, such as quinoa, millet, spelt or bulgar, are more delicate. Store them frozen for up to one year.

Cereals: Keep unopened cereal in the pantry for up to one year; once opened, use within six months.

Oils

When shopping, read the nutrition label and be sure the oil is either monounsaturated or polyunsaturated.

Monounsaturated oils are the healthiest; use canola, extra virgin olive and peanut oil for most of your cooking needs.

Polyunsaturated oils include corn, safflower, soybean, sesame and cottonseed oils.

Cooking sprays are useful for coating your pans and skillets, thus reducing the amount of fat needed for cooking. These sprays contain few calories. If you prefer not to use the store-bought cans, purchase a pump and fill it with your own oil.

Storage

Keep unopened oil in the pantry for up to eight months; once opened, store in a dark, cool place for up to six months. Refrigerate nut oils after opening.

Sauces, condiments and spreads

Read the product labels carefully and avoid sauces and dressings made with butter, cream or excess oil. Choose low-fat versions of salad dressings and mayonnaise. Beware of foods containing high levels of sodium, such as soy sauce, and look for those labeled "low sodium."

Mayonnaise and salad dressings: Just 2 tablespoons of regular bottled salad dressing can contain over 150 calories and 20 grams of fat! Choose the lighter brands and use sparingly.

Salsa: Chopped tomatoes, onions, lemon, herbs and hot peppers are combined in this low-fat condiment. It's great with baked tortilla chips, as a topping for potatoes or burgers and even as a salad dressing.

Vinegars: Stock a variety, such as balsamic, cider, rice and red wine vinegar.

Sauces: Ketchup, barbecue sauce, sweet chili sauce, tomato sauce, hot sauce, plum sauce: most sauces are high in sodium or sugar, so use them in moderation.

Mustards: Dijon mustard is my choice due to its clean, sharp flavor. Mustards are high in sodium but are used sparingly as a flavoring agent.

Peanut butter: Purchase peanut butter made from peanuts only. Read the label: many brands contain icing sugar and are hydrogenated, which means this naturally wonderful food becomes saturated. If the oil rises to the top, just mix firmly until blended.

Jams: Buy pure jams that contain fruit, sugar and pectin only. Fruit preserves I keep on hand include strawberry, blueberry, marmalade and jellies that I use as a garnish over fruit desserts.

Storage

Most unopened condiments can be kept in the pantry for a year or more. Once opened, condiments can be refrigerated for 6 months or longer. Keep peanut butter in the refrigerator for 3 months; replace if it smells rancid.

The Global Pantry

I like to think of my pantry as the "global" pantry—a cupboard that contains the ingredients to create dishes from cuisines around the world. You should be able to find these items in most supermarkets.

Asian

The more common ingredients are long-grain rice, sushi rice, soy sauce, sesame oil, rice wine vinegar, hoisin sauce, oyster sauce, fish sauce, plum sauce, hot chili sauce, black bean sauce, rice noodles, nori (seaweed), wasabi (Japanese horseradish), canned baby corn, canned water chestnuts, canned mandarin oranges, ginger, garlic and sesame seeds.

Mediterranean

A Mediterranean pantry should be stocked with canned tomatoes, tomato paste, black and green olives, roasted red peppers in water, anchovies, Dijon mustard, seasoned breadcrumbs, cornmeal, Arborio rice, sun-dried tomatoes, basil, oregano, bay leaves, a variety of canned beans, olive oil and balsamic vinegar.

Mexican or Latin American

Have on hand a variety of canned beans, as well as jalapeño peppers, baked tortilla chips, avocado, salsa, hot sauce, light sour cream, flour tortillas, rice and low-fat cheeses.

Middle Eastern

Healthy and interesting dishes are easy if you have chickpeas, tahini (sesame paste), bulgar, couscous, brown rice, pitas, cumin and fresh coriander.

North American

Basic ingredients include different kinds of pastas, low-fat cheeses, pasta sauce, lean meats and condiments such as mustard, ketchup, sweet chili sauce, light mayonnaise and low-fat sour cream.

Vegetarian

Though not an ethnic cuisine, vegetarian food is in a category of its own. I love to prepare vegetarian meals occasionally for my family—you don't have to be a vegetarian to enjoy a meatless meal. Have a variety of grains, vegetables, sauces, firm and soft tofu, ground soy and other soy products.

Snacks

Avoid this area of the supermarket if you're hungry. Beverages, candy and cereals top the list of products that contain hidden sugar and empty calories. Cookies, crackers and potato and tortilla chips can contain hydrogenated vegetable fat and excess salt. Crackers can have as much fat as cookies.

Nuts are high in nutrition, but they are loaded with calories and fat grams—approximately 170 calories and 14 grams of fat per ounce (¼ cup). Rather than eating nuts as a snack, which encourages over-consumption, toss a few into your recipes.

Don't feel you can never go down this aisle; just choose snack foods carefully and buy them in moderation. Here are some of the better choices.

- Popcorn (either home-popped or low-fat microwave varieties)
- Pretzels
- Baked tortilla chips
- Fruit bars and lower-fat granola bars
- Cookies such as animal crackers, digestive or arrowroot, which don't have as much sugar and fat as other cookies
- Low-fat crackers such as rye crackers, Melba toast and rice cakes

Food Labels—A Second Language?

Trying to understand product labels is like learning a second language. Never make a food choice based on a product label or marketing campaign. It's important to read between the lines and know what the terms really mean.

Many product claims seem designed to confuse the consumer. Usually it's intended to make a product look healthier and more appealing than it actually is. A food labeled "light" or "low in cholesterol" or one said to contain "no fat" can still be filled with calories and other ingredients that can be harmful to your health. Examine the calories, saturated fat, cholesterol, sodium and fiber content listed on the label, and make sure they're within your guidelines for healthy eating.

Here are some interpretations of the most common food labeling claims.

Free

Many labels include the word "free": fat free, calorie free, cholesterol free, sodium free. What these terms indicate is that one serving of the food contains such a small amount of the substance that it doesn't mean much in the nutritional picture and you don't have to be concerned about it.

Product Dates

These are displayed on most food items. Here's what they mean.

- *The best before date refers to the last day an item should be sold.*

- *The expiration date is the last day that the item should be sold or eaten.*

- *The freshness date is stamped on by the manufacturer to indicate how long freshness is guaranteed.*

- *The pack date is the date the product was packaged or processed by the manufacturer. This date does not indicate how long the food will remain edible.*

Term	Amount (per 100 gram serving)
Fat free	Less than 0.5 g
Calorie free	Less than 1 calorie
Sodium free	No more than 5 mg
Cholesterol free	No more than 3 mg

Light or lite

These terms can be confusing and misleading. When "light" refers to a food product that has been altered, the term means that the food contains one-third fewer calories or half the fat of the regular product. "Lite" can be used to describe the taste, color or texture of the food in which the fat or calories remain the same—so "lite" olive oil may be light in taste, texture or simply color. "Light sodium" means a product contains half the amount of sodium used to make the regular product.

Low or reduced

The word "low" on a label tells you that the product has a reduced level of a specific ingredient. Be aware that a product low in fat may still be high in calories, or vice versa. "Reduced" compares the product with the regular product.

Term	Amount (per 100 gram serving)
Low fat	3 grams or less
Low (in) cholesterol	No more than 20 milligrams
Low calorie	15 calories or less
Low in saturated fat	No more than 2 grams
Low sodium	Less than 40 milligrams; less than 50 percent of the sodium in the regular product
Fat reduced	At least 25 percent less fat than in the regular product
Calorie reduced	50 percent fewer calories than in the regular product

Source

This word indicates that the food product provides a significant amount of a nutrient, such as fiber.

Term	Amount (per 100 gram serving)
Source of fiber	2 grams
High source of fiber	5 grams

Since the Recommended Daily Intake (RDI) for fiber is 25 to 35 grams, you can see that even a very high source of fiber provides only a part of what you need every day. A "high" source must provide 20 percent or more of the RDI for that nutrient per serving. A "good" source must contain between 10 percent and 19 percent of the RDI for that nutrient.

Fresh

The food is raw, unprocessed, has never been frozen, has never been heated and should not contain any preservatives.

Fortified or enriched

The food has a nutrient added to it so that at least 10 percent of the RDI for that nutrient is present. For example, if a food is fortified with iron, then 10 percent of the iron you need in your daily intake is in one serving of this food.

Healthy

This term is not always used appropriately. A healthy food should be low in fat and saturated fat and contain limited amounts of cholesterol and sodium. If it is a single-item food, it must also provide at least 10 percent of one or more of vitamins A or C, iron, calcium, protein or fiber.

Certain raw, canned and frozen fruits and vegetables and certain cereal-grain products can be labeled "healthy" if they do not contain ingredients that change the nutritional profile.

Lean, extra lean

These terms refer to the fat content of meat, fish and chicken. Lean food has less than 10 grams of fat, 4 grams of saturated fat and 95 milligrams of cholesterol per 100 gram serving. Extra lean food contains fewer than 5 grams of fat, 2 grams of saturated fat and 85 milligrams of cholesterol.

Natural or organic

These terms are also used loosely. A natural product contains no artificial ingredient or added color and is only minimally processed, which does not fundamentally alter the raw product. Organic food is produced according to legally regulated standards. For animals it means they were reared without the routine use of antibiotics, growth hormones and artificial ingredients. Fruits and vegetables bearing these designations have been grown with virtually no synthetic pesticides or chemicals. But realize that these regulations can vary in different countries.

100% pure fruit juice

To be 100 percent pure, fruit juice must contain nothing but fruit. But some juice labeled "pure fruit juice" can have as little as 10 to 34 percent fruit content. The rest is made up of water, sugar, color and flavoring. Fruit-flavored drinks have only 10 percent real fruit juice or none at all. Read the labels carefully.

Food Additives

The topic of additives is one of the most confusing areas of all. We have been led to believe that any food product that contains an additive must be harmful to our health. We may even decide that any name we can't pronounce must be bad for us! But some additives actually enhance the nutritional quality of a food. For example, vitamins and minerals are added to enrich foods such as grains, milk, juices, soy products and other foods. If you're worried about additives, a good way to minimize your intake is to eat fresh or minimally processed foods as much as possible. Processed foods always contain the most additives.

Acceptable additives

Beta carotene adds a yellow or orange color to foods such as margarine and cheese. Remember that this nutrient is also a powerful antioxidant.

Calcium propionate supplies some calcium and retards spoilage caused by bacteria, particularly in breads.

Monoglycerides and diglycerides maintain the smooth or soft consistency of foods, such as margarine, ice cream and breads.

Vitamin E is an antioxidant that's added to oils.

Other **vitamins** and **minerals** replace nutrients that are lost when food is processed.

Emulsifiers and **stabilizers** include lecithin, carrageenan and guar gum. They are used to prevent foods such as peanut butter from separating and to improve the consistency and texture of products.

Citric acid/pH control agents prevent botulism in low-acid canned goods.

Questionable additives

BHT and BHA prevent spoilage. They are implicated in increased cholesterol levels, allergic reactions, liver and kidney damage and depletion of vitamin D.

Sulfites, also labeled potassium metabisulfite and sodium metabisulfite, are used in salad bars and to make vegetables look fresher and prevent discoloration. Sulfites are also found in canned and dried food, processed cookies and crackers, frozen shrimp and wine. They can cause allergic reactions and worsen asthma.

Artificial colors, such as reds, yellows, blues and greens, enhance color and are usually found in products such as candy and soft drinks. They are still under review.

Artificial sweeteners are used in soft drinks, yogurts, ice creams and other sweets and are sold in packages as beverage sweeteners. Some artificial sweeteners, used in moderation, pose no serious health risk.

Monosodium glutamate (MSG) is a common additive that modifies the taste and aroma of food without adding color or smell. It is in additives termed hydrolyzed or textured protein, sodium and calcium caseinate, yeast extract, autolyzed yeast and gelatin. It's found in canned soups and vegetables, sauces, snacks, frozen foods and seasonings. Reported side effects include headaches, numbness in the neck and down the spine and tightness in the chest.

Interpreting the Ingredient List

When reading a food label, pay attention to the order of the ingredients on the ingredient list. The first ingredient listed has the most volume by weight in the food. Therefore, if the first ingredient is a form of fat, you know that the product consists mainly of fat. If the label emphasizes whole wheat flour, look at the order of the ingredients to see where whole wheat is on the list. If sugar or fat is the first ingredient and the whole wheat flour is toward the end of the list, you know it's a marketing consideration.

Fat

Butter, lard, vegetable shortening, hydrogenated vegetable oil and partially hydrogenated oil are all forms of fat. "All vegetable oil" on the label does not mean that the food contains no cholesterol, is low in fat or contains healthy fat. The fat could be hydrogenated or saturated, for instance, as in the case of palm or coconut oil.

Sugar

Sucrose, glucose, dextrose, fructose, maltose, lactose, honey, corn syrup and molasses are all forms of sugar. If a label says "no added sugar," the product may still be high in natural sugar, such as concentrated fruit sugar.

Sodium

This can be in the form of salt, onion salt, celery salt, garlic salt, monosodium glutamate (MSG), baking powder, baking soda, benzoate, sodium citrate or sodium phosphate. MSG is also known as hydrolyzed vegetable protein.

Cookware

I'm often asked what cookware is the best. For low-fat cooking, I recommend good-quality non-stick cookware, which allows you to cook using only vegetable spray or a minimal amount of oil, water or stock. Many types are available today, and they range in quality and price. Choose according to your needs. When my children were in their experimental cooking stages, I purchased inexpensive non-stick cookware; when the coating became damaged, I just bought new ones and would generally go through three sets a year. Now that the children are finished experimenting, I own a good-quality set of cookware that will last for years.

Cookware Safety

Materials from your cookware can leach into your foods, especially if the cookware is scratched. Keep these safety facts in mind.

Stainless steel is safe for cooking and storing food and is the most popular type of cookware. Often it is coated with non-stick coatings.

The connection between aluminum cookware and Alzheimer's disease is still unproven. Adults can consume at least 50 milligrams of aluminum daily without harm. Only 1 to 2 milligrams of the aluminum in your cookware would be absorbed.

Copper cookware is coated with another metal to prevent the copper from coming in contact with the food. Do not use copper pots that do not have this coating.

There has been some debate lately on the safety of non-stick pans. High-quality, non- stick cookware presents a very inert surface unless it is misused; this includes overheating, which can cause the release of toxic fumes. To date I believe the advantages outweigh the disadvantages.

Certain glazes used on ceramics, especially those designed to be fired at low temperatures, may release lead and cadmium into food or liquids. Be sure to research the guidelines with respect to using toxic materials in cookware.

When purchasing non-stick cookware, look for carbon-fluorine polymer coatings, which are inert, so nothing sticks to them and they don't react to acids in foods. Choose heavier pans; they'll last longer, conduct and retain heat better and cook evenly, with no hot spots.

Consider a non-stick grill pan or electric grill. You can have the benefits of grilling—great taste and appearance and low fat—but you won't have to step outside in the winter to do the barbecuing.

Don't use metal utensils with non-stick cookware. Once the coating is scratched, food will stick and the coating can enter your food.

For any type of cooking not requiring sautéing, use regular cookware. Cast-iron pans have made a comeback; the most important thing to remember is to season cast-iron cookware before using it. It will cook better and last longer. Brush the inside surfaces of the pan generously with vegetable oil and place in a 350°F oven for 2 hours. Wipe with more vegetable oil and return to the oven, this time with the temperature at 200°F for 1 hour. After cooking, place the pan immediately in hot water and wash it without soap, if possible. Dry the pan and wipe it with a little oil.

The Final Word

Making lifetime changes when it comes to your diet is never an easy task. In the beginning it may feel unnatural and take you completely out of your comfort zone. But when eating and cooking healthier becomes a habit, you'll feel so great you'll never believe you did anything else. Here are my tips for getting started.

1. Work out a master plan that will work for you.

2. Educate yourself about basic nutrition.

3. Make sure you include exercise in your plan. It's part of the healthy living equation.

4. Remember that changing entrenched habits will take you out of your comfort zone, but that is a phase that will end.

5. Avoid fad diets that eliminate certain food groups. Eat everything in moderation.

6. For every excuse you give yourself, come up with a possible solution.

7. Visit a nutritionist or sign up for some healthy cooking classes to get excited about your new direction.

8. Make sure you like what you're eating and cooking to ensure this becomes your new way of life.

Finding the time and the energy to change your eating and exercise habits won't be easy, especially in the beginning. Stick with it. I promise it gets easier and more comfortable as time goes on. Look at your day under a microscope and find a way to make your life healthier. It's the greatest decision you'll ever make.

Breakfast Burrito with Sautéed Onions, Green Peppers, Cheese and Salsa

Take a flour tortilla, stuff it with an egg mixture and roll it, and you have a breakfast burrito. This easily beats fast-food outlet breakfasts—and it's portable! Use any vegetables or cheese of your choice. If you don't have egg substitute, use 2 eggs and ½ cup egg whites.

2 tsp vegetable oil

¾ cup diced onion

1 tsp crushed fresh garlic

½ cup diced green bell pepper

1 cup egg substitute (see page 44)

3 Tbsp low-fat milk

1 Tbsp grated Parmesan cheese

pinch salt and freshly ground black
 pepper

¼ cup medium salsa

2 large wholegrain tortillas
 (or flavor of your choice)

¼ cup grated part-skim mozzarella
 cheese

1. Lightly coat a non-stick skillet with vegetable oil spray, add the oil and place over medium heat. Sauté the onion, garlic and green pepper for 5 minutes, or until the vegetables are softened and lightly browned. Set aside.

2. Whisk the egg, milk, Parmesan cheese, salt and pepper together in a bowl. Spray a clean non-stick skillet with vegetable oil and place over medium-low heat. Add the egg mixture and scramble for 2 minutes or until the eggs are almost set. Fold in the onion mixture and cook for 1 minute. Set aside.

3. Spread the salsa evenly over the 2 tortillas. Divide the egg mixture between the tortillas, placing it in the center, and sprinkle with the cheese. Fold up the bottom of each tortilla. Fold in both sides and continue to roll. Cut in half to serve. If desired, warm in a toaster oven at 400°F for 5 minutes to crisp up the tortilla.

NUTRITIONAL ANALYSIS
PER SERVING
(½ BURRITO)

Calories	185
Protein	14 g
Fat	3 g
Saturated Fat	1 g
Carbohydrates	14 g
Cholesterol	7 mg
Sodium	300 mg
Fiber	3 g

Prep Time:	10 minutes
Cook Time:	8 minutes

Serves 4

41

Multigrain French Toast

NUTRITIONAL ANALYSIS
PER SERVING (1 SLICE)

Calories	107
Protein	6.3 g
Fat	1.3 g
Saturated Fat	0.4 g
Carbohydrates	16 g
Cholesterol	3.8 mg
Sodium	160 mg
Fiber	2.4 g

Prep Time: 5 minutes

Cook Time: 5 minutes

Serves 4

Those pancake houses serve delicious French toast, cooked in loads of oil and smothered with butter and maple syrup. It's not exactly healthy or low in fat, though. My version is delicious and healthy. Using the egg substitute lowers fat, calories and cholesterol.

½ cup egg substitute (see page 44)
  (or 2 large eggs)
3 egg whites
⅓ cup low-fat milk
1 tsp ground cinnamon

1 tsp pure vanilla extract
4 slices multigrain bread
3 Tbsp pure maple syrup
1 Tbsp sifted icing sugar
½ cup sliced strawberries

1. Whisk the eggs, milk, cinnamon and vanilla together in a shallow bowl until well blended. Dip a piece of bread into the mixture, making sure both sides are moistened. Do not leave the bread in the mixture for too long or the bread will fall apart. Repeat with all slices of bread.

2. Spray a large non-stick skillet with vegetable oil and place over medium heat. Cook 2 pieces at a time, browning each side, a total of about 5 minutes.

3. Garnish with a sprinkling of icing sugar, a drizzle of maple syrup and sliced strawberries.

Multigrain French Toast ▶
Photo by Brian MacDonald

Low-Cholesterol Omelet with Oyster Mushrooms, Feta Cheese and Oregano

NUTRITIONAL ANALYSIS
PER SERVING

Calories	146
Protein	13 g
Fat	10 g
Saturated Fat	2.9 g
Carbohydrates	6.2 g
Cholesterol	26 mg
Sodium	300 mg
Fiber	1.4 g

Prep Time:	5 minutes
Cook Time:	6 minutes

Serves 1

This is a tasty and nutritious breakfast or lunch item. Serve it with 2 pieces of whole-grain toast and some sliced fruit for a complete meal. Feel free to use any type of mushroom you like or, if mushrooms aren't a favorite, substitute bell peppers or onions instead. Any cheese can be used: aged cheddar or Swiss cheese is delicious.

1 tsp vegetable oil

1 cup finely diced oyster mushrooms

½ tsp crushed fresh garlic

½ tsp dried oregano

⅓ cup egg substitute (see below)

¼ cup crumbled feta cheese

1. Lightly coat a small non-stick skillet with vegetable oil spray. Heat the oil over medium heat and sauté the mushrooms, garlic and oregano for 4 minutes, until the mushrooms are browned and the liquid has evaporated. Remove the mushroom mixture and set aside.

2. Respray the skillet. Add the egg substitute and cook for 2 minutes, until the eggs begin to set. Sprinkle the mushroom mixture and feta over the eggs and cook for another minute, or just until the omelet is set. Flip one half over the other to serve.

Egg Substitute

Egg substitute is available in cartons and consists of 80% egg whites and 20% egg yolks, with no added color or preservatives. It has a good color, the taste is great, and the nutritional value is better since you're cutting back most of the fat, calories and cholesterol of the whole egg. Egg substitute keeps in the refrigerator for up to about 4 weeks. One egg equals ¼ cup of egg substitute.

Crustless Dill and Spinach Quiche with Mushrooms and Cheese

If you don't have fresh spinach on hand, use 1 package (10 oz) of frozen spinach instead; thaw, drain and squeeze out the moisture. Use aged cheddar for the best flavor, or substitute Swiss cheese or any other strong cheese.

10 oz fresh spinach	2 Tbsp grated Parmesan cheese
2 tsp vegetable oil	2 eggs
1 tsp minced fresh garlic	3 Tbsp chopped fresh dill (or 2 tsp dried)
1 cup chopped onion	1 tsp Dijon mustard
1 cup chopped mushrooms	¼ tsp freshly ground black pepper
1 ⅓ cups smooth light ricotta	⅛ cup goat cheese, crumbled
⅓ cup grated cheddar cheese	

1. Preheat the oven to 350°F. Lightly coat an 8-inch springform pan with vegetable oil spray.

2. Wash the spinach, shake off the excess water and place in a saucepan over high heat. Cook in the water clinging to the leaves until the spinach wilts, approximately 3 minutes. Drain and squeeze out the excess moisture. Chop the spinach and set aside.

3. Heat the oil in a large non-stick skillet over medium heat. Add the garlic, onion and mushrooms and cook until softened, about 8 minutes. Remove from the heat and add the chopped spinach, ricotta, cheddar and Parmesan cheeses, eggs, dill, mustard and pepper. Mix well and pour into the prepared pan. Top with goat cheese.

4. Bake in the center of the oven for 25 to 35 minutes, or until a knife inserted in the center comes out clean. Serve warm.

NUTRITIONAL ANALYSIS PER SERVING

Calories	134
Protein	13 g
Fat	7.6 g
Saturated fat	3.2 g
Carbohydrates	6 g
Cholesterol	54 mg
Sodium	350 mg
Fiber	2 g

Prep Time: 15 minutes

Cook Time: 40 minutes

Make Ahead:
Bake a day in advance and refrigerate in the pan. Reheat in a 300°F oven for 15 minutes.

Serves 6

Frittata with Smoked Salmon, Cream Cheese and Dill

This sensational frittata is a light and healthy alternative to lox and cream cheese on a bagel! Serve alongside wholegrain toast or an English muffin for a complete meal. Smoked salmon freezes well and will keep in the refrigerator for up to one week.

1 tsp vegetable oil

⅓ cup finely diced onion

½ tsp crushed fresh garlic

½ cup egg substitute (see page 44)
  (or 2 large eggs)

3 egg whites

⅓ cup low-fat milk

pinch salt and freshly ground black
  pepper

2 Tbsp low-fat cream cheese, softened

3 Tbsp chopped fresh dill

¼ cup diced smoked salmon

NUTRITIONAL ANALYSIS PER SERVING	
Calories	80
Protein	10 g
Fat	4 g
Saturated Fat	1.2 g
Carbohydrates	6 g
Cholesterol	8 mg
Sodium	412 mg
Fiber	0.7 g

Prep Time:	10 minutes
Cook Time:	9 minutes

Serves 2

1. Lightly coat a small non-stick skillet with vegetable oil spray. Heat the oil over medium heat and sauté the onion and garlic for 3 minutes, or until the onion is tender and lightly browned. Remove from the heat and set aside.

2. Whisk the egg substitute, egg whites, milk, salt and pepper together. Add the onion mixture.

3. Spray a clean 10-inch skillet with vegetable oil, add the egg mixture and cook for 4 minutes, or until nearly set.

4. Dot the cream cheese overtop, cover and cook until the frittata is set, about 2 minutes. Sprinkle with the dill and smoked salmon. Slip the frittata onto a serving platter with a spatula.

5. Cut into wedges and serve immediately.

◀ Frittata with Smoked Salmon, Cream Cheese, and Dill
Photo by Brian MacDonald

Rose's Light Nut and Dried Fruit Granola

NUTRITIONAL ANALYSIS
PER SERVING

Calories	250
Protein	6 g
Fat	9 g
Saturated Fat	0.9 g
Carbohydrates	36 g
Cholesterol	0 mg
Sodium	5 mg
Fiber	4 g

Prep Time: 10 minutes

Cook Time: 35 minutes

Make Ahead:
Keep for up to 1 month in an airtight container.

Serves 8

Ever since I read that the usual serving size of granola, about 3 ounces, contains 360 calories and 18 grams of fat, I decided my goal was to create a delicious, healthier granola recipe. This one is so good I can barely keep it stocked in my pantry. I even send packages by courier to my two children at university! The trick is keeping the oil to a minimum and substituting orange juice for part of the oil. If you prefer dried fruit that is baked—it's much chewier—add it to the granola mixture before baking. If you want the granola crisper, leave it in the oven with the heat off for another two hours. Feel free to substitute any dried fruit you like.

2 cups rolled oats

½ cup all-purpose flour

½ cup brown sugar, packed

1 tsp ground cinnamon

½ tsp ground ginger

3 Tbsp vegetable oil

¼ cup orange juice

3 Tbsp pure maple syrup

½ cup chopped nuts of your choice

¼ cup diced dried apricots

¼ cup diced dried cranberries

1. Preheat the oven to 300°F. Line a baking sheet with aluminum foil and spray with vegetable oil.

2. Combine the oats, flour, sugar, cinnamon, ginger, oil, orange juice, maple syrup and nuts in a mixing bowl; mix thoroughly. Place on the prepared baking sheet and bake for 35 minutes, tossing once to prevent burning.

3. Add the dried fruit. Serve immediately or store in an airtight container.

Rose's Light Nut and Dried Fruit Granola ▶
Photo by Brian MacDonald

Creamy Oatmeal with Maple Syrup, Cinnamon and Dried Cranberries

NUTRITIONAL ANALYSIS
PER SERVING

Calories	150
Protein	5.7 g
Fat	2.3 g
Saturated Fat	0.4 g
Carbohydrates	38 g
Cholesterol	0 mg
Sodium	9 mg
Fiber	5 g

Prep Time:	2 minutes
Cook Time:	5 minutes

Serves 6

One of the best low-glycemic foods (the ones that keep your blood sugar low) is oatmeal. This is the type of "stick-to-your-ribs" food that keeps you full longer. Forget cold cereals or bagels in the morning if you want to stay satisfied until lunch. The nutritional analysis is for oatmeal made with water; the milk adds an extra 45 calories per serving, but it also provides calcium and protein.

1 ⅓ cups quick-cooking rolled oats
2 ¾ cups water or low-fat milk
2 Tbsp pure maple syrup
1 tsp ground cinnamon
⅓ cup dried cranberries

1. Bring the oatmeal and water or milk to a boil in a medium saucepan. Reduce the heat as low as possible, cover and simmer, stirring occasionally, for 5 minutes, or until the oatmeal is cooked and the liquid has been absorbed.

2. Remove from the heat, add the maple syrup, cinnamon and cranberries and serve hot.

Bran, Banana and Raisin Muffins

You can't claim to have a complete repertoire of muffin recipes without including the traditional bran variety. I often find them boring and dry, but the banana and molasses in these muffins boosts the flavor to a new high and simultaneously increases the moisture.

¼ cup vegetable oil

3 Tbsp molasses

1 large egg

1 cup sugar

1 medium ripe banana, mashed (about
    ½ cup)

1 tsp pure vanilla extract

½ cup low-fat plain yogurt

⅓ cup low-fat milk

½ cup wheat bran

¾ cup all-purpose flour

⅓ cup whole wheat flour

1 ½ tsp baking powder

½ tsp baking soda

1 tsp ground cinnamon

pinch salt

⅓ cup raisins

1. Preheat the oven to 375°F. Spray 12 muffin cups with vegetable oil.

2. Combine the oil, molasses, egg, sugar, banana, vanilla, yogurt and milk in a large bowl and mix until well blended.

3. Combine the bran, both flours, baking powder, baking soda, cinnamon, salt and raisins in another bowl and mix well. Add to the wet mixture and stir just until combined. Spoon into the prepared muffin cups and bake in the center of the oven for about 15 minutes, or until the tops are firm to the touch. Turn out and serve immediately or serve at room temperature.

NUTRITIONAL ANALYSIS PER SERVING

Calories	168
Protein	2.4 g
Fat	5.4 g
Saturated Fat	0.6 g
Carbohydrates	28 g
Cholesterol	18 mg
Sodium	129 mg
Fiber	1.8 g

Prep Time: 10 minutes

Cook Time: 15 minutes

Make Ahead:

Bake a day in advance, wrap well and store at room temperature, or freeze for up to 2 weeks.

Makes 12 muffins

Banana Chocolate Chip Muffins

NUTRITIONAL ANALYSIS
PER SERVING

Calories	150
Protein	2g
Fat	6 g
Saturated Fat	1.2 g
Carbohydrates	21 g
Cholesterol	18 mg
Sodium	158 mg
Fiber	1 g

Prep Time: 5 minutes

Cook Time: 15 minutes

Makes 12 muffins

Coffee shop muffins are definitely high in calories and fat—sometimes 600 calories and 30 grams of fat or more! This muffin recipe using mashed bananas and yogurt eliminates the need for a lot of oil. It's perfect for a snack or a lighter dessert.

¾ cup ripe bananas, mashed
   (about 1 ½ medium bananas)
½ cup granulated sugar
¼ cup vegetable oil
1 egg
1 tsp vanilla

1 cup all-purpose flour
1 tsp baking powder
1 tsp baking soda
½ cup low-fat plain yogurt
   (or low-fat sour cream)
¼ cup semi-sweet chocolate chips

1. Preheat oven to 375°F. Spray 12 muffin cups with vegetable oil.

2. Using an electric mixer, beat together bananas, sugar, oil, egg and vanilla in a large bowl until well mixed.

3. In another bowl, combine flour, baking powder and baking soda. Stir the banana and flour mixture together. Stir in the yogurt. Fold in the chocolate chips.

4. Divide the batter among the prepared muffin cups and bake in centre of oven for 15 minutes and a tester inserted in the middle of the muffin comes out clean. Turn out and serve immediately.

Carrot, Apple and Cinnamon Loaf

A loaf containing carrots, apples and raisins is sometimes known as "morning glory" bread. It's a deliciously moist and healthy breakfast loaf that I also serve as a dessert.

¼ cup vegetable oil

2 large eggs

1 cup granulated sugar

1 ½ tsp ground cinnamon

¼ tsp ground nutmeg

1 tsp pure vanilla extract

⅓ cup low-fat plain yogurt

1 ¼ cups grated carrot

⅔ cup peeled, finely chopped apple

⅓ cup raisins

⅔ cup all-purpose flour

½ cup whole wheat flour

1 ½ tsp baking powder

1 tsp baking soda

1 Tbsp brown sugar

1. Preheat the oven to 350°F. Lightly spray an 8½- by 4½-inch loaf pan with vegetable oil.

2. Mix the oil, eggs, granulated sugar, cinnamon, nutmeg, vanilla and yogurt in a large bowl or food processor until well combined. Stir in the carrot, apple and raisins.

3. Combine both flours with the baking powder and baking soda in a separate bowl, mixing well. Add to the egg mixture and stir just until combined. Pour the batter into the prepared loaf pan. Sprinkle with the brown sugar and bake in the center of the oven for 35 to 40 minutes, or until a tester inserted in the middle of the loaf comes out clean.

4. Cool in the pan for 15 minutes, then turn out onto a rack. Serve warm or at room temperature.

NUTRITIONAL ANALYSIS PER SERVING (½ SLICE)

Calories	130
Protein	3.1 g
Fat	5.8 g
Saturated Fat	0.7 g
Carbohydrates	30 g
Cholesterol	36 mg
Sodium	187 mg
Fiber	1.7 g

Prep Time: 10 minutes

Cook Time: 35 minutes

Make Ahead:
Prepare the day before or freeze for up to 2 weeks.

Makes 12 servings

Blueberry and Banana Muffins

NUTRITIONAL ANALYSIS
PER SERVING (1 MUFFIN)

Calories	163
Protein	2.1 g
Fat	6.8 g
Saturated Fat	0.6 g
Carbohydrates	22 g
Cholesterol	18 mg
Sodium	179 mg
Fiber	1.2 g

Prep Time: 10 minutes

Cook Time: 12 minutes

Make Ahead:
Bake a day in advance or freeze for up to 2 weeks.

Makes 12 muffins

The blueberry and banana combination is wonderful in any baked goods, and blueberries freeze beautifully. I always have them in the freezer so I can bake this all year round. Don't thaw the berries before adding them to the batter.

1 ½ medium ripe bananas, mashed (about ¾ cup)
¼ cup vegetable oil
1 large egg
⅔ cup granulated sugar
1 tsp pure vanilla extract
¼ cup low-fat yogurt

¾ cup all-purpose flour
¼ cup whole wheat flour
1 tsp baking powder
1 tsp baking soda
1 tsp ground cinnamon
pinch salt
½ cup blueberries, fresh or frozen

1. Preheat the oven to 375°F. Spray 12 muffin cups with vegetable oil.

2. Beat the bananas, oil, egg, sugar, vanilla and yogurt in a large bowl until well mixed.

3. Combine both flours, baking powder, baking soda, cinnamon and salt in a separate bowl, mixing well. Stir into the liquid ingredients until just mixed. Fold in the blueberries.

4. Pour the batter into the prepared muffin cups and bake for 12 to 15 minutes in the middle of the oven, until the tops are firm to the touch and a tester inserted in the middle of the muffin comes out clean. Turn out and serve immediately.

Strawberry, Banana and Orange Smoothie

If you're in a rush in the morning and need a quick breakfast, try a smoothie. The combination of protein and fruit keeps you satisfied longer. This is also a healthy snack to stave off hunger between meals. Experiment with different fruits, using whatever is in season.

1 cup low-fat milk or soy milk
1 small ripe banana, sliced
1 cup frozen or fresh sliced strawberries
½ cup orange juice
2 Tbsp honey
5 ice cubes

1. Place all the ingredients in a blender and purée. Serve immediately.

NUTRITIONAL ANALYSIS PER SERVING	
Calories	104
Protein	3 g
Fat	0.5 g
Saturated Fat	0.4 g
Carbohydrates	18 g
Cholesterol	3.7 mg
Sodium	34 mg
Fiber	1.6 g
Prep Time:	5 minutes

Serves 4

Frittata with Crab, Red Pepper and Cilantro

NUTRITIONAL ANALYSIS
PER SERVING

Calories	113
Protein	18 g
Fat	2 g
Saturated Fat	0 g
Carbohydrates	6 g
Cholesterol	12 mg
Sodium	230 mg
Fiber	1.2 g

Prep Time: 10 minutes

Cook Time: 14 minutes

Serves 2

A frittata is an open-faced omelet. Using egg whites and egg substitute instead of whole eggs gives this a fraction of the fat, calories and cholesterol in most frittatas. Use any vegetables you like and substitute smoked salmon, prosciutto or diced cooked chicken for the crabmeat.

1 tsp vegetable oil

⅓ cup finely diced onion

½ tsp crushed fresh garlic

⅓ cup finely diced red bell pepper

½ cup egg substitute (see page 44)
   (or 2 large eggs)

3 egg whites

⅓ cup low-fat milk

pinch salt and freshly ground black
   pepper

3 oz finely diced crabmeat (or surimi,
   see page 155)

¼ cup chopped cilantro or parsley

1. Lightly coat a small non-stick skillet with vegetable oil spray. Heat the oil over medium heat and sauté the onion and garlic for 4 minutes, or until the onion is tender and lightly browned. Add the red pepper and sauté for 2 minutes. Remove from the heat.

2. Whisk the egg substitute, egg whites, milk, salt and pepper together. Spray a 10-inch skillet with vegetable oil and place over medium-low heat. Add the egg mixture and the vegetables and cook for 5 minutes, until nearly set.

3. Top with the crabmeat and cilantro. Cover and cook until the frittata is set, about 3 minutes. Use a spatula to slip the frittata onto a serving platter.

4. Cut into wedges and serve immediately.

Seafood Satay

NUTRITIONAL ANALYSIS
PER SERVING

Calories	173
Protein	20 g
Fat	8.4 g
Saturated Fat	1.9 g
Carbohydrates	4.4 g
Cholesterol	161 mg
Sodium	296 mg
Fiber	0.8 g

Prep Time: 10 minutes

Cook Time: 5 minutes

Make Ahead:
Prepare sauce up to
3 days in advance, cover
and refrigerate.

Serves 4

You can substitute fresh, firm fish, such as swordfish, tuna, halibut, haddock or salmon, for the seafood; don't use a fish that will break apart easily when cooked. The light coconut peanut sauce is so creamy you'll never believe it's low in calories and fat—light coconut milk has 3 grams of fat per ¼ cup, compared to the 10 grams of regular coconut milk.

1 lb large peeled shrimp or scallops,
    or a combination
¼ cup light coconut milk
2 Tbsp natural peanut butter
2 tsp low-sodium soy sauce
2 tsp sesame oil
2 tsp rice vinegar

1 tsp honey
1 tsp sesame seeds, toasted
1 tsp minced garlic
½ tsp minced fresh ginger
½ tsp hot Asian chili sauce (or to taste)
3 Tbsp chopped fresh cilantro or parsley

1. Preheat the barbecue or a non-stick indoor grill to medium-high. If using wooden skewers, soak 4 skewers in water for 20 minutes.

2. Thread the seafood on the skewers.

3. For the sauce, purée the coconut milk, peanut butter, soy sauce, sesame oil, vinegar, honey, sesame seeds, garlic, ginger and chili sauce in a blender or small food processor. Divide in half.

4. Brush the skewers with half the sauce. Spray the grill with cooking oil and cook the skewers, turning once, for 5 minutes or until the seafood is just cooked though.

5. Serve with the remaining sauce on the side. Sprinkle with the cilantro and additional sesame seeds, if you like.

Beef Hoisin Mini Meatballs

These are perfect appetizers for a dinner party. Meatballs are usually made from regular ground meat, which has three times the fat and calories of extra-lean. My version compensates for the fat with the addition of a delicious hoisin sauce. For a lighter version, try ground chicken, turkey, pork or veal. The red currant jelly adds a tart-sweet flavor and gives the sauce the thickness it requires.

8 oz extra-lean ground beef

3 Tbsp dry breadcrumbs

2 Tbsp hoisin sauce

1 tsp crushed garlic

1 egg

2 Tbsp minced green onion

⅓ cup hoisin sauce

⅓ cup red currant jelly

1 tsp crushed garlic

½ tsp minced fresh ginger

2 Tbsp water

2 Tbsp chopped green onion

2 Tbsp chopped fresh cilantro or parsley

1. For the meatballs, combine the beef, breadcrumbs, hoisin sauce, garlic, egg and onion. Form into 20 to 24 small meatballs about 1 inch in diameter.

2. Spray a large non-stick skillet with cooking oil and add the meatballs. Cook over medium-high heat for 3 minutes, turning until browned on all sides.

3. For the sauce, combine the hoisin sauce, jelly, garlic, ginger and water in a small bowl. Add to the meatballs and stir well. Cover and simmer on low heat for 10 minutes.

4. Serve garnished with the green onions and cilantro.

NUTRITIONAL ANALYSIS PER SERVING

Calories	150
Protein	8.1 g
Fat	4.2 g
Saturated Fat	1.5 g
Carbohydrates	19.2 g
Cholesterol	52 mg
Sodium	321 mg
Fiber	0.6 g

Prep Time:	15 minutes
Cook Time:	13 minutes

Make Ahead:

Prepare and freeze uncooked meatballs up to 2 weeks in advance. Thaw just before cooking. Can be cooked and refrigerated for up to 2 days. Reheat in a saucepan over low heat until warmed through.

Serves 6

Hot Crab and Artichoke Dip

Calories	69
Protein	8 g
Fat	1.8 g
Saturated Fat	1 g
Carbohydrates	3 g
Cholesterol	25 mg
Sodium	94 mg
Fiber	1.8 g

Prep Time: 10 minutes

Cook Time: 15 minutes

Make Ahead:

Prepare to the baking stage up to 2 days in advance, cover and refrigerate. Bake just before serving, adding an extra 5 minutes until hot.

Serves 8

These hot morsels of artichoke heart, crabmeat, Swiss cheese and dill are outstanding with tasty crackers or flatbread. If you don't have any dill on hand, substitute fresh parsley.

1 can (14 oz) artichoke hearts, drained and halved

4 oz chopped crabmeat or surimi (see page 155)

½ cup shredded part-skim mozzarella

⅓ cup shredded light Swiss cheese

⅓ cup minced fresh dill (or 1 tsp dried dill)

¼ cup low-fat sour cream

3 Tbsp light mayonnaise

1 Tbsp freshly squeezed lemon juice

1 tsp minced garlic

pinch cayenne pepper

1 Tbsp grated Parmesan cheese

1. Preheat the oven to 425°F. Spray a small decorative baking dish with cooking oil.

2. Combine the artichoke hearts, crabmeat, mozzarella and Swiss cheeses, dill, sour cream, mayonnaise, lemon juice, garlic and cayenne pepper in a food processor. Pulse until just combined but still chunky. Place in the prepared baking dish. Sprinkle with Parmesan.

3. Bake in the center of the oven for 10 minutes. Move to the top rack and broil for 3 to 5 minutes, just until the top is slightly browned. Serve warm.

Smoked Fish Spread

This has to be my number-one appetizer spread. I usually serve it with wholegrain crackers, lavash, baked tortilla chips or celery sticks, or use it as a spread in a sandwich. You can now find prepackaged smoked fish in your local supermarket. I buy a few packages at a time and freeze them for later use.

4 oz skinless boneless smoked fish (trout or salmon)

¼ cup light cream cheese, softened

½ cup smooth light ricotta

¼ cup low-fat sour cream

2 Tbsp light mayonnaise

1 Tbsp freshly squeezed lemon juice

pinch freshly ground black pepper

2 Tbsp finely chopped chives or green onions

1. Combine the smoked fish, cream cheese, ricotta, sour cream, mayonnaise, lemon juice and pepper in a food processor and purée until smooth. Stir in the chives.

NUTRITIONAL ANALYSIS PER SERVING (1 TBSP)

Calories	26
Protein	2.2 g
Fat	1.5 g
Saturated Fat	0.6 g
Carbohydrates	0.8 g
Cholesterol	7.2 mg
Sodium	120 mg
Fiber	0 g

Prep Time: 5 minutes

Make Ahead:
Prepare up to 3 days
in advance.

Makes about 1 ½ cups

Bagel Garlic Bread

Calories	90
Protein	2 g
Fat	4 g
Saturated Fat	0.3 g
Carbohydrates	10 g
Cholesterol	0.3 mg
Sodium	109 mg
Fiber	1 g

Prep Time: 5 minutes

Cook Time: 8 minutes

Make Ahead:
Slice bagels and prepare
garlic oil early in the day.
Bake just before serving.

Serves 6

These are as tasty as garlic bread, but without all the calories and fat. Use any herbs and spices you like best.

2 medium wholegrain bagels
2 Tbsp olive oil
1 tsp crushed garlic
2 tsp grated Parmesan cheese
1 Tbsp chopped fresh parsley

1. Preheat the oven to 400°F. Line a baking sheet with foil and spray with cooking oil.

2. Slice each bagel into 5 or 6 very thin rounds. Place on the prepared baking sheet. Combine the olive oil and garlic in a small bowl. Brush over the top of the bagel rounds.

3. Sprinkle with the cheese. Bake for 8 minutes, or until crisp. Sprinkle with parsley.

Smoked Salmon and Goat Cheese Cucumber Slices

This is a great light appetizer at a dinner party. Try smoked trout for an alternative.

3 oz smoked salmon
½ cup goat cheese
3 Tbsp low-fat yogurt
1 tsp freshly squeezed lemon juice
4 tsp chopped fresh dill
24 slices cucumber (¼ inch thick)

1. Combine the goat cheese, yogurt and lemon juice until smooth, using a food processor or by hand.

2. Dice the smoked salmon and set aside 24 small bits for garnish. Add the remaining salmon and the dill to the yogurt-cheese mixture.

3. Divide the mixture evenly among the cucumber slices. Garnish with the reserved salmon bits.

NUTRITIONAL ANALYSIS
PER SERVING

Calories	14
Protein	1 g
Fat	1 g
Saturated fat	0.1 g
Carbohydrates	0 g
Cholesterol	4 mg
Sodium	66 mg
Fiber	0 g

Prep Time: 10 minutes

Make Ahead:
Prepare filling the
day before, cover
and refrigerate.

Serves 6

Smoked Salmon Sushi Squares

My corporate clients vote this their favorite appetizer. It's the perfect solution for those who shy away from sushi because of concern about eating raw fish. The key is cooking the sushi rice properly. I always use a water-to-rice ratio of one-to-one, never stir the rice, and keep it covered even when it's cooling—using a rice cooker is easy, since it can never go wrong. You can find rice wine vinegar already flavored for sushi, so you don't have to add any sugar. Nori is available in good quality supermarkets and Asian food shops.

2 cups sushi rice

2 cups water

¼ cup rice wine vinegar

1 Tbsp granulated sugar

16 thin slices English cucumber
   (unpeeled)

4 oz smoked salmon

1 Tbsp light mayonnaise

½ tsp wasabi (Japanese horseradish)

1 sheet nori (dried seaweed)

1 tsp sesame seeds, toasted

low-sodium soy sauce, wasabi and
   pickled ginger (optional)

1. Combine the rice and water in a saucepan. Bring to a boil and boil for 1 minute. Reduce the heat to low, cover and cook for 12 minutes. Remove from the heat and let stand, covered, for 10 minutes.

2. While the rice cooks, combine the vinegar and sugar in a small saucepan. Bring to a boil, stirring to dissolve the sugar. Remove from the heat.

3. Turn the rice out into a large bowl. Stir in the vinegar and sugar mixture. Cool just until the rice no longer feels hot. Don't let the rice get cold or it will dry out.

4. Line an 8-inch square baking dish with plastic wrap. Cover the bottom with the cucumber slices. Lay the smoked salmon over top. Mix the mayonnaise and wasabi together and spread over the salmon.

5. Place half of the rice over the mayonnaise. Pat it firmly to an even thickness, dipping your fingers in water to prevent the rice from sticking to your hands. Top with the nori. Add the remaining rice, patting it firmly to an even thickness.

6. Invert onto a serving platter and cut into 16 pieces. Sprinkle with the sesame seeds. Serve immediately, or cover with plastic wrap and refrigerate for up to 8 hours. Serve at room temperature, garnished with soy sauce, wasabi and pickled ginger, if desired.

◀ **Smoked Salmon Sushi Squares**
Photo by Lorella Zanetti

NUTRITIONAL ANALYSIS PER SERVING

Calories	97
Protein	3.1 g
Fat	0.9 g
Saturated Fat	0.2 g
Carbohydrates	19 g
Cholesterol	2.0 mg
Sodium	154 mg
Fiber	0.9 g

Prep Time:	15 minutes
Cook Time:	12 minutes

Make Ahead:
Prepare early in the day, cover and refrigerate. If you just want to cook and season the rice earlier in the day, cool before placing in a large plastic bag so it doesn't dry out.

Makes 16 servings

Bruschetta with Minced Olives, Anchovies and Plum Tomatoes

NUTRITIONAL ANALYSIS
PER SERVING (1 SLICE)

Calories	73
Protein	4.2 g
Fat	3 g
Saturated Fat	0.6 g
Carbohydrates	7.6 g
Cholesterol	7 mg
Sodium	365 mg
Fiber	1.4 g

Prep Time: 10 minutes

Cook Time: 11 minutes

Make Ahead:

Prepare topping up to a day in advance and refrigerate.

Makes 12 slices

This twist on bruschetta has a more intense flavor than the regular version. I buy canned sliced olives for convenience; packed in water, they have less fat and fewer calories.

12 slices ½-inch-thick wholegrain French stick

3 Tbsp finely diced black olives

3 Tbsp finely diced green olives

1 tsp crushed fresh garlic

2 minced anchovies

2 tsp olive oil

½ tsp Dijon mustard

½ tsp dried basil

1 cup seeded and diced plum tomatoes

1 Tbsp grated Parmesan cheese

2 Tbsp chopped fresh basil or parsley

1. Preheat the oven to 425°F. Line a baking sheet with foil and spray with cooking oil.

2. Spray both sides of the bread slices with cooking oil. Place on the prepared baking sheet and bake in the center of the oven for 5 minutes per side, or until browned. Remove from the oven. Set the oven to broil.

3. Combine the black and green olives, garlic, anchovies, oil, mustard, dried basil and tomatoes in a small bowl. Mix well and spoon on top of the bread slices. Sprinkle with Parmesan cheese and broil on a rack 6" below the element for 1 minute.

4. Garnish with fresh basil and serve immediately.

English Muffin Tomato Olive Bruschetta

Toasted English muffins are a great alternative to Italian bread, and they keep well in the freezer. In season, try a combination of red and yellow ripe tomatoes. Instead of using a toaster, toast the muffin halves on a baking sheet 3 inches under a preheated broiler for 2 minutes. To avoid excess liquid, seed the tomatoes. Plum tomatoes have a firmer texture.

2 cups diced tomatoes, preferably plum

2 Tbsp olive oil

6 Tbsp chopped fresh basil

1½ tsp minced fresh garlic

¼ cup chopped black olives

1 tsp balsamic vinegar

pinch salt and freshly ground black pepper

3 wholegrain English muffins

3 Tbsp goat cheese, crumbled

1. Preheat the oven to 425°F.

2. Combine the tomatoes, olive oil, 3 Tbsp of the chopped basil, garlic, olives, vinegar and salt and pepper in a bowl. Set aside.

3. Split and toast the English muffins. Place on a baking sheet. Top each muffin half with about ¼ cup of the tomato mixture. Sprinkle the goat cheese over the tomato mixture.

4. Bake in the center of the oven for 8 minutes or until the cheese melts and the topping is warmed through. Cut into quarters, garnish with the remaining 3 Tbsp of basil and serve immediately.

NUTRITIONAL ANALYSIS PER SERVING

Calories	160
Protein	5 g
Fat	6 g
Saturated Fat	0.5 g
Carbohydrates	20 g
Cholesterol	0 mg
Sodium	290 mg
Fiber	1 g

Prep Time: 10 minutes

Cook Time: 8 minutes

Make Ahead:
Prepare tomato mixture early in the day.

Serves 6

Quesadillas with Grilled Chicken, Pesto and Cheese

Calories	203
Protein	15 g
Fat	8.7 g
Saturated Fat	2.5 g
Carbohydrates	16 g
Cholesterol	31 mg
Sodium	263 mg
Fiber	2.1 g

Prep Time: 10 minutes

Cook Time: 21 minutes

Make Ahead:
Make filling up to 2 days
in advance, cover and
refrigerate. Heat gently in
a small skillet until warm.

Serves 6

These make a great appetizer or main meal. I always like to use my own recipe for pesto (see page 342), since it has a lot fewer calories and less fat than the store-bought type. In late summer, when basil is abundant, I make pesto in large batches and freeze it in small containers.

8 oz skinless boneless chicken breast (about 2 breasts)
2 tsp vegetable oil
1 cup chopped onion
2 tsp crushed fresh garlic
¼ cup pesto sauce (homemade or store-bought)

½ cup grated part-skim mozzarella cheese
4 large whole wheat flour tortillas (or any flavor you prefer)

1. Spray a non-stick skillet or grill pan with cooking oil and place over medium-high heat. Sauté the chicken just until cooked, about 6 minutes per side. Set aside. Wipe out the skillet and respray.

2. Heat the oil in a skillet over medium-high heat. Sauté the onion and garlic for 5 minutes, or until the onions are tender and browned. Stir in the pesto and cheese. Dice the chicken and add to the skillet.

3. Divide the mixture among the tortillas, placing it on half of each tortilla. Fold the other half overtop. Heat on a grill pan or in a large skillet for 2 minutes on each side. Cut each tortilla into 3 wedges, making 12 wedges in total.

Smoked Salmon Quesadillas with Baby Spinach

Quesadillas are so versatile—you can serve them as an appetizer, side dish or a main meal. Just be careful not to overcook these (you don't want to cook the smoked salmon). Try smoked trout for a variation.

1 tsp vegetable oil	½ tsp Dijon mustard
1 cup thinly sliced onion	½ tsp crushed fresh garlic
⅓ cup goat cheese	pinch freshly ground black pepper
⅓ cup light cream cheese	3 large tortillas (preferably wholegrain)
¼ cup smooth light ricotta	½ cup baby spinach leaves
1 tsp freshly squeezed lemon juice	2 oz thinly sliced smoked salmon

1. Spray a small non-stick skillet with cooking oil, add the vegetable oil and place over medium-high heat. Sauté the onion for 5 minutes, or until browned. Remove from the heat.

2. Place the goat, cream and ricotta cheeses, lemon juice, mustard, garlic and pepper in the bowl of a small food processor and purée until smooth.

3. Preheat a non-stick grill pan or barbecue to high. Spread the cheese mixture evenly over the tortillas. Distribute the onion mixture, spinach and salmon evenly over half of each tortilla. Fold the other side overtop. Grill for 1 minute per side, just until grill marks appear. Do not overcook. Cut each half into 4 wedges.

NUTRITIONAL ANALYSIS PER SERVING

Calories	184
Protein	11 g
Fat	8.5 g
Saturated Fat	4.4 g
Carbohydrates	20 g
Cholesterol	23 mg
Sodium	385 mg
Fiber	2 g

Prep Time:	15 minutes
Cook Time:	7 minutes

Make Ahead:
Prepare filling up to a day in advance and refrigerate.

Serves 4

Seafood Tortilla Pinwheels

NUTRITIONAL ANALYSIS
PER SERVING

Calories	158
Protein	11 g
Fat	6 g
Saturated Fat	3 g
Carbohydrates	15 g
Cholesterol	51 mg
Sodium	304 mg
Fiber	1 g

Prep Time: 15 minutes

Make Ahead:
Prepare tortillas early in
the day, cover tightly and
keep refrigerate.

Serves 6

The curly edges of green or red leaf lettuce are especially attractive in these pinwheels. Two large tortillas can be used instead of 4 small ones. You can substitute smoked salmon, surimi (see page 155) or smoked trout for the shrimp.

½ cup light cream cheese, softened
½ cup smooth light ricotta
2 Tbsp chopped fresh dill
2 Tbsp chopped green onion
1 Tbsp light mayonnaise
1 Tbsp freshly squeezed lemon juice
½ tsp finely chopped fresh garlic
4 oz chopped cooked shrimp
¼ cup chopped red bell pepper
4 small flour tortillas
Lettuce leaves (optional)

1. Place the cream cheese, ricotta, dill, green onion, mayonnaise, lemon juice and garlic in a bowl and combine thoroughly. Stir in the shrimp and red pepper.

2. Divide the shrimp mixture among the tortillas, spreading it to the edges. Top with lettuce leaves (if using), overlapping them to cover the entire tortilla. Roll up tightly, cover and refrigerate for an hour to chill.

3. Cut each roll crosswise into 6 pieces and serve.

Goat Cheese and Spinach Phyllo Triangles

I love this Greek favorite, but I wanted to enjoy it without the extra calories and fat of the traditional version. To get ½ cup of cooked spinach, cook approximately 4 cups of fresh spinach, drain and squeeze out the excess liquid. Or use half a package of frozen spinach (10 oz) thawed and squeezed dry.

2 tsp vegetable oil
1 cup finely chopped red onion
¾ cup finely chopped red bell pepper
½ cup cooked spinach, drained and
     chopped
½ cup smooth light ricotta

½ cup goat cheese
3 Tbsp chopped fresh dill (or 1 tsp dried)
1½ tsp minced fresh garlic
2 Tbsp grated Parmesan cheese
8 sheets phyllo pastry

1. Preheat the oven to 400°F. Spray a baking sheet with cooking oil.

2. Heat the oil in a non-stick skillet over medium heat; add the onion and sauté for 3 minutes or until softened. Add the red pepper and sauté for 2 minutes. Remove the pan from the heat and stir in the spinach, ricotta, goat cheese, dill, garlic and Parmesan. Mix well.

3. Lay two sheets of phyllo pastry, one on top of the other, on the work surface, with the short side facing you. Cut lengthwise into three strips. Spray with cooking oil. Put 3 Tbsp of filling near the end of one strip. Fold one corner up to enclose the filling and create a triangle-shaped bundle. Flip the bundle up and then continue folding over and up to the end of the phyllo strip. Fill the other two strips in the same manner and place the triangles on the prepared baking sheet. Repeat with the remaining phyllo sheets.

4. Spray the triangles with cooking oil. Bake in the center of the oven for 12 minutes, until browned.

Phyllo Pastry

Phyllo is found in the freezer section of the grocery store.
Thaw at room temperature or overnight in the refrigerator.
The key to working with phyllo is to work quickly. After remov-
ing the number of sheets you need, cover the remaining phyllo
with a wet towel and plastic wrap to prevent drying.

NUTRITIONAL ANALYSIS
PER SERVING
(1 TRIANGLE)

Calories	104
Protein	4 g
Fat	4 g
Saturated Fat	0.8 g
Carbohydrates	12 g
Cholesterol	4 mg
Sodium	107 mg
Fiber	1 g

Prep Time:	15 minutes
Cook Time:	17 minutes

Make Ahead:
These can be prepared, well wrapped and frozen for up to 2 weeks, or refrigerated for up to one day, covered well. Bake an extra 5 to 10 minutes if frozen.

Makes 12

Fingerling Potatoes with Herbed Cheese and Smoked Salmon

NUTRITIONAL ANALYSIS
PER SERVING

Calories	157
Protein	5 g
Fat	1.8 g
Saturated Fat	0.9 g
Carbohydrates	30 g
Cholesterol	5 mg
Sodium	92 mg
Fiber	3.2 g

Prep Time: 10 minutes

Cook Time: 30 minutes

Make Ahead:
Prepare filling up to
2 days in advance, cover
and refrigerate.

Serves 8

Fingerling potatoes are the newest trend for appetizers and side dishes at parties and restaurants. They're a great twist on the standard potato. Most large supermarkets and fruit and vegetable shops carry fingerlings. If you can't find them, use small white potatoes.

8 fingerling potatoes
2 Tbsp light cream cheese
3 Tbsp goat cheese
½ tsp crushed garlic

pinch freshly ground black pepper
1 Tbsp chopped fresh dill
2 oz smoked salmon, diced

1. Preheat the oven to 425°F. Line a baking sheet with foil and spray with cooking oil.

2. Slice the potatoes in half lengthwise and place skin side down on the baking sheet. Spray with cooking oil. Bake approximately 30 minutes or just until tender. Place on a serving dish.

3. Using a small food processor or a whisk, mix both the cheeses with the garlic and pepper until smooth. Stir in the dill. Place a dollop of the mixture on top of each potato and sprinkle with the diced salmon. Serve while still hot.

Fingerling Potatoes with Herbed Cheese and Smoked Salmon ▸
Photo by Lorella Zanetti

Cheesy Pesto Stuffed Mushrooms

NUTRITIONAL ANALYSIS
PER SERVING
(3 MUSHROOMS)

Calories	90
Protein	5 g
Fat	7 g
Saturated Fat	1 g
Carbohydrates	5 g
Cholesterol	5 mg
Sodium	60 mg
Fiber	1 g

Prep Time: 10 minutes

Cook Time: 15 minutes

Make Ahead:
Prepare the filling up to
a day in advance and
refrigerate. Fill the
mushrooms early in the
day and refrigerate. Bake
just before serving.

Serves 5

Substitute fresh parsley or spinach for the basil, especially if it's not in season, or use a combination. Serve these straight from the oven as an appetizer or a vegetable side dish. They also taste great at room temperature and make a great addition to a buffet meal.

15 large cultivated mushrooms

¾ cup packed basil leaves

1 ½ Tbsp olive oil

1 ½ Tbsp pine nuts, toasted

1 Tbsp grated Parmesan cheese

½ tsp minced garlic

2 Tbsp chicken stock or water

¼ cup smooth light ricotta

1. Preheat the oven to 425°F. Spray a baking sheet with cooking oil.

2. Wipe the mushrooms clean and gently remove the stems; reserve for another purpose. Put the mushroom caps on a baking sheet and spray with cooking oil.

3. Process the basil, olive oil, pine nuts, Parmesan and garlic in a food processor until finely chopped, scraping down the sides of the bowl once. Add the stock or water through the feed tube and process until smooth. Add the ricotta and process until mixed.

4. Divide the mixture evenly among the mushroom caps. Bake in the center of the oven for 15 minutes, or until hot and lightly browned.

Mushrooms with Creamy Feta Cheese and Dill Stuffing

This is a great light appetizer, but it can also be served as a vegetable side dish. Try a variety of mushroom sizes. The smaller the mushroom, the more liquid it gives off.

18 medium cultivated mushrooms

1 tsp vegetable oil

1½ tsp minced garlic

⅓ cup finely chopped onion

⅓ cup finely chopped red or green bell pepper

⅓ cup crumbled light feta cheese

3 Tbsp smooth light ricotta

2 Tbsp chopped fresh dill

2 Tbsp finely chopped green onion

1. Preheat the oven to 425°F. Spray a baking sheet with cooking oil.

2. Wipe the mushrooms clean and carefully remove the stems. Set the caps aside and dice the stems.

3. Spray a small non-stick saucepan with cooking oil, add the vegetable oil and place over medium heat. Add the diced mushroom stems, garlic, onion and bell pepper. Cook until softened, about 5 minutes. Remove from the heat.

4. Add the feta and ricotta cheeses, dill and green onion to the pan; mix well. Carefully stuff the mixture into the mushroom caps and place on the prepared baking sheet. Bake for 20 minutes, until hot through and browned.

Toasting Nuts and Seeds

Toasting brings out the flavor of nuts and seeds like sesame seeds, almonds, pecans and pine nuts. Place in a non-stick skillet over medium-high heat and cook for about 2 minutes, or until browned, stirring constantly. They burn easily, so watch them carefully. I do batches of nuts and seeds in advance and freeze them.

NUTRITIONAL ANALYSIS
PER SERVING
(3 MUSHROOMS)

Calories	67
Protein	4 g
Fat	4 g
Saturated Fat	2 g
Carbohydrates	4 g
Cholesterol	14 mg
Sodium	162 mg
Fiber	1 g

Prep Time: 10 minutes

Cook Time: 25 minutes

Make Ahead:
Stuff the mushrooms a day in advance, cover and refrigerate. Bake just before serving.

Serves 6

Hummus

NUTRITIONAL ANALYSIS
PER SERVING (1 TBSP)

Calories	33
Protein	1 g
Fat	2 g
Saturated Fat	0 g
Carbohydrates	2 g
Cholesterol	0 mg
Sodium	20 mg
Fiber	1 g

Prep Time: 5 minutes

Make Ahead:
Cover and refrigerate
for up to 4 days.

Makes 1 cup

This Mediterranean dip is great to serve with pita bread, as a dip for veggies and as a spread for sandwiches or wraps instead of butter or mayonnaise. The store-bought hummus has more oil, increasing the calories and fat. Tahini is made of ground sesame seed and is common in Middle Eastern cooking. It can be purchased in most good-quality supermarkets.

1 cup canned chickpeas, drained and
    rinsed
¼ cup water
¼ cup tahini

2 Tbsp freshly squeezed lemon juice
5 tsp olive oil
1 tsp minced fresh garlic

1. Combine all the ingredients in a food processor. Purée.

Avocado Tomato Salsa

Choose ripe but firm avocados for this salsa. If you're making it ahead, sprinkle the avocado with lemon juice to prevent browning. Serve with crackers or tortilla crisps.

2 cups finely chopped plum tomatoes

½ cup finely chopped avocado

⅓ cup chopped cilantro

¼ cup chopped green onion

1 Tbsp olive oil

1 Tbsp lime or lemon juice

1 tsp minced fresh garlic

½ tsp hot chili sauce (or to taste)

1. Combine all the ingredients in a serving bowl. Let marinate for 1 hour before serving.

NUTRITIONAL ANALYSIS PER SERVING (⅓ CUP)

Calories	53
Protein	1 g
Fat	4 g
Saturated Fat	0.6 g
Carbohydrates	4 g
Cholesterol	0 mg
Sodium	8 mg
Fiber	1 g

Prep Time: 10 minutes

Make Ahead:
Prepare up to 4 hours ahead, cover with plastic wrap and refrigerate. Stir before serving.

Serves 8

Roasted Spiced Chickpeas

NUTRITIONAL ANALYSIS
PER SERVING (⅓ CUP)

Calories	119
Protein	5.6 g
Fat	3.7 g
Saturated Fat	0.7 g
Carbohydrates	16 g
Cholesterol	2 mg
Sodium	21 mg
Fiber	3.4 g

Prep Time: 5 minutes
Cook Time: 60 minutes

Make Ahead:
Prepare up to a week
ahead and store covered
at room temperature.

Serves 6

Everyone is always looking for a great substitute for nuts since they are high in calories and fat, despite being heart healthy. My son created this recipe after being inspired by the Food Network. Chickpeas are low in fat, have no cholesterol and contain protein, dietary fiber and folate. Add some chili or cayenne powder for extra spice. You'll love this tasty alternative to nuts.

2 cups canned chickpeas, drained and
    rinsed
1 Tbsp olive oil
¼ tsp garlic powder

¼ tsp onion powder
pinch paprika
2 Tbsp grated Parmesan cheese

1. Preheat the oven to 350°F. Line a baking sheet with foil and spray with cooking oil.

2. Combine the chickpeas, oil, garlic powder, onion powder, paprika and cheese in a bowl and toss until the chickpeas are evenly coated.

3. Scatter over the prepared baking sheet and bake for 60 to 75 minutes, or until crisp, tossing occasionally.

New Potato and Smoked Salmon Salad with Creamy Dill Dressing

NUTRITIONAL ANALYSIS
PER SERVING

Calories	179
Protein	6.7 g
Fat	6.7 g
Saturated Fat	1.6 g
Carbohydrates	23 g
Cholesterol	11 mg
Sodium	275 mg
Fiber	2.1 g

Prep Time: 15 minutes

Cook Time: 10 minutes

Make Ahead:
Prepare a day in
advance and refrigerate.
Serve chilled.

Serves 8

You've never tasted a potato salad like this before. New potatoes pair beautifully with smoked salmon and dill. Most potato salads are loaded with fat and calories due to the mayonnaise. In this version, the combination of light sour cream, mayonnaise and olive oil reduces the calories. Make sure the potatoes are cool before adding the smoked salmon to avoid cooking the salmon. If small potatoes are not available, cut a regular potato into large cubes before cooking.

1½ lb small new potatoes

6 oz smoked salmon, chopped

½ cup finely chopped snow peas

⅓ cup finely chopped green onion

½ cup low-fat sour cream

¼ cup chopped fresh dill

2 Tbsp light mayonnaise

2 Tbsp olive oil

1 Tbsp freshly squeezed lemon juice

2 tsp Dijon mustard

1 tsp minced fresh garlic

¼ tsp freshly ground black pepper

1. Scrub the potatoes but don't peel them. Place them in a saucepan, add cold water to cover and bring to a boil. Reduce the heat to medium-high. Cook for 10 to 15 minutes, or until tender when pierced with the tip of a knife. Drain and set aside to cool.

2. Slice the potatoes into ¼-inch-thick rounds. Combine the potatoes, smoked salmon, snow peas and green onion in a large bowl.

3. Whisk the sour cream, dill, mayonnaise, oil, lemon juice, mustard, garlic and pepper together in a small bowl. Pour over the potato mixture and toss to coat. Serve immediately or chill.

Grilled Chicken Caesar Salad

Consider this: a not-so-innocent traditional Caesar salad can have over 500 calories and 30 grams of fat per plate! Try this delicious version; you don't need your salad to be swimming in dressing—there is just enough here.

8 oz skinless boneless chicken breast
(about 2 breasts)

2 cups 1-inch Italian bread cubes
1 egg
5 Tbsp grated Parmesan cheese
3 anchovy fillets, minced

1 Tbsp freshly squeezed lemon juice
1 tsp Dijon mustard
1½ tsp minced fresh garlic
pinch freshly ground black pepper
2 Tbsp olive oil
6 cups torn romaine lettuce

1. Preheat the oven to 425°F.

2. Spray a grill or non-stick grill pan with cooking oil and heat to medium-high. Cook the chicken for 6 minutes per side or until cooked through and no longer pink in the center. Dice.

3. Place the bread cubes on a baking sheet. Spray with cooking oil. Bake for 8 to 10 minutes, or until golden.

4. Combine the egg, 3 Tbsp of the Parmesan cheese, anchovies, lemon juice, mustard, garlic and pepper in a small food processor and process until smooth (or use a whisk). Slowly add the olive oil, mixing until thickened.

5. Toss the chicken, croutons and romaine in a large serving bowl. Pour the dressing over the top and toss to coat. Sprinkle with the remaining 2 Tbsp Parmesan cheese.

NUTRITIONAL ANALYSIS PER SERVING

Calories	164
Protein	14 g
Fat	7.9 g
Saturated Fat	1.9 g
Carbohydrates	9.8 g
Cholesterol	61 mg
Sodium	239 mg
Fiber	1.4 g

Prep Time: 15 minutes
Cook Time: 20 minutes

Make Ahead:
Prepare dressing (refrigerate) and croutons (store in a sealed container at room temperature) up to 2 days in advance.

Serves 6

Four-Tomato Salad

The contrasting colors and textures of the tomatoes in this salad are what make it so sensational. If you can find grape tomatoes, they are even sweeter than cherry tomatoes and have a great texture. Don't forget that tomatoes contain lycopene, an antioxidant that helps in the fight against prostate cancer and heart disease.

½ cup sun-dried tomatoes, rehydrated (see page 221)
2 cups sliced field tomatoes
2 cups halved red or yellow cherry tomatoes
2 cups quartered plum tomatoes
1 cup sliced sweet onion, such as Vidalia, Walla Walla or Spanish

½ cup chopped fresh basil or 2 tsp dried basil

3 Tbsp balsamic vinegar
2 Tbsp olive oil
1½ tsp minced fresh garlic
½ tsp granulated sugar
pinch freshly ground black pepper

1. Place the tomatoes, onion and fresh basil in a serving bowl or on a platter.

2. Whisk the vinegar, oil, garlic, sugar and pepper together. Pour over the salad. Serve immediately.

NUTRITIONAL ANALYSIS
PER SERVING

Calories	135
Protein	3 g
Fat	4 g
Saturated Fat	0.8 g
Carbohydrates	18 g
Cholesterol	0 mg
Sodium	130 mg
Fiber	5.2 g

Prep Time: 15 minutes

Make Ahead:
Prepare dressing up to 3 days in advance and refrigerate. Dress salad just before serving.

Serves 4

Four-Tomato Salad
Photo by Mark Shapiro

Bean Salad with Fresh Vegetables and Feta Cheese

NUTRITIONAL ANALYSIS PER SERVING

Calories	220
Protein	8 g
Fat	9 g
Saturated Fat	2 g
Carbohydrates	23 g
Cholesterol	6 mg
Sodium	380 mg
Fiber	6 g

Prep Time: 20 minutes

Make Ahead:
Prepare up to a day in advance and refrigerate.

Serves 4

Beans contain vitamins, minerals and fiber essential to a healthy diet. Use any type you like in this salad, a new take on an old favorite.

¾ cup canned white or red kidney beans, drained and rinsed

¾ cup canned chickpeas, drained and rinsed

1 cup chopped plum tomato

½ cup chopped onion

½ cup chopped celery

½ cup chopped green or red bell pepper

⅓ cup light feta cheese, crumbled

⅓ cup chopped fresh basil or cilantro

2 Tbsp freshly squeezed lemon juice

1 tsp crushed fresh garlic

1 tsp dried basil

½ tsp dried oregano

2 Tbsp olive oil

1. Combine the beans, chickpeas, tomato, onion, celery, green pepper, feta cheese and fresh basil in a serving bowl.

2. Whisk the lemon juice, garlic, dried basil and oregano in a small bowl. Whisk in the oil. Pour the dressing over the salad and stir gently to mix well. Serve immediately at room temperature or chill.

Beans from Scratch

If you want to cook beans from scratch instead of using canned beans, try this method. Bring dried beans and water to a boil and cook for 3 minutes. Remove from the heat and let sit covered for 1 hour. Drain, add fresh water to cover and cook just until tender, approximately 45 minutes (the time will vary, depending on the type of bean).

Broccoli, Snow Pea and Baby Corn Salad with Orange Dressing

This is an outstanding salad to serve at a buffet or as an appetizer before your main meal. If you add some protein, such as chicken, beef or fish, it can be an entire meal. Feel free to substitute any vegetables of your choice, but remember that those with the darkest colors have the most health benefits.

2 cups chopped broccoli florets

1 cup snow peas, cut into 1-inch pieces

½ cup sliced onion

½ medium red bell pepper, sliced

3 cups torn romaine lettuce

¾ cup canned mandarin oranges, drained

½ cup sliced water chestnuts

8 ears canned baby corn, drained and cut in thirds

¼ cup dried cranberries

3 Tbsp olive oil

3 Tbsp orange juice concentrate

1½ tsp balsamic vinegar

½ tsp crushed fresh garlic

4 tsp freshly squeezed lemon juice

1 tsp granulated sugar

1. Steam or microwave the broccoli just until tender-crisp, approximately 2 minutes. Drain and rinse with cold water. Drain again and pat dry. Place in a serving bowl.

2. Add the peas, onion, red pepper, lettuce, mandarin oranges, water chestnuts, corn and cranberries.

3. For the dressing, whisk the oil, juice concentrate, vinegar, garlic, lemon juice and sugar together in a small bowl. Pour over the salad and toss well.

NUTRITIONAL ANALYSIS PER SERVING

Calories	150
Protein	3 g
Fat	8 g
Saturated Fat	0 g
Carbohydrates	19 g
Cholesterol	0 mg
Sodium	16 mg
Fiber	3 g

Prep Time: 20 minutes

Cook Time: 2 minutes

Make Ahead:
Prepare salad and dressing early in the day and refrigerate. Toss together just before serving.

Serves 6

Mango Lettuce Salad with Feta and Olives

NUTRITIONAL ANALYSIS
PER SERVING

Calories	155
Protein	3.3 g
Fat	9.1 g
Saturated Fat	1.7 g
Carbohydrates	15 g
Cholesterol	3.4 mg
Sodium	210 mg
Fiber	2.4 g

Prep Time: 15 minutes

Make Ahead:
Prepare salad and
dressing early in the day
and refrigerate. Toss
together just before serving.

Serves 6

My favorite salads are those combining fruit, an intense cheese and a sweet vinegar dressing—like this one. Mangos contain an abundance of beta carotene and antioxidants, which are thought to prevent disease. You can substitute ripe pears, peaches, strawberries or blueberries (also an antioxidant), for the mango.

4 cups torn, mixed salad greens
1 Belgian endive, sliced
1 small head radicchio, torn
1½ cups diced ripe mango
⅓ cup light feta cheese, crumbled
⅓ cup sliced black olives

2 Tbsp balsamic vinegar
2 Tbsp olive oil
1 Tbsp liquid honey
2 tsp sesame oil
1 tsp minced fresh garlic

1. Toss the greens, endive, radicchio, mango, cheese and olives together in a bowl.

2. Whisk the vinegar, olive oil, honey, sesame oil and garlic together in a small bowl. Pour over the salad and toss to coat.

Mango Lettuce Salad with Feta and Olives ▶
Photo by Lorella Zanetti

Pesto Potato Salad

NUTRITIONAL ANALYSIS
PER SERVING

Calories	154
Protein	4 g
Fat	6 g
Saturated Fat	1 g
Carbohydrates	22 g
Cholesterol	1 mg
Sodium	124 mg
Fiber	3 g

Prep Time: 20 minutes

Cook Time: 20 minutes

Make Ahead:
Prepare entire salad up
to a day in advance, cover
and refrigerate. Toss again
before serving.

Serves 10

You can use ¾ cup store-bought pesto instead of making the pesto here, but keep in mind that calories and fat will be higher. To lessen the calories, substitute 2 Tbsp light sour cream for the same amount of pesto. If fresh basil is unavailable, try a combination of spinach, cilantro and parsley leaves. Grilling the canned corn gives it a barbecued, charred flavor.

2 lb whole red potatoes, scrubbed (unpeeled)

½ cup canned or frozen corn kernels

1¼ cups packed fresh basil leaves

3 Tbsp olive oil

2 Tbsp toasted pine nuts

2 Tbsp grated Parmesan cheese

1 tsp minced fresh garlic

¼ tsp salt

¼ cup chicken stock or water

1 cup halved snow peas

¾ cup finely chopped red onion

¾ cup finely chopped red bell pepper

¾ cup finely chopped green bell pepper

½ cup finely chopped green onion

2 Tbsp pine nuts, toasted

2 Tbsp freshly squeezed lemon juice

1. Put the potatoes in a saucepan with cold water to cover. Bring to a boil and cook for 20 to 25 minutes, or until easily pierced with a sharp knife. Drain and set aside.

2. Spray a non-stick skillet with cooking oil and place over high heat. Sauté the corn until browned, stirring often, about 5 minutes. Set aside.

3. While the potatoes are cooking and cooling, make the pesto. Place the basil, oil, pine nuts, cheese, garlic and salt in a food processor; process until finely chopped. With the motor running, gradually add the stock through the feed tube; process until smooth.

4. Bring a saucepan of water to a boil and blanch the snow peas for 1 or 2 minutes, or until tender-crisp (or use a microwave oven). Immerse in cold water to stop the cooking and drain.

5. Place the snow peas in a large serving bowl. Add the red onion, red and green pepper, green onion, pine nuts and lemon juice. Add the corn and pesto.

6. When the potatoes are cool enough to handle, cut them into wedges and add to the serving bowl. Combine gently and serve immediately.

Mediterranean Barley Salad

This is my variation on traditional Greek salad. I like to have it as a main meal with some protein or as a side dish instead of rice or pasta. You don't have to seed the tomatoes, but removing the seeds eliminates excess liquid.

¾ cups chicken stock or water

¾ cup pearl barley

1½ cups diced cucumber

1½ cups seeded, diced plum tomatoes

¾ cup chopped red onion

¾ cup chopped green bell pepper

⅓ cup sliced black olives

⅓ cup light feta cheese, crumbled

2 Tbsp olive oil

2 Tbsp freshly squeezed lemon juice

1½ tsp minced fresh garlic

1 tsp dried basil

½ tsp dried oregano

⅓ cup chopped fresh basil or parsley

1. Bring the stock to a boil in a medium saucepan and add the barley. Cover, reduce the heat and simmer for 25 to 30 minutes, or just until tender. Do not overcook. Drain well.

2. Place the barley in a large serving bowl. Add the cucumber, tomato, red onion, green pepper, black olives and feta cheese. Toss well.

3. For the dressing, whisk the oil, lemon juice, garlic, dried basil, oregano and fresh basil in a small bowl. Pour the dressing over the salad and toss well. Refrigerate until chilled.

Barley

This nutritious grain is a low-glycemic carbohydrate (see page 16). Pearl barley is not as nutritious as pot barley because the bran has been removed, but it cooks much more quickly. If you prefer pot barley, cook it for 45 minutes or just until tender.

NUTRITIONAL ANALYSIS PER SERVING

Calories	197
Protein	5 g
Fat	8 g
Saturated Fat	2 g
Carbohydrates	29 g
Cholesterol	9 mg
Sodium	290 mg
Fiber	6 g

Prep Time: 15 minutes

Cook Time: 25 minutes

Make Ahead:
Prepare early in the day and refrigerate.

Serves 6

Thai-Style Beef Salad with Orange Sesame Dressing

NUTRITIONAL ANALYSIS
PER SERVING

Calories	166
Protein	11 g
Fat	3.8 g
Saturated Fat	1 g
Carbohydrates	22 g
Cholesterol	24 mg
Sodium	172 mg
Fiber	2.2 g

Prep Time: 20 minutes

Cook Time: 8 minutes

Make Ahead:
Make dressing 3 days in advance and refrigerate. Prepare salad early in the day and refrigerate. Toss together just before serving.

Serves 6

This main course salad has an intriguing Asian-inspired dressing and the thin rice noodles give it a light texture. Use a good-quality steak, making sure you don't over-cook it. Substitute chicken, seafood, or firm tofu for the beef, if you like. Use the dressing as a marinade for chicken, pork or fish. Rice vermicelli is available in higher quality supermarkets or Asian markets. It is made with rice flour and comes in different thicknesses. It's great for those who are allergic to wheat.

8 oz boneless grilling steak

2 oz thin rice vermicelli

4 cups torn, mixed salad greens

1 cup finely chopped snow peas

1 cup thinly sliced red bell pepper

½ cup sliced canned water chestnuts, drained

½ cup canned mandarin oranges, drained

⅓ cup chopped sweet onion

¼ cup chopped green onion

2 Tbsp orange juice concentrate

1½ Tbsp packed brown sugar

2 Tbsp rice vinegar

2 Tbsp low-sodium soy sauce

2 tsp sesame oil

1 tsp minced fresh garlic

½ tsp minced fresh ginger

½ tsp hot Asian chili sauce

pinch salt

⅓ cup chopped cilantro or parsley

1. Spray a non-stick grill pan with cooking oil and place over medium heat. Cook the steak for 5 to 8 minutes, or until done to your taste, turning once. (Or grill on a barbecue preheated to medium-high.) Cool. Slice thinly.

2. Pour boiling water over the rice noodles. Let stand for 5 minutes. Drain and rinse with cold water.

3. Combine the rice noodles, salad greens, snow peas, red pepper, water chestnuts, mandarin oranges, sweet onion, green onion and sliced steak in a large serving bowl.

4. To make the dressing, whisk the juice concentrate, sugar, vinegar, soy sauce, oil, garlic, ginger, chili sauce and salt in a small bowl.

5. Pour the dressing over the salad and toss to mix well. Garnish with cilantro.

Tex-Mex Macaroni Salad with Charred Corn and Black Beans

Serve this delicious salad either at room temperature or chilled. It's perfect in a baked tortilla shell. Purchase a tortilla baking pan from a kitchen store, fit it with a large tortilla and bake it at 400°F for 10 minutes or until crisp. If you don't have cider vinegar, substitute balsamic or another fruit vinegar.

8 oz elbow macaroni

1 cup canned corn kernels, drained

1½ cups chopped seeded plum tomatoes

1 cup canned black beans, rinsed and drained

½ cup chopped green onion

⅓ cup chopped fresh cilantro or parsley

⅓ cup barbecue sauce

2 Tbsp cider vinegar

1 Tbsp molasses

1 tsp minced, seeded jalapeño pepper or hot chili sauce to taste

1. Bring a saucepan of water to a boil and cook the macaroni for 8 to 10 minutes, or until tender but firm. Drain, rinse and drain again. Place in a large serving bowl.

2. Spray a non-stick skillet with cooking oil and set over high heat. Cook the corn, stirring often, until slightly charred, about 8 minutes. Add to the macaroni, along with the tomatoes, beans, onion and cilantro. Toss to combine.

3. To make the dressing, whisk the barbecue sauce, cider vinegar, molasses and jalapeño together in a small bowl. Pour the dressing over the macaroni mixture and toss to coat. Serve immediately or chill.

NUTRITIONAL ANALYSIS
PER SERVING

Calories	229
Protein	7.4 g
Fat	11 g
Saturated Fat	2.4 g
Carbohydrates	25 g
Cholesterol	5 mg
Sodium	400 mg
Fiber	4.3 g

Prep Time:	15 minutes
Cook Time:	8 minutes

Make Ahead:
Make early in the day and refrigerate. Best served at room temperature.

Serves 8

Spinach Salad with Candied Pecans, Pears and Brie
Photo by Brian MacDonald

Spinach Salad with Candied Pecans, Pears and Brie

This is the number-one salad in my catering company. The sweet and savory combination of cinnamon-sugared pecans, ripe pears and small morsels of brie is sensational. There is very little oil in this, but you won't miss it. You can easily make this a main meal salad by adding some grilled chicken or shrimp.

⅓ cup pecan halves

3 Tbsp icing sugar

¼ tsp cinnamon

⅛ tsp allspice

⅛ tsp nutmeg

2 Tbsp orange juice concentrate, thawed

2 Tbsp olive oil

1 Tbsp balsamic vinegar

1 tsp minced garlic

½ tsp liquid honey

½ tsp Dijon mustard

8 cups baby spinach leaves

1 cup diced radicchio

1 large ripe pear, peeled, cored and diced

2 oz brie, diced

1. Preheat the oven to 350°F. Spray a baking sheet with cooking oil.

2. Rinse the pecans with cold water. Drain, but do not let them dry. Combine the icing sugar, cinnamon, allspice and nutmeg in a small bowl. Dip the pecans in the sugar mixture, coating them well. Spread on the prepared baking sheet.

3. Bake for 15 minutes in the center of the oven. Remove and cool. When they're cool enough to handle, chop coarsely.

4. Combine the spinach, radicchio, pear and brie in a large serving bowl.

5. Whisk the juice concentrate, oil, vinegar, garlic, honey and mustard together in a small bowl. Pour the dressing over the salad and toss to coat. Garnish with the candied pecans.

NUTRITIONAL ANALYSIS
PER SERVING

Calories	189
Protein	4.2 g
Fat	12 g
Saturated Fat	2.7 g
Carbohydrates	13 g
Cholesterol	9 mg
Sodium	105 mg
Fiber	2.6 g

Prep Time:	15 minutes
Cook Time:	15 minutes

Make Ahead:

Prepare pecans 2 weeks in advance and store in an airtight container. Prepare salad and dressing early in the day and refrigerate. Toss together and garnish just before serving.

Serves 8

Coleslaw with Thai-Style Dressing, Dried Cranberries and Apricots

NUTRITIONAL ANALYSIS
PER SERVING

Calories	65
Protein	1.6 g
Fat	0.7 g
Saturated Fat	0.5 g
Carbohydrates	13 g
Cholesterol	0 mg
Sodium	129 mg
Fiber	2.6 g

Prep Time: 20 minutes

Make Ahead:
Prepare salad ingredients
and dressing early in the
day and refrigerate. Toss
together just before serving.

Serves 8

Now here's a coleslaw that will be the hit of your next get-together. Brightly colored vegetables and fruit give it eye appeal, and the sweet Asian-style dressing is a wonderful complement. It even tastes great the next day.

3 cups thinly sliced green cabbage

3 cups thinly sliced red cabbage

1 cup sliced snow peas

1 cup sliced red bell pepper

½ cup chopped green onion

⅓ cup dried cranberries

⅓ cup diced dried apricots

⅓ cup light coconut milk

⅓ cup chopped cilantro or parsley

2 tsp fish or oyster sauce

2 tsp packed brown sugar

1 Tbsp freshly squeezed lemon juice

1 tsp minced fresh garlic

½ tsp minced fresh ginger

1 tsp minced jalapeño peppers (seeded)
or to taste

1. Combine the green and red cabbage, snow peas, red pepper, green onion, cranberries and apricots in a large bowl and mix well.

2. For the dressing, whisk the coconut milk, cilantro, fish sauce, brown sugar, lemon juice, garlic, ginger and jalapeño together in a small bowl. Pour the dressing over the cabbage mixture and toss to coat.

Asian Rice Noodle Salad with Coconut Ginger Dressing

Rice noodles have a denser texture and creamier taste than wheat noodles. Combine them with a coconut-peanut dressing and a variety of vegetables to make this great appetizer or main course. Light coconut milk is now available in most supermarkets, and it's a real find at 75 percent less fat and calories than regular coconut milk.

8 oz medium-thick rice noodles, broken in half

1½ cups finely chopped snow peas

1½ cups finely chopped red bell pepper

½ cup finely chopped green onion

⅓ cup chopped cilantro or parsley

¼ cup chopped peanuts

½ cup light coconut milk

3 Tbsp natural peanut butter

2 Tbsp low-sodium soy sauce

2 Tbsp rice vinegar

1 Tbsp sesame oil

1 Tbsp sesame seeds, toasted

2 tsp minced fresh garlic

2 Tbsp brown sugar

1 tsp minced fresh ginger

1 tsp hot chili sauce, or to taste

1. Bring a large saucepan of water to a boil and cook the noodles for 3 to 5 minutes or until tender. Drain. Rinse under cold running water and drain again.

2. Combine the noodles, snow peas, red pepper, green onion, cilantro and peanuts in a large serving bowl.

3. For the dressing, combine the coconut milk, peanut butter, soy sauce, vinegar, sesame oil, sesame seeds, garlic, brown sugar, ginger and chili sauce in a bowl or a small food processor. Whisk or process the mixture until smooth.

4. Pour the dressing over the vegetable-noodle mixture and toss to coat.

NUTRITIONAL ANALYSIS PER SERVING

Calories	214
Protein	6.8 g
Fat	7.9 g
Saturated Fat	1.3 g
Carbohydrates	28 g
Cholesterol	0 mg
Sodium	116 mg
Fiber	2.2 g

Prep Time: 20 minutes

Cook Time: 5 minutes

Make Ahead:
Prepare the vegetables, make the dressing and cook the noodles early in the day and refrigerate. Rinse the noodles with room-temperature water just before tossing with the other ingredients.

Serves 8

Wild and Brown Rice Pilaf with Dried Fruit and Pecans

NUTRITIONAL ANALYSIS
PER SERVING

Calories	258
Protein	6.4 g
Fat	9.5 g
Saturated Fat	1.4 g
Carbohydrates	33 g
Cholesterol	1.9 mg
Sodium	107 mg
Fiber	3.5 g

Prep Time: 15 minutes

Cook Time: 35 minutes

Make Ahead:
Prepare up to a day in advance and refrigerate. Bring to room temperature before serving.

Serves 8

This rice dish is amazingly versatile. I serve it as a side salad at meals, put it on a buffet table or use it to stuff roasted chicken or turkey. Very little oil is needed because of the flavors in the salad.

¾ cup wild rice

¾ cup brown rice

4 cups vegetable or chicken stock

½ cup chopped pecans, toasted

⅓ cup chopped green onion

⅓ cup dried cranberries

⅓ cup dried chopped apricots

⅓ cup chopped cilantro or parsley

1 Tbsp olive oil

1 Tbsp orange juice concentrate, thawed

1 Tbsp freshly squeezed lemon juice

2 tsp low-sodium soy sauce

2 tsp raspberry or balsamic vinegar

1½ tsp sesame oil

1 tsp minced fresh garlic

1. Combine the wild and brown rice with the stock in a saucepan. Bring to a boil. Reduce the heat to a simmer, cover and cook for 35 to 40 minutes, or just until the rice is tender. Drain off the excess liquid. Place the rice in a large serving bowl and set aside to cool.

2. Stir the pecans, green onion, cranberries, apricots and cilantro into the cooled rice.

3. Whisk the olive oil, juice concentrate, lemon juice, soy sauce, vinegar, sesame oil and garlic together in a small bowl. Pour the dressing over the salad and toss to coat.

Wild and Brown Rice Pilaf with Dried Fruit and Pecans ▶
Photo by Lorella Zanetti

Wheat Berry and Charred Corn Salad

**NUTRITIONAL ANALYSIS
PER SERVING**

Calories	167
Protein	5.4 g
Fat	5 g
Saturated Fat	1 g
Carbohydrates	21 g
Cholesterol	1.9 mg
Sodium	118 mg
Fiber	3.7 g

Prep Time: 10 minutes

Cook Time: 45 minutes

Make Ahead:
Prepare up to a day in
advance and refrigerate.
Serve at room temperature.

Serves 6

Wheat berry is a husked whole kernel of wheat with its nutritious bran intact. It's a nice break from pasta or rice. I buy it in bulk and keep it in my freezer, where it will last for over a year. Most supermarkets carry wheat berries, and you can always find them at a health food store.

3 cups chicken or vegetable stock

1 cup wheat berries

1 cup canned corn kernels, drained

1 cup diced broccoli

1 cup diced red bell pepper

1 Tbsp olive oil

2 tsp liquid honey

1½ tsp sesame oil

1 tsp minced fresh garlic

⅓ cup chopped fresh cilantro or parsley

2 Tbsp orange juice concentrate, thawed

2 Tbsp rice vinegar

1. Bring the stock to a boil in a saucepan. Stir in the wheat berries. Reduce the heat to a simmer, cover and cook just until tender, about 45 to 50 minutes. Do not overcook. Drain off the excess liquid. Place the wheat berries in a serving bowl.

2. Spray a non-stick skillet with cooking oil and place over medium heat. Cook the corn, stirring frequently, until it begins to char, about 5 minutes over medium heat. Stir in the broccoli and red pepper. Cook for 4 minutes, or just until the vegetables begin to soften. Transfer to the bowl with the wheat berries.

3. Whisk the juice concentrate, vinegar, olive oil, honey, sesame oil and garlic in a small bowl. Pour the dressing over the wheat berry mixture and toss to coat. Garnish with the cilantro.

Shrimp and Macaroni Salad with Creamy Russian Dressing

This can be served as a main meal or as a side dish, and it's great on a buffet table. You can substitute another shellfish or even fresh fish such as cooked salmon for the shrimp. Always be sure to weigh your shrimp after it's been peeled. For each pound of peeled shrimp you need to purchase approximately 1¼ pounds of shrimp in the shell.

8 oz macaroni or any small shell pasta

12 oz peeled and deveined raw shrimp

⅓ cup light mayonnaise

⅓ cup low-fat sour cream

¼ cup sweet tomato chili sauce or ketchup

½ cup minced green bell pepper

½ cup minced red bell pepper

½ cup minced red onion

⅓ cup chopped fresh dill or parsley

pinch freshly ground black pepper

1. Cook the macaroni in a pot of boiling water for 8 to 10 minutes, or until tender but firm.

2. Drain, rinse under cold running water and drain thoroughly.

3. If using large or jumbo shrimp, cut them into halves. Spray a non-stick skillet with cooking oil and place over medium-high heat. Cook the shrimp until pink, about 2 minutes.

4. Combine the mayonnaise, sour cream, and chili sauce in a small bowl and mix well.

5. Combine the green and red pepper, onion, dill, pepper, pasta, shrimp and dressing in a serving bowl. Toss to coat well. Chill before serving.

NUTRITIONAL ANALYSIS PER SERVING

Calories	394
Protein	22 g
Fat	9 g
Saturated Fat	2.8 g
Carbohydrates	54 g
Cholesterol	99 mg
Sodium	283 mg
Fiber	3 g

Prep Time: 15 minutes

Cook Time: 8 minutes

Make Ahead:
Prepare up to a day in advance and refrigerate.

Serves 4

Shrimp, Avocado and Feta Salad

This amazing salad is so filling you'll need only a small portion. Dice the avocado just before you're ready to serve, or squeeze some lemon juice over it to prevent browning if you prepare it earlier in the day. Always be sure to weigh your shrimp after it's been peeled. For each pound of peeled shrimp you need to purchase approximately 1¼ pounds of shrimp in the shell. Purchase cooked cocktail shrimp if you don't want to bother cooking raw shrimp.

16 oz large shrimp, peeled and deveined

3 cups diced and seeded plum tomatoes

1 cup diced ripe avocado

⅓ cup chopped cilantro or parsley

¼ cup diced red onion

½ cup light feta cheese, crumbled

2 Tbsp olive oil

2 Tbsp freshly squeezed lemon juice

1½ tsp minced fresh garlic

1 tsp minced jalapeño pepper or 1 tsp hot sauce

pinch salt and freshly ground black pepper

1. Spray a non-stick skillet with cooking oil and place over medium-high heat. Cook the shrimp just until pink, about 3 minutes. Remove from the heat, cool and dice.

2. Combine the shrimp with the remaining ingredients in a large serving bowl and mix thoroughly. Serve immediately.

NUTRITIONAL ANALYSIS
PER SERVING

Calories	229
Protein	19 g
Fat	13 g
Saturated Fat	3.6 g
Carbohydrates	6 g
Cholesterol	127 mg
Sodium	334 mg
Fiber	2.6 g

Prep Time:	15 minutes
Cook Time:	3 minutes

Make Ahead:
Prepare a day in advance, omitting the avocado, cover and refrigerate. Add avocado just before serving.

Serves 6

Shrimp, Avocado and Feta Salad
Photo by Brian MacDonald

Spinach and Oyster Mushroom Salad with Mandarin Oranges and Pecans

Calories	131
Protein	2.6 g
Fat	8.5 g
Saturated Fat	1.1 g
Carbohydrates	11 g
Cholesterol	1.9 mg
Sodium	55 mg
Fiber	1.9 g

Prep Time:	15 minutes
Cook Time:	8 minutes

Serves 8

Popeye was right! Spinach is one of the best vegetables you could possibly consume in terms of nutrition. It's loaded with iron and folate, as well as vitamins A and C. One cup has only 40 calories. It also tastes great, particularly in this salad, where it's combined with sautéed mushrooms and a light mayonnaise dressing. The oyster mushrooms are especially nice, but you can always substitute ordinary cultivated mushrooms.

1 tsp vegetable oil

2 cups sliced oyster mushrooms

8 cups baby spinach

1 cup canned mandarin oranges, drained

½ cup sliced canned water chestnuts, drained

½ cup sliced red onion

⅓ cup chopped toasted pecans

2 Tbsp olive oil

2 Tbsp low-fat sour cream

1 Tbsp light mayonnaise

1 Tbsp balsamic vinegar

2 tsp liquid honey

½ tsp minced fresh garlic

1. Heat the vegetable oil in a non-stick skillet over medium-high heat. Cook the mushrooms for 8 minutes, or until browned.

2. Combine the spinach, mandarin oranges, water chestnuts, onion, pecans and warm mushrooms in a large serving bowl.

3. Whisk the olive oil, sour cream, mayonnaise, vinegar, honey and garlic together in a small bowl. Pour the dressing over the spinach mixture and toss to coat well.

Greek Pasta Salad

If you're tired of traditional Greek salads, try this. The addition of pasta makes it a great side dish. Add some grilled chicken or shrimp and you have a main meal. Fresh oregano is always a treat but it's not always easy to find—basil and parsley are fine substitutes. Penne, rotini or medium shell pasta can be used instead of the bow-ties. When it's in season, use delicious sweet Vidalia onion in place of the red onion.

12 oz bow-tie pasta

2¾ cups diced plum tomatoes

1 cup diced cucumber

1 cup diced green bell pepper

¾ cup sliced red onion

⅔ cup light feta cheese, crumbled

⅓ cup sliced black olives

⅓ cup chopped fresh oregano

3 Tbsp olive oil

3 Tbsp freshly squeezed lemon juice

2 Tbsp water

2 Tbsp balsamic vinegar

2 tsp crushed fresh garlic

pinch freshly ground black pepper

1. Cook the pasta in a large pot of boiling water according to the package instructions, or until firm to the bite, about 10 minutes. Drain and rinse with cold water. Drain well and place in a serving bowl.

2. Add the tomatoes, cucumber, green pepper, onion, feta cheese, olives and oregano to the serving bowl.

3. Combine the oil, lemon juice, water, vinegar, garlic and black pepper in a bowl and whisk to mix. Pour the dressing over the pasta and toss well.

NUTRITIONAL ANALYSIS
PER SERVING

Calories	299
Protein	9 g
Fat	9 g
Saturated Fat	3 g
Carbohydrates	47 g
Cholesterol	10 mg
Sodium	224 mg
Fiber	5 g

Prep Time: 15 minutes

Cook Time: 10 minutes

Make Ahead:

Prepare salad up to a day in advance. Toss with the oregano just before serving.

Serves 8

Italian Bean Pasta Salad

NUTRITIONAL ANALYSIS
PER SERVING

Calories	333
Protein	11 g
Fat	9 g
Saturated Fat	2 g
Carbohydrates	53 g
Sodium	420 mg
Cholesterol	8 mg
Fiber	7 g

Prep Time: 15 minutes

Make Ahead:
Prepare salad and
dressing early in the day
and refrigerate. Toss
together up to 2 hours
before serving.

Serves 8

Serve this as a side dish, salad or main course. The beans and pasta form a complete protein, so it's perfect for the vegetarian. Use any combination of canned cooked beans you like. Fresh cooked beans are excellent if you have the time (see page 84). It tastes great at room temperature or chilled.

12 oz medium shell pasta

2 ½ cups chopped plum tomatoes

¾ cup diced green bell pepper

¾ cup diced red onion

⅔ cup canned red kidney beans, drained and rinsed

⅔ cup canned white kidney beans, drained and rinsed

⅔ cup canned chickpeas, drained and rinsed

½ cup light feta cheese, crumbled

⅓ cup fresh chopped basil or parsley

¼ cup freshly squeezed lemon juice

3 Tbsp olive oil

1 Tbsp balsamic vinegar

2 tsp crushed fresh garlic

2 ½ tsp dried basil

1 ½ tsp dried oregano

1. Cook the pasta in boiling water according to package directions, or until firm to the bite, about 10 minutes. Rinse with cold water. Drain well and place in a serving bowl.

2. Add the tomatoes, green pepper, onion, red and white kidney beans, chickpeas, feta cheese and basil to the serving bowl.

3. Combine the lemon juice, oil, vinegar, garlic, basil and oregano in a small bowl. Mix well. Pour the dressing over the pasta and toss.

Italian Bean Pasta Salad ▶
Photo by Lorella Zanetti

Three-Bean, Avocado and Charred Corn Salad with Lime Dressing

NUTRITIONAL ANALYSIS
PER SERVING

Calories	180
Protein	6 g
Fat	7.4 g
Saturated Fat	0.95 g
Carbohydrates	26 g
Cholesterol	0 mg
Sodium	420 mg
Fiber	7.5 g

Prep Time: 15 minutes
Cook Time: 10 minutes

Make Ahead:
Prepare dressing and salad early in the day, reserving the avocado and cilantro, and refrigerate. Add just before serving and toss with the dressing.

Serves 6

This salad has nutrition galore and makes a great side salad or buffet dish. Often I'll add some grilled chicken or fish and make it a main meal. Cut the avocado just before serving, or add some lemon juice to it to prevent discoloration.

8 oz green beans
1 cup canned corn kernels, drained
1 cup canned black beans, drained and rinsed
1 cup canned chickpeas, drained and rinsed
¾ cup diced red bell pepper
½ cup diced red onion
½ cup diced ripe avocado

1½ tsp lime or lemon zest
3 Tbsp freshly squeezed lime or lemon juice
2 Tbsp olive oil
1 tsp minced fresh garlic
1 tsp minced fresh ginger
1 tsp minced jalapeño or ½ tsp hot sauce (or to taste)
Pinch salt and freshly ground black pepper
⅓ cup chopped fresh cilantro, basil or parsley

1. Steam the green beans just until bright green and still crisp, about 3 minutes. Place immediately under cold water and rinse until the beans are no longer warm. Place in a serving bowl.

2. Spray a small non-stick skillet with cooking oil and place over medium heat. Sauté the corn, stirring frequently, until browned, approximately 8 minutes. Add to the serving bowl, along with the black beans, chickpeas, bell pepper, onion and avocado.

3. Whisk the zest, juice, oil, garlic, ginger, jalapeño, salt and pepper together in a small bowl.

4. Pour the dressing over the salad and toss to mix well. Garnish with the cilantro.

Three-Bean, Avocado and Charred Corn Salad with Lime Dressing
Photo by Lorella Zanetti

Quinoa Greek Salad

NUTRITIONAL ANALYSIS
PER SERVING

Calories	208
Protein	7.6 g
Fat	9.1 g
Saturated Fat	1.8 g
Carbohydrates	24 g
Cholesterol	3.4 mg
Sodium	250 mg
Fiber	2.5 g

Prep Time: 15 minutes

Cook Time: 15 minutes

Make Ahead:
Prepare up to a day in advance and refrigerate. Serve chilled or at room temperature.

Serves 6

Quinoa

Some people like to rinse quinoa before cooking to rid it of a somewhat mineral taste. I don't bother if the quinoa is fresh. Toasting the quinoa in a non-stick skillet for about 2 minutes just until lightly browned gives it a nutty flavor.

You'll love this new version of a Greek salad. Quinoa, pronounced "keen-wah," is the most nutritious grain in town. It's a complete protein, which is especially important to vegetarians. It's also high in calcium and iron. You can find it in most large supermarkets or health food stores. It's the only grain that is allowed on the Jewish holiday of Passover, because it is not actually a true grain.

2 cups chicken or vegetable stock

1 cup quinoa

½ cup diced red bell pepper

½ cup diced green bell pepper

½ cup diced English cucumber, skin on

¼ cup chopped green onion

¼ cup sliced black olives

¼ cup diced red onion

⅔ cup light feta cheese, crumbled

1½ tsp grated lemon zest

¼ cup freshly squeezed lemon juice

2 Tbsp olive oil

1 tsp minced fresh garlic

1 tsp dried basil

½ tsp dried oregano

pinch freshly ground black pepper

⅓ cup chopped fresh basil or parsley

1. Bring the stock to a boil in a saucepan. Stir in the quinoa. Reduce the heat to medium-low, cover and cook for 15 minutes, or until the quinoa is tender and the liquid has been absorbed. Transfer to a large serving bowl and set aside to cool.

2. Add the red and green pepper, cucumber, green onion, olives, red onion and feta cheese to the cooled quinoa.

3. Whisk the lemon zest and juice, oil, garlic, dried basil, oregano and pepper in a small bowl. Pour the dressing over the quinoa mixture and toss to coat well. Garnish with fresh basil.

Jicama and Orange Salad with Ginger Dressing

Jicama (pronounced "heek-a-ma") is a round vegetable with a beige skin and crisp white flesh that tastes like a cross between an apple and a pear. It's a staple in Central American cuisine and is usually eaten raw. It's very low in calories. This is a visually beautiful salad.

2 cups peeled jicama sliced into strips
    ½ inch wide by 3 inches long
6 cups baby spinach
1 cup thinly sliced red bell pepper
½ cup thinly sliced red onion
1 large orange, peeled, membranes removed and cut into thin strips

4 tsp rice vinegar
1 Tbsp brown sugar

2 ½ tsp sesame oil
2 ½ tsp low-sodium soy sauce
1 ½ tsp olive oil
1 ½ tsp water
1 tsp minced fresh garlic
1 tsp minced fresh ginger

1 ½ tsp sesame seeds, toasted
¼ cup chopped cilantro or parsley

NUTRITIONAL ANALYSIS PER SERVING

Calories	137
Protein	2.9 g
Fat	3.9 g
Saturated Fat	0.5 g
Carbohydrates	24 g
Cholesterol	0 mg
Sodium	12 mg
Fiber	5.3 g

Prep Time: 20 minutes

Make Ahead:
Prepare salad and dressing early in the day and refrigerate; toss together just before serving

Serves 6

1. Place the jicama, spinach, red pepper, onion and orange slices in a large serving bowl.

2. Whisk the vinegar, sugar, sesame oil, soy sauce, olive oil, water, garlic and ginger together in a small bowl.

3. Pour the dressing over the salad and toss to combine. Garnish with sesame seeds and cilantro.

Oven-Roasted Caesar Potato Salad

NUTRITIONAL ANALYSIS
PER SERVING

Calories	174
Protein	4.3 g
Fat	7.3 g
Saturated Fat	1.1 g
Carbohydrates	23 g
Cholesterol	5 mg
Sodium	139 mg
Fiber	2 g

Prep Time: 15 minutes

Cook Time: 30 minutes

Make Ahead:
Prepare dressing and salad ingredients up to a day in advance and refrigerate. Toss salad with dressing and add garnishes just before serving.

Serves 6

This is the perfect potato salad when you're bored with the traditional mayonnaise-based version. Omit the prosciutto if you want to keep it meatless. If you can't find small potatoes, use larger ones and cut them into quarters before baking.

1 ¼ lb small red potatoes

1 large red onion, cut into 8 wedges

5 large cloves garlic, wrapped in foil

1 Tbsp freshly squeezed lemon juice

3 anchovies

1 tsp Dijon mustard

3 Tbsp Parmesan cheese

2 Tbsp light mayonnaise

2 Tbsp olive oil

3 Tbsp water

1 oz diced prosciutto

⅓ cup diced green onion

⅓ chopped fresh parsley

1. Preheat the oven to 425°F. Line a baking sheet with foil and spray with cooking oil.

2. Place the potatoes, onion wedges and garlic on the prepared baking sheet. Spray the potatoes and onion with cooking oil. Roast for approximately 25 minutes. Turn the onion and potatoes over and roast for another 5 minutes, until soft. Remove from the oven and set aside to cool.

3. When the vegetables are cool, cut the potatoes into quarters and dice the onions. Peel and chop the garlic. Place the roasted vegetables in a serving bowl.

4. Combine 2 Tbsp of the Parmesan cheese, mayonnaise, oil, water, lemon juice, anchovies and mustard in the bowl of a small food processor. Purée until smooth.

5. Toss the dressing with the salad. Garnish with the remaining 1 Tbsp cheese, prosciutto, green onion and fresh parsley.

Fresh Fig, Prosciutto and Goat Cheese Salad

I was served a salad similar to this at a formal dinner party and it inspired me to create this version. It's simple to make, yet the flavor combinations are outstanding and it presents beautifully. Be sure the figs are soft and ripe. For those who prefer not to eat meat, substitute smoked salmon for the prosciutto. Mesclun is sold as a salad mix at supermarkets, but you can use any lettuce you like.

4 cups mesclun

8 fresh black figs, each cut into 8 wedges

1 Tbsp olive oil

1½ tsp balsamic vinegar

1 oz prosciutto, chopped

¼ cup crumbled goat cheese

¼ cup chopped fresh basil or parsley

1. Place the mesclun and fig wedges in a bowl and drizzle with oil and vinegar. Mix until well coated.

2. Place on individual serving plates and scatter the prosciutto, cheese and basil overtop.

NUTRITIONAL ANALYSIS
PER SERVING

Calories	194
Protein	4.5 g
Fat	7.2 g
Saturated Fat	1.9 g
Carbohydrates	31 g
Cholesterol	9 mg
Sodium	218 mg
Fiber	4.6 g

Prep Time: 10 minutes

Serves 4

Edamame Salad

Edamame is all the rage today. These soy beans are a great source of protein, an excellent source of fiber and loaded with vitamins and minerals. You can eat them on their own or toss them into a salad.

3 cups frozen edamame beans

1 cup canned corn kernels, drained

½ diced water chestnuts

½ cup diced red bell pepper

¼ cup chopped green onions

¼ cup chopped cilantro

2 Tbsp low-sodium soy sauce

1½ Tbsp rice vinegar

1 tbsp sesame oil

2 tsp honey

1 tsp crushed garlic

½ tsp minced ginger

1 tsp toasted sesame seeds

NUTRITIONAL ANALYSIS PER SERVING

Calories	257
Protein	17 g
Fat	7.9 g
Saturated Fat	0.5 g
Carbohydrates	29 g
Cholesterol	0 mg
Sodium	398 mg
Fiber	3.6 g

Prep Time: 10 minutes

Cook Time: 8 minutes

Make Ahead:
This can be made a day in advance. It is best to add the cilantro just before serving.

Serves 4

1. Boil edamame beans just until bright green, approximately 3 minutes. Drain and rinse with cold water. Place in serving bowl.

2. In non-stick skillet sprayed with vegetable oil, sauté corn just until browned, approximately 5 minutes. Add to edamame along with water chestnuts, bell pepper, green onions and cilantro.

3. Mix soy sauce, rice vinegar, sesame oil, honey, garlic and ginger and pour over salad. Garnish with toasted sesame seeds.

Edamame Salad
Photo by Lorella Zanetti

Tabbouleh with Mint, Feta and Avocado

NUTRITIONAL ANALYSIS
PER SERVING

Calories	223
Protein	8.3 g
Carbohydrate	28 g
Fat	10 g
Saturated Fat	2.4 g
Cholesterol	5 mg
Sodium	258 mg
Fiber	8.2 g

Prep Time: 15 minutes

Cook Time: 15 minutes

Make Ahead:
Make up to a day in
advance, cover and
refrigerate.

Serves 6

Tabbouleh is a classic Middle Eastern dish made primarily with bulgar, parsley, garlic and mint. My version adds some new flavors and uses less oil than the traditional dish.

1 cup bulgar

1 cup water or stock

½ cup finely chopped red onion

1 cup diced cucumber

1½ cups diced plum tomatoes

2 green onions, thinly sliced

¼ cup pitted black olives

⅔ cup light feta cheese, crumbled

⅔ cup diced avocado

½ cup chopped fresh parsley

½ cup chopped fresh mint

¼ cup freshly squeezed lemon juice

2 Tbsp olive oil

2 tsp crushed fresh garlic

2 tsp minced jalapeño pepper, or to taste

1. Bring the water to a boil. Add bulgar, cover and remove from the heat and let sit for 15 minutes. Fluff with a fork, place in a serving bowl and set aside to cool.

2. Add the red onion, cucumber, tomatoes, green onions, olives, feta and avocado to the bulgar; mix well.

3. Combine the parsley, mint, lemon juice, oil, garlic, and jalapeño; pour over the bulgar mixture. Toss to mix well. Serve either at room temperature or chilled.

Orzo Soup with Caramelized Onions and Cheese

NUTRITIONAL ANALYSIS
PER SERVING

Calories	168
Protein	8 g
Fat	5 g
Saturated Fat	2 g
Carbohydrates	24 g
Cholesterol	10 mg
Sodium	290 mg
Fiber	1 g

Prep Time: 10 minutes

Cook Time: 35 minutes

Make Ahead:
Prepare onions and stock
a day in advance and
refrigerate. Reheat, add
and cook orzo; garnish
with cheese and parsley
just before serving.

Serves 6

French onion soup is a popular choice in restaurants, but the cheese topping contains a lot of fat and calories. Here's a great-tasting onion soup with orzo and a grating of Swiss cheese for flavor. The brown sugar enhances the natural sweetness of slow-cooked onions.

2 tsp vegetable oil

2 large white onions, thinly sliced

1 Tbsp packed brown sugar

2 tsp minced fresh garlic

6 cups vegetable or chicken stock

1 tsp dried thyme

⅔ cup orzo or other small pasta

pinch salt and freshly ground black
   pepper

½ cup shredded light Swiss or
   mozzarella cheese

3 Tbsp chopped fresh parsley

1. Spray a saucepan with cooking oil, add the vegetable oil and place over medium heat. Add the onions and sauté for 5 minutes. Stir in the brown sugar and garlic. Reduce the heat to medium-low and cook, uncovered, for 20 minutes, or until browned and tender, stirring occasionally.

2. Stir in the stock and thyme and bring to a boil. Add the pasta, salt and pepper and reduce the heat to medium. Cover and cook for 10 minutes or until the pasta is tender.

3. Ladle the soup into bowls and sprinkle evenly with the cheese and parsley. Serve immediately.

Gazpacho with Baby Shrimp

Gazpacho is always appreciated during the warmer months, and the baby shrimp add another dimension to this classic dish.

2 ½ cups tomato juice

4 tsp balsamic vinegar

2 tsp crushed fresh garlic

1 cup diced green bell pepper

1 cup diced red or yellow bell pepper

1 ¼ cups diced tomatoes

1 cup diced cucumber

1 cup chopped green onion

1 cup diced celery

¼ cup chopped cilantro or parsley

2 Tbsp chopped fresh basil

2 Tbsp freshly squeezed lemon juice

3 oz cooked baby shrimp

2 tsp minced jalapeño pepper or hot chili paste, to taste

pinch salt and freshly ground black pepper

2 Tbsp low-fat sour cream

1. Combine the tomato juice, vinegar and garlic in a large bowl.

2. Combine the bell pepper, tomatoes, cucumber, green onion and celery in a separate bowl and mix well. Add half the vegetable mixture to the bowl with the tomato juice. Purée the other half in a food processor or blender until smooth. Add to the bowl.

3. Add the cilantro, basil, lemon juice, shrimp, jalapeño, salt and pepper to the bowl. Stir gently to combine well. Refrigerate until completely chilled. To serve, garnish each bowl with a little sour cream.

NUTRITIONAL ANALYSIS PER SERVING

Calories	58
Protein	4 g
Fat	0.5 g
Saturated fat	0 g
Carbohydrates	11 g
Cholesterol	18 mg
Sodium	413 mg
Fiber	3 g

Prep Time: 20 minutes

Make Ahead:
Prepare up to a day in advance and refrigerate until serving time.

Serves 6

Curried Squash and Sweet Potato Soup

NUTRITIONAL ANALYSIS
PER SERVING

Calories	188
Protein	7 g
Fat	4 g
Saturated Fat	0.1 g
Carbohydrates	30 g
Cholesterol	2 mg
Sodium	200 mg
Fiber	4 g

Prep Time: 15 minutes

Cook Time: 25 minutes

Make Ahead:
Prepare up to 2 days in advance and refrigerate. Reheat over low heat, adding more stock if too thick.

Serves 4

Squash and sweet potatoes are both low-glycemic vegetables—that is, they raise your blood sugar level slowly so you stay full longer. To save time, try to find squash that's already peeled and cut.

2 tsp vegetable oil
1 tsp crushed fresh garlic
1 cup chopped onion
1 cup sliced mushrooms
1½ cups peeled, seeded and cubed butternut squash
1½ cups chopped peeled sweet potato

3¼ cups chicken stock
½ tsp ground ginger
1 tsp curry powder
2 Tbsp honey
¼ cup 2 percent evaporated milk
2 Tbsp low-fat yogurt or sour cream
¼ cup chopped cilantro or parsley

1. Spray a large non-stick saucepan with cooking oil, add the vegetable oil and place over medium-high heat. Add the garlic, onion and mushrooms and sauté until softened, approximately 5 minutes.

2. Add the squash, sweet potato, stock, ginger and curry powder. Reduce the heat, cover and simmer for 20 minutes, or until the vegetables are tender.

3. Transfer to a food processor and purée until creamy and smooth. Return to the saucepan. Stir in the honey and milk, blending well.

4. Ladle into individual bowls and garnish each serving with a dollop of yogurt and a sprinkle of cilantro.

Dill Carrot Soup

A well-made carrot soup is delicious and so simple you can prepare it any night of the week. I add some honey in case the carrots aren't that sweet, but taste and judge for yourself. The evaporated milk gives the texture of cream without the excess fat and calories.

2 tsp vegetable oil	1 cup peeled diced potatoes
2 tsp crushed fresh garlic	⅓ cup 2 percent evaporated milk
1 cup chopped onion	2 Tbsp honey
6 to 8 medium carrots, peeled and thinly sliced	pinch ground nutmeg
	¼ cup chopped fresh dill
3 ½ cups chicken stock	

1. Spray a non-stick skillet with cooking oil, add the vegetable oil and place over medium heat. Sauté the garlic and onion until softened, approximately 5 minutes. Add the carrots, stock and potatoes; cover and simmer for 25 minutes.

2. Transfer to a food processor and purée until smooth, working in batches if necessary.

3. Return to the saucepan and stir in the milk, honey, nutmeg and dill. Serve immediately.

NUTRITIONAL ANALYSIS PER SERVING

Calories	96
Protein	5 g
Fat	3 g
Saturated Fat	0.6 g
Carbohydrates	12 g
Cholesterol	2 mg
Sodium	220 mg
Fiber	3 g

Prep Time:	15 minutes
Cook Time:	30 minutes

Make Ahead:
Prepare up to 2 days in advance and refrigerate. Reheat over low heat, adding more stock if too thick.

Serves 6

Curried Carrot Orange Soup

NUTRITIONAL ANALYSIS
PER SERVING

Calories	119
Protein	2 g
Fat	1 g
Saturated Fat	0.1 g
Carbohydrates	26 g
Cholesterol	0 mg
Sodium	180 mg
Fiber	3 g

Prep Time: 15 minutes

Cook Time: 28 minutes

Make Ahead:
Prepare up to 2 days in advance and refrigerate. Reheat over low heat, adding more stock if too thick.

Serves 6

The curry adds an intriguing quality to this tasty vegetable soup. Use the juice from the orange you zest. The sweeter the carrots, the better tasting the soup. You can adjust the honey accordingly.

1 tsp vegetable oil

1½ tsp minced fresh garlic

1 tsp curry powder

1 cup chopped onion or sliced leeks

6 medium carrots, peeled and thinly sliced

3¾ cups vegetable or chicken stock

1 cup peeled diced sweet potato

2 tsp grated orange zest

½ cup freshly squeezed orange juice

2 Tbsp honey

⅓ cup chopped cilantro or parsley

1. Spray a non-stick saucepan with cooking oil, add the vegetable oil and place over medium heat. Add the garlic, curry and onion; cook until softened, about 3 minutes.

2. Add the carrots, stock and sweet potato. Bring to a boil, then reduce the heat to low. Cover and simmer for 20 to 25 minutes, until the vegetables are tender.

3. Transfer to a food processor or blender and purée, working in batches if necessary. Return to the saucepan and stir in the zest, juice and honey.

4. Ladle into individual bowls and garnish with cilantro.

Potato Cheddar Cheese Soup

The evaporated milk is what makes this soup creamy. For maximum flavor, use aged cheddar cheese.

1 tsp vegetable oil

1 tsp minced fresh garlic

1 cup chopped onion

3 ½ cups peeled diced potato

3 cups chicken stock

1 cup shredded light aged cheddar cheese

¼ cup 2 percent evaporated milk

1 tsp Dijon mustard

pinch salt

¼ tsp ground black pepper

⅓ cup chopped fresh parsley or dill

1. Spray a non-stick saucepan with cooking oil, add the vegetable oil and place over medium heat. Add the garlic and onion; cook until softened, about 4 minutes. Add the potatoes and stock. Bring to a boil, then reduce the heat to low. Cover and simmer until the potatoes are tender, about 20 minutes.

2. Transfer to a food processor or blender and purée, working in batches if necessary. Return the puréed soup to the saucepan.

3. Reserve 2 Tbsp of the cheese. Stir the remaining cheese, milk, mustard, salt and pepper into the soup. Simmer for 2 minutes or until the cheese melts. Garnish each bowl with parsley and a sprinkle of the reserved cheese.

NUTRITIONAL ANALYSIS PER SERVING

Calories	253
Protein	10 g
Fat	9 g
Saturated Fat	5 g
Carbohydrates	33 g
Cholesterol	25 mg
Sodium	357 mg
Fiber	3 g

Prep Time: 10 minutes

Cook Time: 26 minutes

Make Ahead:
Prepare up to a day in advance and refrigerate. Reheat gently over low heat, adding more stock if too thick.

Serves 4

Red and Yellow Bell Pepper Soup

Calories	99
Protein	3 g
Fat	2 g
Saturated Fat	0.2 g
Carbohydrates	19 g
Cholesterol	0 mg
Sodium	175 mg
Fiber	3 g

Prep Time: 15 minutes

Cook Time: 28 minutes

Make Ahead:
Roast peppers and refrigerate for up to 3 days or freeze for up to 4 months. Prepare soups early in the day, cover and refrigerate. Reheat in separate saucepans over low heat until warmed through.

Serves 6

This soup is so elegant and dramatic, yet simple to prepare. For a more intense flavor, add the cilantro before puréeing. To save time, purchase roasted peppers in a jar (just make sure they're packed in water).

2 tsp vegetable oil
2 tsp minced fresh garlic
1½ cups chopped onion
1¼ cups chopped carrot
½ cup chopped celery
4 cups chicken or vegetable stock
1½ cups peeled diced potato
freshly ground black pepper to taste
2 red bell peppers, roasted
2 yellow bell peppers, roasted
¼ cup chopped cilantro, dill or basil

1. Spray a non-stick saucepan with cooking oil, add the vegetable oil and place over medium heat. Add the garlic, onion, carrot and celery. Cook for 8 minutes or until the vegetables are softened, stirring occasionally.

2. Add the stock and potato. Bring to a boil, then reduce the heat to low. Cover and simmer for 20 to 25 minutes, or until the carrots and potatoes are tender.

3. Purée the red peppers in a food processor until smooth. Add half the soup mixture and process until smooth. Season with black pepper and pour into a serving bowl.

4. Rinse out the food processor. Purée the yellow peppers until smooth. Add the remaining soup to the yellow pepper purée and process until smooth. Season with black pepper and pour into another serving bowl.

5. To serve, ladle some of the red pepper soup into one side of an individual serving bowl while, at the same time, ladling some of the yellow pepper soup into the other side of the bowl. Garnish with a sprinkle of cilantro.

Roasting Bell Peppers

Cut bell peppers in half and remove ribs and seeds. Lay the peppers out on a baking sheet and place (6 inches) under the broiler for 15 to 20 minutes, turning several times until charred on all sides. Alternatively, you can use a barbecue on medium-high heat. Place in a bowl and cover tightly with plastic wrap; let cool and remove skin.

Red and Yellow Bell Pepper Soup
Photo by Mark Shapiro

Cauliflower, Leek and Spicy Sausage Soup

NUTRITIONAL ANALYSIS
PER SERVING

Calories	152
Protein	6 g
Fat	6 g
Saturated Fat	3 g
Carbohydrates	14 g
Cholesterol	16 mg
Sodium	389 mg
Fiber	2 g

Prep Time: 10 minutes

Cook Time: 35 minutes

Make Ahead:
Prepare up to a day ahead
and refrigerate. Reheat
gently over low heat before
serving, adding more
stock if too thick.

Serves 6

If hot spices aren't to your taste, use sweet sausage. Substitute broccoli for the cauliflower, if you like—both belong to the same vegetable family. Leeks can have a lot of soil hidden between the layers. To clean them, slice them in half lengthwise and wash under cold running water.

4 oz spicy sausage, chopped and casing removed
2 tsp vegetable oil
2 tsp minced fresh garlic
2 cups chopped leek
4 cups chicken stock
3 cups cauliflower florets
1 cup peeled diced potato

1. Spray a small non-stick skillet with cooking oil and sauté the sausage over medium heat just until browned and cooked through, approximately 5 minutes. Drain off the fat and set aside.

2. Spray a non-stick saucepan with cooking oil, add the vegetable oil and place over medium heat. Add the garlic and leek and cook for 5 minutes or until softened.

3. Add the stock, cauliflower and potato and bring to a boil. Cover, reduce the heat to low and simmer for 25 minutes, or until the potato is tender.

4. Transfer to a food processor and purée until smooth. Add the sausage and serve immediately.

Charred Corn, Wild Rice and Roasted Pepper Soup

When I began to sauté corn kernels, it was like I'd discovered a new vegetable! It tastes like corn right off the barbecue. I serve this soup all year round; it makes an elegant starter at a dinner party.

1 can (12 oz) corn kernels, drained, or 2 cups frozen corn, thawed

2 tsp vegetable oil

1 cup chopped onion

1½ tsp minced fresh garlic

4 cups vegetable or chicken stock

⅓ cup wild rice

1 cup peeled diced sweet potato

pinch salt and freshly ground black pepper

¾ cup 2 percent evaporated milk

2 Tbsp all-purpose flour

⅓ cup chopped roasted red bell pepper (see page 122)

⅓ cup chopped fresh basil or dill

1. Spray a large non-stick skillet with cooking oil and place over medium-high heat. Sauté the corn for about 8 minutes, until it is lightly charred. Set aside.

2. Spray large saucepan with cooking oil, add the vegetable oil and place over medium heat. Add the onion and garlic; sauté for 5 minutes, just until the onion is lightly browned.

3. Add the stock, rice, sweet potato, salt, pepper and corn. Cover and simmer for 30 minutes or just until the rice is tender.

4. Combine the milk and flour in a small bowl until smooth. Stir into the soup and add the red peppers. Simmer for 2 minutes or just until slightly thickened. Ladle into individual bowls and garnish with basil.

NUTRITIONAL ANALYSIS PER SERVING

Calories	197
Protein	8.5 g
Fat	3.4 g
Saturated Fat	0.8 g
Carbohydrates	29 g
Cholesterol	3.7 mg
Sodium	274 mg
Fiber	3.4 g

Prep Time: 10 minutes

Cook Time: 45 minutes

Make Ahead:
Prepare soup up to a day in advance, adding more stock if too thick.

Serves 6

Udon Noodle Soup with Chicken and Shrimp

Udon noodles are long, round noodles with a wonderfully dense texture. You can often find them prepackaged in the produce section of your supermarket or an Asian food shop. This soup is an all-time favorite—it's not only delicious, but also quick to make. To keep bean sprouts fresh longer, store them in water in the refrigerator.

4 oz skinless boneless chicken breast (about 1 breast), diced

2 tsp minced fresh ginger

2 tsp minced fresh garlic

6 cups chicken or beef stock

2 Tbsp low-sodium soy sauce

6 oz fresh udon noodles

2 cups sliced bok choy

½ cup sliced snow peas

8 oz raw shrimp, peeled, deveined and chopped

1 cup bean sprouts

2 large green onions, chopped

2 tsp sesame oil

3 Tbsp chopped cilantro or parsley

1. Spray a non-stick wok or large non-stick saucepan with cooking oil. Add the chicken and cook over medium-high heat for 4 minutes, or until the meat is barely cooked through. Add the ginger and garlic and cook for 1 minute. Set aside.

2. Bring the stock and soy sauce to a boil in a large saucepan. Add the noodles and return to a boil. Reduce the heat to medium-high and cook for 4 minutes, or until the noodles are tender. Add the bok choy, snow peas and shrimp. Cook for 2 minutes, or until the shrimp are pink and the snow peas are tender-crisp.

3. Add the chicken, bean sprouts and green onions. Cook just until heated through. Ladle into individual bowls and garnish each serving with a drizzle of sesame oil and a sprinkle of cilantro.

NUTRITIONAL ANALYSIS PER SERVING

Calories	207
Protein	12 g
Fat	7 g
Saturated Fat	2.1 g
Carbohydrates	23 g
Cholesterol	46 mg
Sodium	380 mg
Fiber	1 g

Prep Time: 15 minutes

Cook Time: 12 minutes

Make Ahead:
Prepare up to a day in advance and refrigerate. Reheat over low heat, adding garnish just before serving. Udon noodles do not freeze well.

Serves 6

Udon Noodle Soup with
Chicken and Shrimp
Photo by Mark Shapiro

Butternut Squash, Cinnamon and Ginger Soup

NUTRITIONAL ANALYSIS
PER SERVING

Calories	178
Protein	4.7 g
Fat	3.5 g
Saturated Fat	1.2 g
Carbohydrates	25 g
Cholesterol	5.1 mg
Sodium	97 mg
Fiber	6.1 g

Prep Time: 12 minutes

Cook Time: 23 minutes

Make Ahead:
Prepare soup up to
2 days in advance and
refrigerate. Reheat in
a saucepan over low
heat, adding more stock
if too thick.

Serves 6

Butternut squash, sweet, smooth and creamy, makes a soup that tastes like it's loaded with butter. Squash is also a low-glycemic food, which means it releases sugars slowly and helps to keep you feeling full longer. The molasses and spices give this soup its distinctive flavor. To save time, look for squash that's already peeled and chopped. Make sure to wash leeks well to remove all the dirt between the leaves. I cut and separate the leaves before washing.

2 tsp vegetable oil

1½ tsp minced fresh garlic

1½ cups sliced leek

5 cups peeled and diced butternut
   squash (about 1 large whole squash)

4 cups chicken stock

1 cup diced carrot

1 tsp ground cinnamon

½ tsp ground ginger

pinch salt and freshly ground black
   pepper

2 Tbsp molasses

2 Tbsp honey

3 Tbsp low-fat yogurt or sour cream

1. Spray a non-stick saucepan with cooking oil, add the vegetable oil and place over medium-low heat. Stir in the garlic and leeks. Cover and cook until softened, about 3 minutes.

2. Stir in the squash, stock, carrot, cinnamon, ginger, salt and pepper. Bring to a boil, then reduce the heat to medium-low. Cover and cook for 15 to 20 minutes, or until the vegetables are tender. Add the molasses and honey.

3. Transfer the soup to a food processor or blender. Purée until smooth, working in batches if necessary.

4. Ladle into individual bowls and garnish with a dollop of yogurt.

Green and Yellow Split Pea Soup

There is no better comfort food than split pea soup. There are many versions of this traditional soup in my cookbooks, so for this one I've combined both green and yellow split peas. The flavors are amazing and the texture is smooth as cream.

2 tsp vegetable oil	1 cup peeled diced potatoes
1 cup chopped onion	⅓ cup dried yellow split peas
1 cup chopped carrot	⅓ cup dried green split peas
1 cup chopped celery	pinch salt and freshly ground black
2 tsp minced fresh garlic	pepper
1 tsp Dijon mustard	¼ cup finely chopped green onion
4 ½ cups chicken or vegetable stock	¼ cup low-fat yogurt

1. Spray a non-stick saucepan with cooking oil, add the vegetable oil and place over medium-high heat. Add the onion, carrot, celery and garlic. Sauté for 8 minutes or until the vegetables are softened and starting to brown.

2. Stir in the mustard, stock, potatoes, yellow and green split peas, salt and pepper. Bring to a boil, then reduce the heat to medium-low. Cover and cook for 30 to 35 minutes or until the split peas are soft.

3. Transfer the soup to a blender or food processor and purée, working in batches if necessary.

4. Ladle into individual bowls and garnish with a sprinkle of green onion and a dollop of yogurt.

NUTRITIONAL ANALYSIS
PER SERVING

Calories	167
Protein	12 g
Fat	4.1 g
Saturated Fat	0.7 g
Carbohydrates	24 g
Cholesterol	0 mg
Sodium	275 mg
Fiber	8.1 g

Prep Time: 10 minutes

Cook Time: 43 minutes

Make Ahead:
Prepare up to 2 days in advance and refrigerate. Reheat in a saucepan over low heat, adding more stock if too thick.

Serves 6

Sweet Pea Soup

NUTRITIONAL ANALYSIS
PER SERVING

Calories	146
Protein	7.7 g
Fat	3.2 g
Saturated Fat	0.9 g
Carbohydrates	21.5 g
Cholesterol	4 mg
Sodium	215 mg
Fiber	5.4 g

Prep Time: 10 minutes

Cook Time: 20 minutes

Make Ahead:
Make up to 2 days in
advance and refrigerate.
Reheat gently over
low heat, adding more
stock if too thick.

Serves 6

Frozen peas allow you to enjoy the sweet, fresh flavor of this soup all year round. Chopped frozen onions, now sold in supermarkets, are handy if you're in a hurry. Keeping a jar of minced garlic in your refrigerator is also a good idea. I use double the amount I would if using fresh garlic since the purchased minced garlic is less intense.

2 tsp vegetable oil

1 cup chopped onion

1½ tsp minced fresh garlic

4 cups frozen green peas

3 cups chicken or vegetable stock

1 cup peeled diced potatoes

pinch salt and freshly ground black
    pepper

2 Tbsp low-fat sour cream

¼ cup chopped fresh mint or parsley

1. Spray a non-stick saucepan with cooking oil, add the vegetable oil and place over medium heat. Sauté the onion and garlic for 5 minutes or until the onion is soft and lightly browned.

2. Stir in the peas, stock, potatoes, salt and pepper. Bring to a boil, then reduce the heat to a simmer. Cover and cook for 15 minutes.

3. Transfer the soup to a blender or food processor and purée until smooth, working in batches if necessary.

4. Ladle into individual bowls and garnish with a dollop of sour cream and a sprinkle of mint.

Black Bean Soup

This creamy, rich-tasting soup is very nutritious. I like to serve it garnished with low-fat sour cream, diced plum tomatoes or a sprinkle of shredded cheddar cheese. If you can't find canned black beans, cook your own using the quick-soak method (see page 84). You'll need 1 cup of dried beans and they'll take about 40 minutes to cook.

2 tsp vegetable oil

1 cup chopped onion

1 cup chopped carrot

2 tsp minced fresh garlic

1 can (19 oz) black beans, drained
    and rinsed

2 ½ cups chicken or vegetable stock

½ tsp granulated sugar

¾ tsp cumin

¼ cup chopped cilantro or parsley

1. Spray a non-stick saucepan with cooking oil, add the vegetable oil and place over medium heat. Cook the onion, carrot and garlic, stirring occasionally, for 5 minutes, or until softened.

2. Set aside ½ cup of the black beans. Add the remaining beans, stock, sugar and cumin to the vegetable mixture. Bring to a boil, then reduce the heat to medium-low. Cover and cook for 15 minutes, or until the carrots are tender.

3. Purée the soup in a blender or food processor, working in batches if necessary. Return the purée to the saucepan. Stir in the reserved beans.

4. Ladle into individual bowls and garnish with chopped cilantro.

NUTRITIONAL ANALYSIS PER SERVING

Calories	140
Protein	8.2 g
Fat	3.2 g
Saturated Fat	0.2 g
Carbohydrates	25 g
Cholesterol	0 mg
Sodium	390 mg
Fiber	7.1 g

Prep Time: 10 minutes
Cook Time: 20 minutes

Make Ahead:
Make up to 2 days in advance and refrigerate. Reheat in a saucepan over low heat, adding more stock if too thick.

Serves 4

White Kidney Bean Purée with Prosciutto

NUTRITIONAL ANALYSIS
PER SERVING

Calories	205
Protein	12 g
Fat	3.8 g
Saturated Fat	0.2 g
Carbohydrates	31 g
Cholesterol	4 mg
Sodium	420 mg
Fiber	8 g

Prep Time: 5 minutes

Cook Time: 15 minutes

Make Ahead:
Prepare soup up to
2 days in advance and
refrigerate. Reheat over
low heat, adding more
stock if too thick. Garnish
just before serving.

Serves 6

This soup has a creamy texture without the fat and calories. You can substitute 2 ounces of smoked salmon or sautéed spicy or sweet sausage for the prosciutto.

2 tsp vegetable oil

1½ cups chopped onion

2 tsp chopped fresh garlic

2 cans (19 oz each) white kidney beans. drained and rinsed

2½ cups chicken stock

pinch freshly ground black pepper

1 oz prosciutto, chopped

2 Tbsp chopped fresh parsley

1. Spray a non-stick saucepan with cooking oil, add the vegetable oil and place over medium heat. Cook the onions and garlic, stirring occasionally, for 5 minutes, or until the onions are softened and begin to brown.

2. Reserve ½ cup of the beans. Add the remainder, along with the stock and pepper, to the pan. Bring to a boil, then lower the heat and simmer for 10 minutes.

3. Transfer the soup to a food processor or blender and purée, working in batches if necessary. Return to the saucepan and add the reserved ½ cup of beans and the prosciutto and heat to warm the beans. Garnish with parsley and serve immediately.

Pasta and Bean Soup (Fagioli)

This classic Italian soup is a medley of vegetables, beans and pasta. Serve it with some Italian bread for a wonderful lunch. The beans and pasta combine to make this soup a complete protein. Use any variety of beans you prefer, such as chickpeas, white kidney beans or white navy beans. If you like the taste of freshly cooked beans instead of canned, use the quick soak and cook method, (see page 84). Try adding a teaspoon of pesto as a garnish.

2 tsp vegetable oil
½ cup chopped onion
⅓ cup chopped carrot
⅓ cup chopped celery
2 tsp minced fresh garlic
3 ½ cups vegetable or chicken stock
1 can whole tomatoes (19 oz)
2 tsp granulated sugar
1 ½ tsp dried basil

1 tsp dried oregano
dash salt and freshly ground black
    pepper
3 cups canned red kidney beans, drained
    and rinsed
½ cup elbow macaroni or small shell
    pasta
3 Tbsp grated Parmesan cheese
¼ cup chopped fresh basil or parsley

1. Spray a large non-stick saucepan with cooking oil, add the vegetable oil and place over medium heat. Sauté the onions, carrots, celery and garlic for 5 minutes.

2. Stir in the stock, tomatoes, sugar, dried basil, oregano, salt, pepper and 2 cups of the beans. Mash the remaining 1 cup beans and stir into the mixture. Bring to a boil, crushing the tomatoes with the back of a spoon. Reduce the heat to a simmer and cook covered for 15 minutes, stirring occasionally.

3. Stir in the pasta. Cook for 5 to 8 minutes, until the pasta is tender but firm. Ladle into individual bowls and sprinkle with Parmesan and basil.

NUTRITIONAL ANALYSIS
PER SERVING

Calories	260
Protein	14 g
Fat	3.6 g
Saturated Fat	0.6 g
Carbohydrates	43 g
Cholesterol	2.5 mg
Sodium	638 mg
Fiber	13 g

Prep Time: 15 minutes
Cook Time: 28 minutes

Make Ahead:
Prepare the soup up to
the point of adding the
pasta and refrigerate for
up to 2 days. Bring to a boil,
add the pasta and cook,
adding more stock
if too thick. Garnish
before serving.

Serves 6

Tortilla, Sautéed Corn and Plum Tomato Soup

NUTRITIONAL ANALYSIS
PER SERVING

Calories	150
Protein	6.8 g
Fat	4.1 g
Saturated Fat	1.1 g
Carbohydrates	20 g
Cholesterol	4.1 mg
Sodium	375 mg
Fiber	4.3 g

Prep Time: 20 minutes

Cook Time: 22 minutes

Make Ahead:
Prepare up to a day
in advance, omitting the
garnishes. Reheat gently
over low heat and garnish
just before serving.

Serves 6

The garnishes for this soup make it a real Tex-Mex favorite, as well as a beautiful looking soup. It's a great starter to a main course of fajitas, burritos or quesadillas. I buy flavored tortillas in bulk and freeze them. To defrost, place the entire package in the microwave oven and heat on High for 30 seconds, or just until you can break away the number you need. Refreeze the remainder. The different colors add interest to any meal.

2 tsp vegetable oil

1 cup chopped onion

½ cup chopped green bell pepper

2 tsp minced fresh garlic

¾ cup canned corn kernels, drained

4 cups chicken or vegetable stock

¾ cup canned black beans, drained and rinsed

3 Tbsp basmati rice

1 tsp hot chili paste

1 cup diced plum tomatoes

¼ tsp salt and freshly ground black pepper

2 ½ tsp cornstarch

1 cup thinly sliced flavored flour tortillas

⅓ cup chopped cilantro or parsley

¼ cup low-fat sour cream

1. Spray a non-stick saucepan with cooking oil, add the vegetable oil and place over medium heat. Cook the onion, green pepper and garlic, stirring occasionally, for 5 minutes or until the onions are golden. Stir in the corn and cook for 5 minutes, or until the corn begins to brown.

2. Stir in the stock, black beans, rice and chili paste. Bring to a boil, reduce the heat to a simmer and cook for 12 minutes.

3. Add the tomatoes, cornstarch (dissolved in 1 Tbsp of water) and salt and pepper. Simmer for 2 minutes until slightly thickened.

4. Ladle the soup into individual bowls and garnish each serving with tortilla strips, fresh herbs and sour cream.

Tortilla, Sautéed Corn
and Plum Tomato Soup
Photo by Lorella Zanetti

Wild Mushroom and Barley Soup

NUTRITIONAL ANALYSIS
PER SERVING

Calories	173
Protein	6 g
Fat	3 g
Saturated Fat	0.3 g
Carbohydrates	33 g
Cholesterol	0 mg
Sodium	236 mg
Fiber	7 g

Prep Time: 10 minutes

Cook Time: 35 minutes

Make Ahead:
Prepare up to 2 days in
advance and refrigerate.
Reheat gently over
low heat, adding more
stock if too thick.

Serves 6

Oyster or cremini mushrooms are best, but if they're unavailable, you can substitute cultivated white mushrooms. Use pot barley if you prefer, but you will need to cook it longer (see page 89).

2 tsp vegetable oil	½ cup pearl barley
2 tsp minced fresh garlic	1½ tsp dried basil or thyme leaves
1 cup chopped onion	¼ tsp freshly ground black pepper
3½ cups vegetable or chicken stock	4½ cups wild mushrooms, sliced
1 can (19 oz) tomatoes, crushed	3 Tbsp chopped fresh basil or parsley

1. Spray a non-stick saucepan with cooking oil, add the vegetable oil and place over medium heat. Add the garlic and onions and cook for 4 minutes or until softened.

2. Stir in the stock, tomatoes, barley, dried basil and pepper. Bring to a boil, then reduce the heat to medium-low. Cover and simmer for 30 minutes, or until the barley is tender.

3. Meanwhile, spray a non-stick skillet with cooking oil and place over high heat. Cook the mushrooms, stirring frequently, for 8 minutes or until browned.

4. Stir the mushrooms into the soup. Ladle into individual bowls, sprinkle with fresh basil and serve immediately.

Lima Bean Soup with Sautéed Sausage

I don't often use lima beans in my cooking, but I found this soup has a great flavor—resembling split peas. Substitute any other canned bean of your choice.

4 oz spicy chicken or turkey sausage

2 tsp vegetable oil

1½ cups chopped onion

2 tsp crushed fresh garlic

½ cup chopped carrot

3½ cups vegetable or chicken stock

1 cup peeled diced potato

2½ cups canned lima beans, drained
  and rinsed

¼ cup chopped cilantro or parsley

1. Remove the sausage casings and crumble the meat. Spray a non-stick skillet with cooking oil and sauté the sausage over medium heat for approximately 5 minutes, or until cooked through and browned. Set aside.

2. Heat the oil in a non-stick saucepan over medium heat. Add the onion and garlic and sauté for 5 minutes, or just until lightly browned. Add the carrot and sauté for 3 minutes.

3. Add the stock, potato and 2 cups of the lima beans, reserving ½ cup for garnish. Bring to a boil, cover and simmer for 20 minutes.

4. Transfer the soup to the bowl of a food processor or blender and purée until smooth, working in batches if necessary. Return to the saucepan. Add the reserved ½ cup lima beans and the cooked sausage and return to the heat briefly to reheat. Garnish with cilantro just before serving.

NUTRITIONAL ANALYSIS
PER SERVING

Calories	196
Protein	10 g
Fat	5.9 g
Saturated Fat	1.1 g
Carbohydrates	26 g
Cholesterol	20 mg
Sodium	541 mg
Fiber	4.7 g

Prep Time: 10 minutes

Cook Time: 33 minutes

Make Ahead:
Prepare up to 2 days in advance and refrigerate. Reheat over low heat, adding more stock if too thick. Garnish just before serving.

Serves 6

Red Split Pea Soup

NUTRITIONAL ANALYSIS
PER SERVING

Calories	164
Protein	8.6 g
Fat	3.3 g
Saturated Fat	0.8 g
Carbohydrates	25 g
Cholesterol	2 mg
Sodium	190 mg
Fiber	8.3 g

Prep Time: 5 minutes

Cook Time: 20 minutes

Make Ahead:
Prepare up to 2 days in advance and refrigerate. Reheat over low heat, adding more stock if too thick. Garnish just before serving.

Serves 6

We tend to use green or yellow split peas in soups, but the red version has a distinct flavor that makes a nice change. They're readily available, but you can always substitute the other varieties.

2 tsp vegetable oil

1 cup chopped onion

⅔ cup chopped carrot

2 tsp chopped fresh garlic

3 cups chicken or vegetable stock

¾ cup dried red split peas

pinch freshly ground black pepper

¼ cup crumbled goat cheese

2 Tbsp chopped fresh parsley

1. Spray a non-stick saucepan with cooking oil, add the vegetable oil and place over medium heat. Cook the onion, carrot and garlic for 5 minutes, stirring occasionally, until the vegetables are softened and beginning to brown.

2. Add the stock, peas and pepper. Bring to a boil, then reduce the heat and simmer for 15 minutes. Transfer to a food processor or blender and purée until smooth, working in batches if necessary.

3. Ladle into individual bowls and garnish each serving with goat cheese and parsley.

Butternut Squash and Apple Purée

This combination of sweet and tart flavors is incredible. To save time, shop for squash that has been peeled and cubed.

2 tsp vegetable oil

2 cups chopped onion

2 tsp chopped fresh garlic

2 tsp chopped fresh ginger

3 ½ cups vegetable or chicken stock

2 lb butternut squash, peeled and cubed
    (approximately 6 ½ cups)

1 medium green apple, peeled and diced

⅓ cup apple juice concentrate

¼ tsp freshly ground black pepper

3 Tbsp low-fat sour cream

3 Tbsp chopped fresh parsley

1. Spray a non-stick saucepan with cooking oil, add the vegetable oil and place over medium heat. Cook the onion, garlic and ginger for 8 minutes, stirring frequently, until softened and beginning to brown.

2. Add the stock, squash, apple, apple juice concentrate and pepper. Bring to a boil, then reduce the heat and simmer for 15 minutes, or until the squash is tender.

3. Transfer to a food processor or blender and purée until smooth, working in batches if necessary.

4. Ladle into individual bowls and garnish with a dollop of sour cream and a sprinkle of parsley.

NUTRITIONAL ANALYSIS PER SERVING

Calories	112
Protein	3.2 g
Carbohydrates	22 g
Fat	1.9 g
Saturated Fat	0.4 g
Carbohydrates	22 g
Cholesterol	2 mg
Sodium	155 mg
Fiber	3.7 g

Prep Time: 15 minutes
Cook Time: 23 minutes

Make Ahead:
Prepare up to 2 days in advance and refrigerate. Reheat gently over low heat, adding more stock if too thick. Garnish just before serving.

Serves 8

Hoisin Glazed Salmon

This has to be the easiest and most delicious salmon dish you'll ever prepare. As an alternative to baking the salmon, grill it and serve the sauce overtop. I like to serve this alongside plain couscous, rice or rice noodles. The sauce in this dish is also wonderful with chicken or pork. I often make a triple batch and refrigerate or freeze it for later use.

¼ cup hoisin sauce

2 tsp low-sodium soy sauce

2 tsp sesame oil

1 tsp honey

1 tsp minced fresh garlic

½ tsp minced fresh ginger

four 4-oz skinless salmon fillets

2 tsp sesame seeds

3 Tbsp chopped fresh cilantro or parsley

1. Preheat the oven to 425°F. Stir the hoisin sauce, soy sauce, sesame oil, honey, garlic and ginger together in a bowl.

2. Place the salmon on a rimmed baking sheet. Spoon half the hoisin mixture over the salmon. Sprinkle with the sesame seeds. Bake in the center of the oven for 10 minutes per inch of thickness of fish, or until the fish flakes easily when pierced with a fork.

3. Garnish with cilantro and serve with the remaining sauce on the side.

Hoisin

Hoisin is a thick brown sauce made from soybeans, garlic, sugar, chili peppers, various spices and often sweet potatoes. It has a fairly strong flavor and is often combined with low-sodium soy sauce, sesame oil and some honey to make a great baste for fish, chicken or pork. Hoisin is available in the Asian section of supermarkets.

NUTRITIONAL ANALYSIS PER SERVING

Calories	232
Protein	24 g
Fat	11 g
Saturated Fat	1.7 g
Carbohydrates	9.2 g
Cholesterol	64 mg
Sodium	398 mg
Fiber	0.7 g

Prep Time: 5 minutes
Cook Time: 10 minutes

Make Ahead:
Prepare sauce up to 4 days in advance and refrigerate.

Serves 4

Salmon with Orange-Miso Glaze
Photo by Brian MacDonald

Salmon with Orange-Miso Glaze

You can either bake this fish or barbecue it on a cedar plank. The planks are available at fish stores, supermarkets or lumberyards. Presoak them in water for at least 8 hours to prevent burning. You can reuse the planks a couple of times.

2 Tbsp yellow miso	½ tsp grated orange peel
¼ cup orange juice concentrate	four 4-oz skinless salmon fillets
2 tsp low-sodium soy sauce	2 tsp sesame seeds
2 tsp sesame oil	3 Tbsp diced green onions
5 tsp brown sugar	2 Tbsp chopped cilantro

1. Preheat the oven to 425°F. Spray a baking sheet with cooking oil (or have ready a pre-soaked cedar plank and preheat the barbecue to high).

2. To make the glaze, combine the miso, orange juice, soy sauce, oil, sugar and orange peel in a small bowl.

3. Remove 2 Tbsp of the glaze and brush lightly over the salmon. Sprinkle with the sesame seeds.

4. Place the salmon on the prepared baking sheet or cedar plank and bake or grill for 10 minutes per inch of thickness of fish, or until the fish flakes easily when pierced with a fork.

5. Serve with the remaining sauce on the side. Garnish each serving with a sprinkling of green onions and cilantro.

Miso

Miso is a fermented soybean paste that comes in various colors and flavors; the lighter the color, the less pungent the taste. I like to use the milder yellow or white miso, but if you want a stronger flavor, try the red or brown variety. In the past it was a challenge to obtain miso paste, but today it can be found in major supermarkets, health food stores and Asian food stores.

NUTRITIONAL ANALYSIS PER SERVING

Calories	321
Protein	38 g
Fat	13 g
Saturated Fat	2.5 g
Carbohydrates	12 g
Cholesterol	77 mg
Sodium	551 mg
Fiber	0.6 g

Prep Time: 5 minutes

Cook Time: 10 minutes

Make Ahead:
Prepare sauce up to 2 days in advance and refrigerate. Salmon can be cooked up to a day before, refrigerated and served at room temperature.

Serves 4

Salmon Stuffed with Mixed Olives and Sun-Dried Tomatoes

Calories	386
Protein	37 g
Fat	13 g
Saturated Fat	2.2 g
Carbohydrates	7.5 g
Cholesterol	112 mg
Sodium	436 mg
Fiber	2.1 g

Prep Time: 10 minutes

Cook Time: 10 minutes

Make Ahead:
Prepare filling up to 3 days
in advance and refrigerate.

Serves 4

This olive and sun-dried tomato mixture is incredible with salmon, but it also goes well with halibut or sea bass. If you don't have both types of olives on hand, remember that green have a more intense flavor and black are milder. If you like, add some thinly sliced olives as a garnish. Serve over Sweet Potato Mash (page 279) with grilled vegetables on the side.

3 Tbsp chopped black olives

3 Tbsp chopped green olives

3 Tbsp chopped rehydrated sun-dried
    tomatoes (see page 221)

2 Tbsp seasoned breadcrumbs

2 tsp olive oil

1 tsp crushed fresh garlic

1 tsp Dijon mustard

four 4-oz skinless salmon fillets

3 Tbsp chopped fresh parsley or basil

1. Preheat the oven to 425°F. Spray a baking sheet with cooking oil.

2. Finely chop the olives, sun-dried tomatoes, breadcrumbs, oil, garlic and mustard, either by hand or using a small food processor.

3. Make a ¼-inch vertical slit through the top of each salmon fillet to within ¼ inch of each end. Divide the filling and stuff the fish. Bake in the center of the oven for 10 minutes per inch of thickness. Garnish with fresh parsley or basil.

Salmon Stuffed with Mixed Olives and Sun-Dried Tomatoes
Photo by Brian MacDonald

Honey-Nut Coated Salmon

NUTRITIONAL ANALYSIS
PER SERVING

Calories	293
Protein	23 g
Fat	13 g
Saturated Fat	2.7 g
Carbohydrates	21 g
Cholesterol	69 mg
Sodium	87 mg
Fiber	0.6 g

Prep Time:	5 minutes
Cook Time:	16 minutes

Make Ahead:
Prepare sauce up to
a day in advance and
refrigerate; reheat in a
skillet over low heat.

Serves 4

The pecan and maple syrup sauce gets thick and sticky—almost candy-like—upon cooling. If you like the sauce looser, heat it just before serving. Salmon has a higher fat content than other fish, but it contains good omega-3 fatty acids that help lower bad cholesterol.

3 Tbsp finely chopped pecans

3 Tbsp liquid honey

2 Tbsp maple syrup

2 tsp butter or margarine

½ tsp Dijon mustard

four 4-oz skinless salmon fillets

3 Tbsp chopped cilantro or fresh parsley

1. Heat the oven to 425°F. Spray a non-stick baking pan or grill pan with cooking oil.

2. Place the pecans in a small non-stick skillet and toast over medium-high heat for 3 minutes or until golden and fragrant. Stir in the honey, maple syrup and butter. Reduce the heat to low and cook for 3 minutes or until slightly thickened. Whisk in the mustard.

3. Grill or bake the salmon, cooking for 10 minutes per inch thickness of the fish, or until the fish flakes easily when pierced with a fork.

4. Serve the fish with the sauce overtop and garnish with cilantro.

Salmon over White and Black Bean Salsa

Use swordfish or tuna instead of salmon, if you like, or substitute other varieties of beans. If you'd like to cook your own beans instead of using the canned ones, 1 cup of dried beans yields 3 cups cooked. (See page 84.)

1 cup canned black beans, drained and
    rinsed
1 cup canned white kidney or navy
    beans, drained and rinsed
¾ cup chopped tomatoes
½ cup chopped green bell pepper
¼ cup chopped red onion
⅓ cup chopped fresh cilantro or basil

2 Tbsp white or red balsamic vinegar
2 Tbsp freshly squeezed lemon juice
1 Tbsp olive oil
1½ tsp minced fresh garlic
1 tsp hot chili paste, or to taste
1 lb salmon fillets
3 Tbsp chopped cilantro or basil

NUTRITIONAL ANALYSIS
PER SERVING

Calories	319
Protein	32 g
Fat	9 g
Saturated Fat	2 g
Carbohydrates	29 g
Cholesterol	56 mg
Sodium	313 mg
Fiber	9 g

Prep Time: 10 minutes
Cook Time: 10 minutes

Make Ahead:
Prepare the bean mixture
earlier in the day and
refrigerate. Bring to room
temperature before serving.

Serves 4

1. Preheat the barbecue to high, or set the oven to 425°F and line a baking sheet with foil sprayed with cooking oil.

2. To make the salsa, combine the black beans, white beans, tomatoes, green pepper, onion and cilantro. Whisk the vinegar, lemon juice, olive oil, garlic and chili paste together. Pour over the bean mixture and toss to combine.

3. Barbecue the fish, or bake uncovered in the center of the oven, for approximately 10 minutes for each inch of thickness, or until the fish flakes when pierced with a fork.

4. To serve, spoon the bean salsa on a plate or platter and place the fish overtop.

Salmon Teriyaki

This is the number-one choice for clients of my catering company. As an alternative, grill the fish and serve the sauce separately. Use the sauce over chicken as well.

¼ cup packed brown sugar

2 Tbsp low-sodium soy sauce

1 Tbsp water

2 Tbsp rice vinegar

2 tsp sesame oil

2 tsp cornstarch

2 tsp minced fresh garlic

1½ tsp minced fresh ginger

four 4-oz skin-on salmon fillets

2 tsp sesame seeds

3 Tbsp chopped cilantro or parsley

1. Preheat the oven to 425°F. Line a rimmed baking sheet with foil and spray with cooking oil.

2. Whisk the brown sugar, soy sauce, water, vinegar, oil, cornstarch, garlic and ginger together in a small saucepan. Cook over medium heat until thickened and smooth. Remove from the heat.

3. Place the salmon, skin-side down, on the prepared baking sheet. Spoon half the sauce over the salmon. Sprinkle with sesame seeds. Bake in the center of the oven for 10 minutes per inch thickness of fish, or until the fish flakes easily when pierced with a fork.

4. Garnish with cilantro and serve with the remaining sauce on the side.

NUTRITIONAL ANALYSIS PER SERVING

Calories	250
Protein	24 g
Fat	10 g
Saturated Fat	1.6 g
Carbohydrates	16 g
Cholesterol	64 mg
Sodium	323 mg
Fiber	0.3 g

Prep Time:	5 minutes
Cook Time:	13 minutes

Make Ahead:
Cook sauce up to 3 days in advance and refrigerate. Reheat in a small skillet over low heat just until warmed through.

Serves 4

Salmon Teriyaki
Photo by Lorella Zanetti

Salmon and Rice Wrapped with Banana Leaves in Black Bean Sauce

NUTRITIONAL ANALYSIS
PER SERVING

Calories	484
Protein	43 g
Fat	17 g
Saturated Fat	2.5 g
Carbohydrates	38g
Cholesterol	107 mg
Sodium	400 mg
Fiber	1.4 g

Prep Time: 15 minutes
Cook Time: 40 minutes

Make Ahead:
Prepare fish packets early
in the day and refrigerate.
Add an extra 5 minutes
to the cooking time.

Serves 4

One of my favorite dishes in Thai restaurants is fish wrapped in banana leaves. I experimented at home and found it was easy to do, and it's so dramatic looking! The leaves are available in many Asian stores and they can be frozen for later use.

½ cup brown rice

1½ cups chicken or fish stock

¼ cup packed brown sugar

¼ cup ketchup or sweet chili sauce

3 Tbsp black bean sauce

1 Tbsp rice vinegar

2 tsp sesame oil

1 tsp minced fresh garlic

1 tsp minced fresh ginger

four 8- by 8-inch banana leaves

four 4-oz skinless salmon fillets

1 Tbsp sesame seeds, toasted

¼ cup chopped fresh cilantro or parsley

1. Preheat the oven to 425°F. Line a baking sheet with foil and spray with cooking oil.

2. Combine the rice and stock in a small saucepan and bring to a boil. Cover and simmer for 25 minutes, just until the rice is cooked. Do not overcook. Remove from the heat and keep covered another 10 minutes. Drain any excess liquid and set aside to cool.

3. To make the sauce, whisk the brown sugar, ketchup, black bean sauce, vinegar, oil, garlic and ginger together in a small bowl.

4. Divide the rice among the banana leaves, placing it in the center of the leaf. Place a salmon fillet over the rice. Divide the sauce in half and pour half over the salmon pieces.

5. Fold the banana leaves around the salmon (tie with a thin strip of banana leaf) and place on the prepared baking sheet. Bake for approximately 15 minutes, or until the fish is just cooked. (You will have to open one packet to test for doneness; the fish should flake when pierced with a fork.)

6. To serve, open the banana leaves, drizzle with the remaining sauce and garnish with the sesame seeds and cilantro.

Orange Soy-Glazed Swordfish with Mushrooms

Wild mushrooms, especially the oyster mushrooms in this dish, are a special taste treat. Substitute any firm fish, such as tuna, orange roughy or halibut, for the swordfish.

2 Tbsp low-sodium soy sauce

2 Tbsp orange juice concentrate

2 Tbsp honey

2 Tbsp water

1 tsp minced fresh garlic

1 tsp minced fresh ginger

¾ tsp cornstarch

four 4-oz swordfish steaks

1 tsp vegetable oil

½ lb mushrooms, sliced

3 Tbsp finely chopped green onion

3 Tbsp chopped cilantro or parsley

1. Preheat the oven to 425°F. Spray a 9-inch baking dish with cooking oil.

2. To make the glaze, whisk the soy sauce, juice concentrate, honey, water, garlic, ginger and cornstarch together in a small saucepan. Bring to a boil, then simmer over medium heat until thickened, about 2 minutes.

3. Put the swordfish in a single layer in the prepared baking dish. Pour the sauce overtop and bake uncovered for 10 minutes per inch of thickness, or until the fish flakes easily when pierced with a fork.

4. While the fish bakes, heat the oil in a skillet sprayed with cooking oil. Add the mushrooms and cook over medium-high heat until browned, about 8 minutes.

5. Scatter the mushrooms over the fish. Garnish with green onions and cilantro.

NUTRITIONAL ANALYSIS
PER SERVING

Calories	201
Protein	24 g
Fat	6 g
Saturated Fat	1 g
Carbohydrates	13 g
Cholesterol	44 mg
Sodium	553 mg
Fiber	1 g

Prep Time: 10 minutes

Cook Time: 20 minutes

Make Ahead:

Prepare sauce up to a day in advance and refrigerate. Reheat andadd more water if too thick.

Serves 4

Swordfish with Mango Salsa

NUTRITIONAL ANALYSIS
PER SERVING

Calories	175
Protein	22 g
Fat	5 g
Saturated Fat	0 g
Carbohydrates	11 g
Cholesterol	43 mg
Sodium	101 mg
Fiber	2 g

Prep Time: 15 minutes

Cook Time: 10 minutes

Make Ahead:
Make salsa early in the
day and refrigerate.

Serves 6

Any firm fish will work with this recipe; try tuna or shark. The key to perfect fish is never to overcook it—fish is best when slightly undercooked. Parsley or dill can be substituted for the cilantro, and pineapple, papaya or peaches for the mango. The salsa is also delicious with chicken or pork.

six 4-oz swordfish steaks

1½ cups finely diced mango

¾ cup finely diced red bell pepper

½ cup finely diced green bell pepper

½ cup finely diced red onion

¼ cup chopped cilantro

2 Tbsp orange juice concentrate

1 Tbsp freshly squeezed lemon juice

2 tsp olive oil

1 tsp minced fresh garlic

½ tsp granulated sugar

1. Preheat the barbecue to high or set the oven to 425°F. Line a baking sheet with foil and spray with cooking oil.

2. Barbecue or bake the fish for 10 minutes per inch of thickness, or until it flakes easily when pierced with a fork.

3. While the fish is cooking, combine the mango, red and green peppers, onion, cilantro, juice concentrate, lemon juice, oil, garlic and sugar in a bowl. Mix thoroughly. Serve the fish with the salsa spooned overtop.

Swordfish with Mango Salsa ▶
Photo by Mark Shapiro

Pecan-Coated Swordfish with Lemon Sauce

NUTRITIONAL ANALYSIS
PER SERVING

Calories	341
Protein	27 g
Fat	15 g
Saturated Fat	3 g
Carbohydrates	17 g
Cholesterol	99 mg
Sodium	228 mg
Fiber	1 g

Prep Time:	10 minutes
Cook Time:	16 minutes

Serves 4

Nuts and fish make a great combination. Nuts contain a healthy fat, but the key is moderation, since they are high in calories. The trick to getting the nuts to adhere to the fish is chopping them finely. Try almonds or cashews instead of pecans and substitute tuna, shark, marlin or any firm white fish for the swordfish. Be careful not to overcook the fish or it will be dry (especially swordfish and tuna, which are easier to overcook than other fish).

½ cup pecans

2 Tbsp seasoned breadcrumbs

1 egg

3 Tbsp 2 percent milk

1 lb swordfish

2 tsp vegetable oil

⅔ cup fish or low-sodium chicken stock

2 Tbsp freshly squeezed lemon juice

4 tsp sugar

2 tsp cornstarch

1½ tsp grated lemon zest

2 Tbsp chopped fresh parsley

1. Preheat the oven to 425° F. Spray a 9-inch baking dish with cooking oil.

2. Place the pecans and breadcrumbs in the bowl of a small food processor and process until finely chopped. Transfer to a shallow bowl.

3. Whisk the egg and milk together in a shallow bowl. Dip the fish in the egg mixture, then coat with the pecan mixture.

4. Spray a large non-stick skillet with cooking oil. Add the vegetable oil and place over medium heat. Cook the fish until golden, about 2 minutes per side.

5. Place in the prepared baking dish. Bake uncovered in the center of the oven for 10 minutes per inch of thickness, or until the fish flakes easily when pierced with a fork.

6. While the fish bakes, whisk the stock, lemon juice, sugar, cornstarch and lemon zest together in a small saucepan. Cook over medium heat for approximately 2 minutes, or until the sauce thickens slightly.

7. Pour the sauce over the fish and sprinkle with the parsley.

Sole Rolled with Crab and Garlic Breadcrumbs

Sole is one of the few fish that is difficult to over bake. This is a plus for those intimidated by cooking fish. The tasty stuffing adds flavor to this delicate fish. Sole can be gently reheated the next day and still stay moist.

NUTRITIONAL ANALYSIS
PER SERVING

Calories	215
Protein	39 g
Fat	4.6 g
Saturated Fat	1.2 g
Carbohydrates	3.4 g
Cholesterol	109 mg
Sodium	354 mg
Fiber	0.6 g

4 oz crabmeat (or surimi)

2 Tbsp light mayonnaise

1 Tbsp freshly squeezed lemon juice

¼ cup chopped green onion

2 Tbsp chopped fresh dill or parsley

2 Tbsp seasoned breadcrumbs

1 tsp olive oil

½ tsp crushed fresh garlic

four 4-oz sole fillets

2 Tbsp chopped fresh dill or parsley

Prep Time: 10 minutes

Cook Time: 10 minutes

Make Ahead:
Prepare stuffing up to a day
in advance and refrigerate.

Serves 4

1. Preheat the oven to 425°F. Spray a baking dish with cooking oil.

2. To make the stuffing, combine the crabmeat, mayonnaise, lemon juice, green onion and dill or parsley in the bowl of a food processor. Pulse just until still chunky. Alternatively, finely chop by hand.

3. For the topping, combine the breadcrumbs, oil and garlic.

4. Divide the filling over the sole fillets. Roll them up and fasten with a toothpick. Sprinkle the crumb mixture overtop. Place in the prepared baking dish and bake in the center of the oven for 10 minutes or until fish flakes and is no longer opaque. Remove toothpicks.

5. Garnish with dill or parsley and serve immediately.

Surimi

Surimi is made from precooked fish, usually pollock and whiting, seasoned to imitate crab or lobster. It's a very economical alternative to these seafoods and is available in sticks and flakes. Surimi is a low-fat, low-cholesterol food with only 70 to 80 calories per 3 oz serving. It keeps for up to two months unopened in the refrigerator, and lasts about four days once unsealed. It's available fresh or frozen.

Grilled Tuna Niçoise

There's nothing tastier than a niçoise salad made with freshly seared tuna. The trick to properly searing tuna is to cook it on high heat for the time specified—and no more. If you're not going to eat immediately, place it in the refrigerator to stop the cooking process, otherwise the tuna will be overcooked. Instead of fresh tuna, you can use two small cans of flaked white tuna packed in water (not oil).

2 small red potatoes

1 cup green beans, trimmed, steamed, rinsed with cold water and cut into 2-inch pieces

½ cup diced cucumber

½ cup halved cherry tomatoes

⅓ cup diced red onion

¼ cup sliced black olives

⅓ cup chopped fresh dill

2 Tbsp olive oil

2 Tbsp freshly squeezed lemon juice

4 anchovies, minced

1 tsp crushed fresh garlic

½ tsp Dijon mustard

pinch salt and freshly ground black pepper

1 lb raw tuna

1. Boil the potatoes until tender, approximately 15 minutes. Drain, cool and dice. Place in a serving bowl. Add the steamed beans, cucumber, tomatoes, onion, olives and dill.

2. To make the dressing, stir the oil, lemon juice, anchovies, garlic, mustard, salt and pepper together until well mixed. Pour over the potato mixture. Place three-quarters of the potato mixture on a serving platter, leaving the remainder for garnish.

3. Heat a non-stick grill pan or barbecue to high and grill the tuna for approximately 1½ minutes per side for seared, or until done to your preference, but do not overcook. Place the tuna, either whole or sliced, over the potato mixture and scatter the reserved mixture overtop or along the side.

NUTRITIONAL ANALYSIS PER SERVING

Calories	353
Protein	42 g
Fat	10 g
Saturated Fat	1.8 g
Carbohydrates	21 g
Cholesterol	83 mg
Sodium	382 mg
Fiber	3.6 g

Prep Time:	15 minutes
Cook Time:	18 minutes

Make Ahead:
Prepare salad and dressing early in the day and refrigerate. Bring to room temperature before serving.

Serves 4

Grilled Tuna Niçoise
Photo by Lorella Zanetti

Tilapia with Cashew Crust

Calories	294
Protein	37 g
Fat	14 g
Saturated Fat	3 g
Carbohydrates	5.1 g
Cholesterol	85 mg
Sodium	143 mg
Fiber	0.6 g

Prep Time: 5 minutes

Cook Time: 10 minutes

Make Ahead:
Prepare the nut mixture
up to a day in advance,
cover and refrigerate.

Serves 4

I created this recipe for the Pickle Barrel restaurant chain in Toronto. It's a real winner for fish lovers. The mild taste of tilapia goes well with nuts, and this lemon-nut combination is outstanding. If you want to substitute another fish, try sole. Serve this over a bed of fresh grilled vegetables.

⅓ cup chopped toasted cashews

4 Tbsp grated Parmesan cheese

1 Tbsp olive oil

1 Tbsp freshly squeezed lemon juice

½ tsp crushed fresh garlic

four 4-oz tilapia fillets

3 Tbsp chopped fresh dill or basil

lemon wedges

1. Preheat the oven to 425°F. Line a baking sheet with foil and spray with cooking oil.

2. Place the cashews, cheese, oil, juice and garlic in the bowl of a food processor and process just until coarsely ground. Do not purée. Alternatively, finely chop by hand.

3. Place the fish on the prepared baking sheet and divide the nut mixture overtop, pressing it onto the fillets to help it adhere. Bake for 10 minutes per inch of thickness, or until the fish flakes when pierced with a fork. Garnish with the dill and lemon wedges.

Tilapia with Cashew Crust ▶
Photo by Brian MacDonald

Tilapia with Pineapple Mango Salsa

NUTRITIONAL ANALYSIS
PER SERVING

Calories	215
Protein	35 g
Fat	5.4 g
Saturated Fat	1.3 g
Carbohydrates	7.6 g
Cholesterol	85 mg
Sodium	91 mg
Fiber	0.8 g

Prep Time: 15 minutes

Cook Time: 10 minutes

Make Ahead:
Prepare salsa early in the day and refrigerate.

Serves 4

Tilapia is a mild-tasting fish that I like to serve with a tasty sauce or salsa. It's perfect for those who don't like strong-tasting fish. Substitute other fresh fruit of your choice, such as peaches, plums or nectarines. If you want a spicy flavor, add hot sauce to taste.

½ cup fresh diced pineapple

½ cup diced mango

3 Tbsp finely diced onion

3 Tbsp finely diced red bell pepper

3 Tbsp finely diced green bell pepper

¼ cup finely chopped cilantro or basil

1 Tbsp freshly squeezed lemon juice

2 tsp orange juice concentrate

2 tsp honey

2 tsp olive oil

four 4-oz tilapia fillets

1. Place the pineapple, mango, onion, red and green pepper, cilantro, lemon juice, orange juice concentrate, honey and oil in a bowl and mix to combine.

2. Spray a non-stick skillet or grill pan with cooking oil and heat to medium-high. Cook the tilapia for approximately 5 minutes per side, or just until it is no longer opaque and the fish flakes. Do not overcook.

3. Place the fish on a serving platter and spoon half the salsa overtop. Serve with the remaining salsa on the side.

Tilapia with Tomato, Olive and Cheese Topping

Tilapia is very popular—delicious and affordable—but you can use any firm white fish, such as halibut, snapper or haddock, with this tasty topping. When cooking fish with a topping, make sure you include the topping when calculating the thickness for baking times.

1 cup chopped plum tomatoes

½ cup shredded part-skim mozzarella
    cheese

¼ cup chopped black olives

¼ cup crumbled goat cheese

1 tsp minced fresh garlic

1 tsp dried basil

1 lb tilapia fillets

3 Tbsp chopped fresh basil or parsley

1. Preheat the oven to 425°F. Line a baking sheet with foil and spray with cooking oil.

2. Combine the tomatoes, mozzarella cheese, olives, goat cheese, garlic and basil in a bowl; mix well.

3. Place the tilapia on a rimmed baking sheet. Top with the tomato mixture. Bake for 10 minutes per inch of thickness of the fish and topping, or until the fish flakes easily when pierced with a fork. Garnish with the basil before serving.

Tilapia

Tilapia is a white-fleshed fish that is sometimes slightly pinkish in color. It is an excellent choice for grilling and broiling and is easily adapted to most types of cooking. This fish is very low in fat, free of saturated fat and high in protein. It's also an excellent alternative to other, over-fished species.

NUTRITIONAL ANALYSIS PER SERVING

Calories	198
Protein	27 g
Fat	8.5 g
Saturated Fat	3.6 g
Carbohydrates	3.3 g
Cholesterol	60 mg
Sodium	255 mg
Fiber	0.5 g

Prep Time: 10 minutes

Cook Time: 15 minutes

Make Ahead:
The topping can be prepared up to a day in advance and refrigerated.

Serves 4

Mussels with Tomatoes, Basil and Garlic
Photo by Brian MacDonald

Mussels with Tomatoes, Basil and Garlic

This simple and delicious mussel dish can be either an appetizer or a main meal. Serve it with a wholegrain French or Italian loaf to mop up the flavorful juices.

2 lb mussels in the shell

1½ tsp vegetable oil

¾ cup finely diced onion

¾ cup thinly sliced red bell pepper

½ cup thinly sliced zucchini (optional)

2 tsp crushed fresh garlic

1 can (14 oz) tomatoes, drained and chopped

⅓ cup dry white wine or fish stock

2 Tbsp tomato paste

1½ tsp dried basil

1 tsp dried oregano

⅓ cup chopped fresh basil or parsley

NUTRITIONAL ANALYSIS PER SERVING

Calories	108
Protein	10 g
Fat	2 g
Saturated fat	0 g
Carbohydrates	8 g
Cholesterol	22 mg
Sodium	351 mg
Fiber	2 g

Prep Time: 10 minutes

Cook Time: 20 minutes

Make Ahead:
Prepare sauce up to a day in advance and refrigerate. Bring to a boil and cook the mussels just before serving.

Serves 4

1. Discard any mussels that don't close when tapped. Scrub the mussels under cold water and pull off the beards. Set the mussels aside.

2. Spray a large non-stick saucepan with cooking oil, add the vegetable oil and place over medium-high heat. Add the onions, bell pepper, zucchini (if using) and garlic; sauté for 5 minutes. Add the tomatoes, wine, tomato paste, dried basil and oregano; cook on medium heat for 10 minutes, stirring occasionally until sauce thickens slightly.

3. Add the mussels. Cover and cook until the mussels are fully open, 4 to 5 minutes. Discard any that do not open.

4. Arrange the mussels in individual bowls and pour the sauce overtop. Garnish with the fresh basil.

Squid Rings with Creamy Tomato Dip

NUTRITIONAL ANALYSIS
PER SERVING

Calories	248
Protein	20 g
Fat	8 g
Saturated Fat	2 g
Carbohydrates	22 g
Cholesterol	257 mg
Sodium	399 mg
Fiber	1 g

Prep Time: 10 minutes

Cook Time: 8 minutes

Make Ahead:

Prepare breaded squid early in the day, cover and refrigerate; add 5 minutes to the baking time. Prepare sauce up to 48 hours in advance and refrigerate.

Serves 4

Instead of breadcrumbs, use crushed cornflake crumbs for a crunchier texture. Be sure not to overbake the squid or it will become rubbery. Undercooking it slightly is perfect.

12 oz cleaned squid, fresh or frozen (body only)

3 Tbsp all-purpose flour

1 egg

2 Tbsp low-fat milk

¾ cup seasoned breadcrumbs

¼ cup grated Parmesan cheese

1 tsp garlic powder

1 tsp chili powder

3 Tbsp light mayonnaise

1½ Tbsp tomato paste

1½ Tbsp low-fat yogurt

1½ Tbsp water

1 tsp minced fresh garlic

¾ tsp dried basil

3 Tbsp chopped fresh parsley

1. Preheat the oven to 425°F. Spray a baking sheet with cooking oil.

2. Cut entire squid crosswise into ½-inch-wide rings. Dust with the flour.

3. Whisk the egg and milk together in a shallow bowl. Combine the breadcrumbs, Parmesan cheese, garlic powder and chili powder in a shallow dish and mix well. Dip the squid rings in the egg mixture, then coat with the breadcrumb mixture. Place on the prepared baking sheet and bake in the center of the oven for 5 to 8 minutes, or until just done at the center and browned.

4. While the squid is cooking, make the dip by combining the mayonnaise, tomato paste, yogurt, water, minced garlic and basil. Garnish the squid with fresh parsley and serve with the tomato dip on the side.

Thai Seafood Stew

Serve this wonderful stew with a salad and a French baguette for dipping. You can substitute fish such as salmon, halibut, swordfish or tilapia for any of the seafood. Fish stock can be bought fresh or in powdered form, but clam juice is a great substitute. If you have neither, use low-sodium chicken stock. If you prefer, cut the lemon grass into larger pieces and remove it before serving. Be sure not to overcook this dish.

2 tsp vegetable oil

1 cup chopped onions

2 tsp minced garlic

2 cups chopped plum tomatoes

½ cup fish stock or clam juice

1 Tbsp fish sauce or oyster sauce

1 Tbsp packed brown sugar

1 stalk lemon grass, finely chopped,
    or 2 tsp grated lemon rind

16 mussels in the shell, scrubbed and
    debearded

8 oz peeled and deveined shrimp

8 oz scallops

½ cup light coconut milk

1 tsp Asian hot sauce

¼ cup chopped fresh cilantro or parsley

1. Spray a large non-stick saucepan with cooking oil, add the vegetable oil and place over medium heat. Add the onions and garlic and cook for 5 minutes, stirring occasionally.

2. Stir in the tomatoes, stock, fish sauce, brown sugar and lemon grass. Bring to a boil. Reduce the heat to a simmer, cover and cook for 5 minutes.

3. Stir in the seafood, cover and cook for 3 minutes, or just until the mussels open and the seafood is barely cooked. Do not overcook. Stir in the coconut milk and hot sauce; cook for 1 minute.

4. Sprinkle with cilantro and serve immediately.

NUTRITIONAL ANALYSIS PER SERVING

Calories	258
Protein	31 g
Fat	7.5 g
Saturated Fat	2.2 g
Carbohydrates	16 g
Sodium	435 mg
Cholesterol	123 mg
Fiber	2.1 g

Prep Time:	10 minutes
Cook Time:	15 minutes

Make Ahead:
Make the sauce up to a day in advance and refrigerate. Cook the seafood and finish the stew just before serving.

Serves 4

Light Coconut Milk

Light coconut milk is a delicious and healthy substitute for regular coconut milk. It has a creamy, smooth texture and flavor and contains 75 percent less fat and calories than regular coconut milk. It has 3 grams of fat per ¼ cup, whereas the same amount of regular coconut milk contains 11 grams.

Pesto Shrimp and Scallop Kabobs

Calories	229
Protein	25 g
Fat	11 g
Saturated Fat	2.3 g
Carbohydrates	5 g
Cholesterol	110 mg
Sodium	211 mg
Fiber	2.1 g

Prep Time: 10 minutes

Cook Time: 5 minutes

Make Ahead:
Prepare pesto up to 2 days
in advance and refrigerate.

Serves 4

These shellfish kabobs make a great appetizer or an entrée when served over rice or couscous. If shellfish isn't what you like, fish such as salmon and halibut are equally delicious. Feel free to use any combination of vegetables (as in photo). If you're using wooden skewers, soak them for at least 20 minutes in water before barbecuing.

8 oz medium scallops

8 oz peeled and deveined large shrimp

16 cherry tomatoes (or a combination of
   bell pepper and red onion)

1 cup packed fresh basil leaves

2 Tbsp grated Parmesan cheese

1 Tbsp toasted pine nuts

2 Tbsp light cream cheese

1 tsp minced fresh garlic

3 Tbsp low-sodium chicken stock or
   water

2 Tbsp olive oil

1. Thread the scallops, shrimp and tomatoes evenly onto 4 large or 8 small skewers.

2. To make the pesto, purée the basil, Parmesan, pine nuts, cream cheese, garlic, stock and oil in the bowl of a small food processor until smooth. Brush half the pesto over the kabobs.

3. Preheat a grill to high, or spray a non-stick skillet with cooking oil and place over high heat. Grill or sauté the kabobs on both sides just until cooked, about 5 minutes. Serve with the remaining pesto.

Pesto Shrimp and ▶
Scallop Kabobs
Photo by Brian MacDonald

Asian Crab and Shrimp Cakes

I love the traditional fried crab cakes served in restaurants, but are they ever high in calories and fat! Here I've used a combination of baby shrimp and crabmeat and sautéed them in a very small amount of oil. The low-fat mayonnaise sauce goes beautifully with these delicate cakes.

6 oz chopped crabmeat (or surimi, see page 155)

4 oz baby shrimp (cooked)

3 Tbsp light mayonnaise

2 Tbsp freshly squeezed lemon juice

¼ cup chopped green onion

¼ cup chopped cilantro

½ cup dry unseasoned breadcrumbs

1 large egg

1 tsp crushed fresh garlic

½ tsp crushed fresh ginger

1 tsp Dijon mustard

2 tsp vegetable oil

1 Tbsp light mayonnaise

2 Tbsp low-fat sour cream

1 tsp sesame oil

1 tsp low-sodium soy sauce

¼ cup finely diced red bell pepper

1. To make the cakes, combine the crabmeat, shrimp, mayonnaise, lemon juice, green onion, cilantro, breadcrumbs, egg, garlic, ginger and mustard in a food processor. Finely chop until the mixture just comes together. Don't purée. Alternatively, chop by hand.

2. Form into 6 cakes.

3. Spray a non-stick skillet with cooking oil. Add the vegetable oil and place over medium heat. Sauté the cakes for about 5 minutes per side, or just until browned and hot.

4. To make the sauce, combine the mayonnaise, sour cream, sesame oil and soy sauce in a serving bowl. Whisk until smooth.

5. Garnish the cakes with the diced red pepper and serve the sauce alongside.

NUTRITIONAL ANALYSIS PER SERVING

Calories	99
Protein	12 g
Fat	5.8 g
Saturated Fat	1.7 g
Carbohydrates	6.4 g
Cholesterol	91 mg
Sodium	384 mg
Fiber	0.6 g

Prep Time: 20 minutes

Cook Time: 10 minutes

Make Ahead:
Prepare the cakes to the cooking stage up to a day in advance and refrigerate. Sauté just before serving.

Serves 6

Asian Crab and Shrimp Cakes
Photo by Brian MacDonald

Shrimp with Plum Tomatoes, Feta and Basil

NUTRITIONAL ANALYSIS
PER SERVING

Calories	262
Protein	37 g
Fat	7.6 g
Saturated Fat	1.9 g
Carbohydrates	8.1 g
Cholesterol	277 mg
Sodium	490 mg
Fiber	2 g

Prep Time: 10 minutes

Cook Time: 6 minutes

Make Ahead:
Prepare tomato mixture
early in the day.

Serves 4

I like to use large-sized shrimp for this dish. The combination of flavors is great and this dish also has visual appeal. It's pretty enough to bring to the table in your best decorative serving dish.

1 ½ lb peeled and deveined shrimp

3 cups diced and seeded plum tomatoes

¼ cup chopped cilantro or parsley

1 ½ tsp crushed fresh garlic

1 tsp dried basil

½ tsp dried oregano

1 tsp minced jalapeño peppers or 1 tsp
  hot chili paste (or to taste)

pinch salt and freshly ground black
  pepper

½ cup crumbled light feta cheese

1 Tbsp olive oil

2 tsp freshly squeezed lemon juice

2 Tbsp chopped cilantro or basil

1. Preheat the oven to broil and spray an 8-inch baking dish with cooking oil. Preheat a non-stick grill pan or barbecue to medium-high.

2. Grill the shrimp for approximately 4 minutes, turning halfway through the cooking time. Do not overcook. Place in the prepared baking dish.

3. Combine the tomatoes, cilantro, garlic, dried basil, oregano, jalapeño pepper, salt and pepper. Mix well and pour over the shrimp. Sprinkle with the feta. Broil for 2 minutes or just until browned. Remove from the oven.

4. Combine the oil and lemon juice and drizzle over the top. Garnish with the cilantro and serve.

Olive, Feta and Parsley-Stuffed Chicken Breasts

NUTRITIONAL ANALYSIS
PER SERVING

Calories	254
Protein	33 g
Fat	8.2 g
Saturated Fat	2.3 g
Carbohydrates	12 g
Cholesterol	124 mg
Sodium	390 mg
Fiber	0.8 g

Prep Time: 15 minutes

Cook Time: 12 minutes

Make Ahead:
Prepare to the baking stage up to a day in advance and refrigerate. Bake just before serving, adding an extra 5 to 10 minutes to the baking time. You can also bake them a day in advance, refrigerate and serve at room temperature.

Serves 4

This savory stuffing is a delicious way to dress up boneless chicken breasts. The trick to enjoying olives is to have them in moderation. Although they contain heart-healthy monounsaturated fat, eating too many can raise your calorie intake.

4 skinless boneless chicken breasts (about 1 lb)

⅓ cup crumbled light feta cheese

3 Tbsp chopped fresh parsley

2 Tbsp chopped black olives

½ tsp dried basil

1 egg

2 Tbsp water (or low-fat milk)

½ cup dry seasoned breadcrumbs

2 tsp vegetable oil

1. Preheat the oven to 425°F. Spray a baking sheet with cooking oil.

2. Working with one at a time, place the chicken breasts between two sheets of waxed paper and pound to an even ¼-inch thickness.

3. Stir the feta, parsley, olives and basil together in a bowl. Place one-quarter of the mixture near the end of each chicken breast. Roll the chicken up and secure with toothpicks or small skewers.

4. Beat the egg and water together in a shallow bowl. Place the breadcrumbs on a plate.

5. Spray a large non-stick skillet with cooking oil, add the vegetable oil and place over medium-high heat. Dip each chicken roll in the egg mixture, then coat with the breadcrumbs. Brown the rolls, turning occasionally, for 3 minutes or until done on all sides. Transfer to the prepared baking sheet.

6. Bake for 12 to 14 minutes or until the chicken is cooked through and no longer pink in the center. Remove the toothpicks and serve whole or cut the rolls into medallions.

Chicken Bruschetta

I've always loved bruschetta in Italian restaurants, so I adapted the topping for chicken. It's outstanding and dramatic looking. The trick is not to overcook the tomato topping. If you prepare the chicken ahead of time, pop it in the oven for 10 minutes to warm it up before adding the bruschetta topping. Plum tomatoes are best, but if you have to use field tomatoes, seed them first to reduce the amount of liquid. You can replace the basil with fresh parsley or even cilantro.

4 skinless boneless chicken breasts (about 1 lb)

¼ cup all-purpose flour

1 egg

2 Tbsp low-fat milk

½ cup dry seasoned breadcrumbs

2 tsp vegetable oil

1½ cups diced plum tomatoes

¼ cup chopped green onion

1 Tbsp olive oil

1 tsp minced fresh garlic

pinch salt and freshly ground black pepper

3 Tbsp grated Parmesan cheese

¼ cup chopped fresh basil

NUTRITIONAL ANALYSIS PER SERVING

Calories	320
Protein	36 g
Fat	11 g
Saturated Fat	2.6 g
Carbohydrates	27 g
Cholesterol	123 mg
Sodium	300 mg
Fiber	2.4 g

Prep Time: 15 minutes

Cook Time: 11 minutes

Make Ahead:
Prepare chicken up to a day in advance, cover and refrigerate. Add the topping and cook just before serving.

Serves 4

1. Preheat the oven to 425°F. Line a baking sheet with foil and coat lightly with cooking oil.

2. Working with one at a time, place the chicken breasts between two sheets of waxed paper and pound to an even ½-inch thickness.

3. Place the flour on a plate. Beat the egg and milk together in a shallow bowl. Place the breadcrumbs on a separate plate.

4. Spray a large non-stick skillet with cooking oil, add the vegetable oil and place over medium-high heat.

5. Coat each flattened chicken breast in flour, dip in the egg mixture, then coat in the breadcrumbs. Cook for 3 minutes per side, or until browned and almost cooked through. Transfer to the prepared baking sheet.

6. Stir the tomatoes, onions, oil, garlic, salt and pepper together in a bowl. Spoon over the chicken breasts. Sprinkle with the Parmesan. Bake in the center of the oven for 5 minutes, or until the chicken is cooked through and the tomato topping is hot. Sprinkle the basil overtop and serve immediately.

Chicken Paella with Sausage, Shrimp and Mussels

NUTRITIONAL ANALYSIS PER SERVING

Calories	407
Protein	49 g
Fat	7.3 g
Saturated Fat	2.2 g
Carbohydrates	36 g
Cholesterol	139 mg
Sodium	624 mg
Fiber	3 g

Prep Time: 20 minutes

Cook Time: 45 minutes

Make Ahead:

Prepare early in the day up to where the seafood is added; cover and refrigerate. Reheat, add the seafood and cook just before serving. This can be frozen without mussels for up to 6 weeks.

Serves 6

This is my light version of paella. The key to this dish is the arborio rice, which gives it a wonderful, creamy texture.

12 oz skinless boneless chicken breast (about 3 breasts), cubed

3 Tbsp all-purpose flour

2 tsp vegetable oil

6 oz mild Italian sausage, cut into ½-inch pieces

1 cup chopped onion

2 tsp minced fresh garlic

1 cup chopped red bell pepper

1 cup chopped green bell pepper

1 cup short-grain arborio rice

2 ½ cups chicken stock

2 cups chopped plum tomatoes

2 tsp dried basil

1 tsp dried oregano

1 bay leaf

½ tsp crumbled saffron threads (optional)

pinch salt and freshly ground black pepper

6 oz peeled and deveined shrimp

12 mussels, scrubbed and beards removed

¼ cup chopped fresh parsley

1. Dust the chicken with flour. Lightly coat a large non-stick skillet with cooking oil, add the vegetable oil and place over medium-high heat. Brown the chicken on all sides, about 3 minutes. Remove from the pan and set aside.

2. Respray the pan with cooking oil. Add the sausage and cook over medium-high heat for 5 minutes, or until cooked through. Remove from the pan with a slotted spoon, draining as much fat as possible. Set aside.

3. Wipe out the pan and respray. Cook the onions and garlic over medium-high heat for 4 minutes, or until softened. Stir in the red and green peppers; cook for 3 minutes. Stir in the rice and cook for 1 minute. Add the sausage, chicken stock, tomatoes, basil, oregano, bay leaf, saffron (if using), salt and pepper. Bring to a boil. Cover, lower the heat to a simmer and cook for 25 minutes, stirring occasionally.

4. If the shrimp are large or jumbo, cut them in half. Add the shrimp, mussels and reserved chicken to the sausage mixture. Increase the heat to medium-high and cook for 5 minutes, or until the rice is soft and the mussels have opened. (If the rice begins to stick to the bottom, add another ½ cup stock.) Discard the bay leaf and any mussels that do not open. Distribute evenly among large individual bowls, garnish with parsley and serve immediately.

Chicken Paella with Sausage, Shrimp and Mussels
Photo by Brian MacDonald

Lemon Chicken with Nutty Coating

NUTRITIONAL ANALYSIS
PER SERVING

Calories	269
Protein	30 g
Fat	12 g
Saturated fat	2 g
Carbohydrates	15 g
Cholesterol	66 mg
Sodium	253 mg
Fiber	3 g

Prep Time: 10 minutes

Cook Time: 14 minutes

Make Ahead:
Prepare chicken up
to the cooking stage
a day in advance, cover and
refrigerate. Cook just before
serving, adding an extra
5 to 10 minutes to the
baking time. Prepare sauce
a day ahead and refrigerate;
reheat in a saucepan over
low heat, adding extra
stock if too thick.

Serves 4

Lemon chicken is a favorite, but in restaurants it's usually deep-fried and has excess salt—definitely not a healthy choice. My sautéed version has a coating of breadcrumbs and chopped almonds, cutting back the fat and calories. The lemon sauce goes beautifully with the chicken.

4 skinless boneless chicken breasts (about 1 lb)
½ cup dry breadcrumbs
¼ cup finely chopped almonds
pinch salt and freshly ground black pepper
1 egg
2 Tbsp water or low-fat milk

2 tsp vegetable oil
½ cup chopped mushrooms
½ cup chicken stock
2 Tbsp freshly squeezed lemon juice
1 tsp grated lemon rind
1 tsp cornstarch dissolved in 2 tsp water
1 tsp honey
3 Tbsp chopped fresh parsley

1. Working with one at a time, place the chicken breasts between 2 sheets of waxed paper and pound to an even ½-inch thickness.

2. Combine the breadcrumbs, nuts, salt and pepper in the bowl of a small food processor and process until finely ground. (The finer the nuts, the better they will stick to the chicken.) Place on a plate. Whisk the egg and water or milk together in a shallow bowl.

3. Dip the chicken into the egg mixture, then coat well with the breadcrumb mixture.

4. Spray a non-stick skillet with cooking oil, add the vegetable oil and place over medium heat. Sauté the chicken until browned on both sides and no longer pink inside, approximately 8 minutes. Place in a serving dish, cover and keep warm.

5. Spray the same skillet with cooking oil and sauté the mushrooms until softened, approximately 3 minutes. Add the stock, lemon juice, rind, dissolved corstarch and honey and reduce the heat to low.

6. Simmer for 3 minutes, until the liquid is reduced and the sauce thickened.

7. Pour the sauce over the chicken and garnish with parsley.

Chicken and Eggplant Parmesan

Eggplant, a healthy vegetable, is often loaded with fat and calories from the amount of oil used in frying or sautéing. This baked version omits the oil, and it turns out great! Purchase fresh young eggplant; when overripe, it becomes bitter. If the skin doesn't spring back when pressed, then it's too old.

1 egg

2 Tbsp water or low-fat milk

¾ cup dry seasoned breadcrumbs

3 Tbsp chopped fresh parsley

1 Tbsp grated Parmesan

1 tsp minced fresh garlic

4 crosswise slices of eggplant, skin on, approximately ½ inch thick

4 skinless boneless chicken breasts (about 1 lb)

2 tsp vegetable oil

½ cup tomato-based pasta sauce

⅓ cup shredded part-skim mozzarella cheese

1. Preheat the oven to 425°F. Spray a baking sheet with cooking oil.

2. Whisk the egg with the water in a small bowl. Combine the breadcrumbs, parsley, parmesan and garlic on a plate, mixing well. Dip the eggplant in the egg mixture, then coat with the breadcrumb mixture. Place on the prepared pan. Bake, turning once, for 20 minutes or until tender.

3. While the eggplant is baking, prepare the chicken. Working with one at a time, place the chicken breasts between two sheets of waxed paper and pound to an even ¼-inch thickness. Spray a large non-stick skillet with cooking oil, add the vegetable oil and place over medium-high heat. Dip the chicken in the egg mixture, then coat with the remaining breadcrumb mixture. Cook the chicken, turning once, for 4 minutes or until golden brown and almost cooked through.

4. Spread 1 Tbsp of the tomato sauce on each baked eggplant slice. Place a chicken breast on top of each eggplant slice. Spread another 1 Tbsp tomato sauce on each chicken piece. Sprinkle with mozzarella cheese. Bake for 5 minutes, or until the cheese is golden and the chicken fully cooked.

NUTRITIONAL ANALYSIS PER SERVING

Calories	312
Protein	37 g
Fat	8.4 g
Saturated Fat	2.8 g
Carbohydrates	22 g
Cholesterol	129 mg
Sodium	450 mg
Fiber	2.7 g

Prep Time:	10 minutes
Cook Time:	29 minutes

Make Ahead:

Cook the eggplant and chicken early in the day and refrigerate. Bake just before serving, adding an extra 5 minutes to the baking time.

Serves 4

Chicken Supreme Stuffed with Sun-Dried Tomatoes and Goat Cheese

NUTRITIONAL ANALYSIS
PER SERVING

Calories	328
Protein	59 g
Fat	6.5 g
Saturated Fat	2.9 g
Carbohydrates	6.3 g
Cholesterol	143 mg
Sodium	302 mg
Fiber	1.9 g

Prep Time: 5 minutes

Cook Time: 30 minutes

Make Ahead:
Stuff chicken up to a day in advance, wrap well and refrigerate. Bake an extra 10 minutes.

Serves 4

Chicken supreme refers to a boneless breast of chicken with the wing tip attached. It's often served this way at more formal dinners. If your supermarket or butcher doesn't have this cut, you can just use a boneless chicken breast. The stuffing is the surprise when you slice into this tender chicken. Cook it with the skin on to retain moisture, but remove the skin before eating.

½ cup rehydrated sun-dried tomatoes (see page 221)
½ cup crumbled goat cheese
½ tsp dried basil
4 chicken supremes
3 Tbsp chopped fresh basil or parsley

1. Preheat the oven to 400°F. Spray a baking sheet with cooking oil.

2. Finely chop the sun-dried tomatoes, goat cheese and dried basil by hand, or place in the bowl of a small food processor and chop briefly, just until still slightly coarse.

3. Make a horizontal slit about 2 inches long through each chicken supreme to make a pocket. Stuff each chicken evenly with the cheese mixture and secure with a toothpick.

4. Spray a non-stick skillet or grill pan with cooking oil and heat over medium-high heat.

5. Sear the chicken on both sides until browned, about 5 minutes. Place on the prepared baking sheet and bake for about 25 minutes, until the internal temperature reaches 170°F and the meat is no longer pink in the center. Don't overcook. Garnish with basil or parsley.

Chicken Satay with Hoisin, Oyster and Apricot Glaze

I like to serve these chicken skewers over a pilaf of rice or couscous. Be sure to divide the sauce in half before brushing over the chicken to avoid any transfer of bacteria. You can substitute peach jam for the apricot if you prefer.

¼ cup apricot jam

1 Tbsp oyster sauce

3 Tbsp hoisin sauce

1 lb skinless boneless chicken breasts

2 tsp sesame seeds, toasted

3 Tbsp chopped fresh parsley or cilantro

1. If using wooden skewers, soak 12 medium skewers in water for 20 minutes. Spray a barbecue or non-stick grill pan with cooking oil and preheat to hot.

2. For the sauce, combine the jam, oyster sauce and hoisin sauce by hand. Divide into 2 equal portions, one for basting the skewers and the other to serve with the cooked satays.

3. Cut the chicken into 12 strips about 4 inches long and 1 inch wide. Thread the chicken strips on the skewers. Brush one portion of the sauce over the satays. Grill for about 3 minutes per side, until the chicken is no longer pink in the center.

4. Serve with the remaining portion of sauce on the side.

NUTRITIONAL ANALYSIS PER SERVING

Calories	208
Protein	27 g
Fat	2.7 g
Saturated Fat	0.6 g
Carbohydrates	18 g
Cholesterol	66 mg
Sodium	305 mg
Fiber	0.9 g

Prep Time: 5 minutes

Cook Time: 6 minutes

Make Ahead:
Make sauce up to 2 days in advance and refrigerate. Bring to room temperature before serving.

Serves 4

Pesto-Stuffed Chicken Rolls

This delicious, elegant and simple dish is one of my favorites for entertaining. The rolls can be left whole, sliced in half or cut into medallions. Making your own lower-fat pesto (see page 342) is always preferable, but for this small amount the store-bought version is fine. Buy roasted red peppers packed in water, not oil, or make your own (see page 122).

4 skinless boneless chicken breasts
(about 1 lb)
2 Tbsp light cream cheese, softened
1 Tbsp pesto
2 Tbsp chopped, roasted red pepper

1 egg
2 Tbsp water or low-fat milk
½ cup seasoned breadcrumbs
2 tsp vegetable oil

1. Preheat the oven to 425°F. Line a baking sheet with foil and spray with cooking oil.

2. Working with one at a time, place the chicken breasts between two sheets of waxed paper and pound to an even ¼-inch thickness.

3. Stir the cream cheese and pesto together in a small bowl until smooth. Divide the mixture among the chicken breasts, spreading it thinly over the surface. Scatter the red pepper overtop. Starting at the short end, roll up each chicken breast and secure with a toothpick or small skewer.

4. Beat the egg and water together in a shallow bowl. Place the breadcrumbs on a plate.

5. Spray a large non-stick skillet with cooking oil, add the oil and place over medium-high heat. Dip each chicken roll in the egg mixture, then coat in the breadcrumbs. Cook, turning occasionally, for 3 minutes or until well browned on all sides. Transfer to the prepared baking sheet.

6. Bake for 12 to 14 minutes, or until the chicken is cooked through and no longer pink in the center. Remove the toothpicks and serve whole or slice the rolls into medallions.

NUTRITIONAL ANALYSIS PER SERVING

Calories	242
Protein	31 g
Fat	7.8 g
Saturated Fat	1.9 g
Carbohydrates	12 g
Cholesterol	123 mg
Sodium	369 mg
Fiber	0.8 g

Prep Time:	15 minutes
Cook Time:	15 minutes

Make Ahead:
Prepare to the baking stage up to a day early, cover and refrigerate; bake just before serving, adding an extra 5 to 10 minutes to the baking time. Prepare a day early, refrigerate and bring to room temperature before serving.

Serves 4

Pesto-Stuffed Chicken Rolls
Photo by Lorella Zanetti

Chicken Fagioli

NUTRITIONAL ANALYSIS PER SERVING

Calories	316
Protein	33 g
Fat	7 g
Saturated Fat	1 g
Carbohydrates	31 g
Cholesterol	92 mg
Sodium	538 mg
Fiber	8 g

Prep Time: 10 minutes

Cook Time: 40 minutes

Make Ahead:
Make up to a day in advance (reserving the Parmesan and fresh basil garnish), cover and refrigerate. Reheat over low heat in a covered skillet for about 10 minutes. Garnish just before serving.

Serves 4

The tomato sauce, beans and herbs give this dish a true Mediterranean flavor. Use different types of beans for variety. This is even better the next day when the tastes have combined.

2 tsp vegetable oil

4 medium chicken quarters cut into legs and thighs

¼ cup all-purpose flour

2 tsp minced fresh garlic

½ cup chopped onion

⅓ cup chopped carrots

⅓ cup chopped celery

1½ cups canned red kidney beans, drained and rinsed

1 cup canned tomato purée

¾ cup chicken stock

2 tsp dried basil

2 tsp chili powder

1½ tsp brown sugar

1½ tsp dried oregano

2 bay leaves

¼ tsp dried chili flakes, or to taste

¼ cup chopped fresh basil or parsley

2 Tbsp grated Parmesan cheese

1. Spray a large non-stick skillet with cooking oil, add 1 tsp of the vegetable oil and place over high heat. Dust the chicken with the flour and brown on all sides, about 6 minutes. Set the chicken aside and pour off any excess fat from pan. Wipe the skillet clean and respray.

2. Place the skillet over medium heat and add the remaining 1 tsp of oil. Cook the garlic, onion, carrots and celery, stirring frequently, for 5 minutes or until softened.

3. Mash ½ cup of the kidney beans; add the mashed and whole beans, tomato purée, stock, dried basil, chili powder, brown sugar, oregano, bay leaves and chili flakes to the skillet. Bring to a boil, then reduce the heat to medium-low.

4. Add the browned chicken, cover and cook for 30 minutes, or until the juices run clear when the legs are pierced at the thickest point. Turn the chicken a couple of times during cooking and stir occasionally.

5. Garnish with fresh basil and Parmesan cheese. (Remove the skin before eating.)

Chicken with Rice, Green Olives and Tomato Sauce

This is a fantastic one-dish meal that's great for the family or even for entertaining. It's got all the elements of a well-balanced meal, with protein, rice and vegetables. You can substitute wild rice and brown rice, or use a combination; just increase the stock to 2 cups.

3 tsp vegetable oil

4 medium chicken quarters cut into thighs and drumsticks

¼ cup all-purpose flour

2 tsp minced fresh garlic

1½ cups chopped onion

1½ cups chopped green bell peppers

1 cup white rice

1 can (19 oz) tomato purée

1¾ cups chicken stock

½ cup sliced stuffed green olives

1 Tbsp drained capers

2 tsp dried basil

2 tsp chili powder

1½ tsp dried oregano

1 bay leaf

¼ cup chopped fresh parsley or cilantro

NUTRITIONAL ANALYSIS PER SERVING

Calories	422
Protein	34 g
Fat	10 g
Saturated Fat	2 g
Carbohydrates	76 g
Cholesterol	92 mg
Sodium	564 mg
Fiber	8 g

Prep Time: 10 minutes

Cook Time: 36 minutes

Make Ahead:
Prepare the dish a day in advance, cover and refrigerate. It's great reheated in a 300°F oven for 15 minutes or until warm.

Serves 4

1. Preheat the oven to 400°F. Spray a 13- by 9-inch baking dish with cooking oil.

2. Spray a large non-stick skillet with cooking oil, add 2 tsp of the vegetable oil and place over medium heat. Dust the chicken with the flour. Brown on all sides, about 6 minutes.

3. Transfer to the prepared baking dish.

4. Remove the fat from the skillet, wipe it clean and respray with cooking oil.

5. Heat the remaining 1 tsp oil over medium heat. Add the garlic, onion and green pepper and cook, stirring frequently, for 4 minutes or until softened.

6. Stir in the rice, tomatoes, stock, olives, capers, basil, chili powder, oregano and bay leaf.

7. Bring to a boil, cook for 1 minute and pour over the chicken. Cover tightly with foil and bake for 30 minutes, stirring a couple of times, until the juices run clear when the leg is pierced at the thickest point and the rice is tender. Remove the skin and bay leaf before eating. Garnish with parsley or cilantro.

Lemon Chicken on a Bed of Red Peppers and Snow Peas

NUTRITIONAL ANALYSIS
PER SERVING

Calories	290
Protein	29 g
Fat	10 g
Saturated Fat	1 g
Carbohydrates	20 g
Cholesterol	66 mg
Sodium	31 mg
Fiber	2 g

Prep Time: 15 minutes

Cook Time: 11 minutes

Make Ahead:
Prepare sauce early in the day and reheat in a saucepan over low heat, adding a little water if too thick.

Serves 4

This is a beautiful looking dish. If you substitute vegetables, try to keep the contrasting colors. You can replace the chicken with turkey, veal or pork scaloppini. Serve this with a fragrant basmati rice.

4 skinless boneless chicken breasts (about 1 lb)

¼ cup all-purpose flour

2 tsp vegetable oil

1½ cups thinly sliced red peppers

1½ cups sugar snap peas or halved snow peas

⅔ cup chicken stock

2 Tbsp freshly squeezed lemon juice

4 tsp granulated sugar

1 Tbsp cornstarch

1½ tsp sesame oil

1½ tsp grated lemon zest

½ tsp minced fresh garlic

3 Tbsp chopped fresh parsley

1. Working with one at a time, place the chicken breasts between sheets of waxed paper and pound to an even ¼-inch thickness. Dust with flour.

2. Spray a large non-stick skillet with cooking oil, add 1 tsp of the vegetable oil and heat to medium-high. Sauté the chicken until browned on both sides and just cooked, approximately 6 to 8 minutes. Cover with foil to keep warm.

3. Spray a large non-stick skillet with cooking oil, add the remaining 1 tsp of vegetable oil and heat to medium. Sauté the red peppers and peas until tender-crisp, about 3 minutes.

4. Place in a serving dish and arrange the chicken on top.

5. Combine the stock, lemon juice, sugar, cornstarch, sesame oil, lemon zest and garlic in a saucepan, whisking to blend. Bring to a boil and cook over medium heat for 2 to 3 minutes, or until thickened.

6. Drizzle some of the sauce over the chicken. Sprinkle with parsley. Serve the extra sauce on the side.

Chicken with Roasted Pepper and Prosciutto

You can serve these chicken breasts whole or, for a pretty presentation, slice them crosswise into medallions and fan them out on the plate. If prosciutto is unavailable, use thin slices of smoked ham. For a more intense flavor, use a stronger-tasting cheese, such as Swiss.

4 skinless boneless chicken breasts (about 1 lb)

1 oz sliced prosciutto (4 thin slices)

½ cup grated part-skim mozzarella cheese

1 small roasted red pepper (see page 122), cut into strips, or ½ cup store-bought roasted peppers

1 egg

2 Tbsp water or low-fat milk

½ cup dry seasoned breadcrumbs

2 tsp vegetable oil

NUTRITIONAL ANALYSIS PER SERVING

Calories	225
Protein	34 g
Fat	6 g
Saturated Fat	1.6 g
Carbohydrates	14 g
Cholesterol	78 mg
Sodium	350 mg
Fiber	0 g

Prep Time:	15 minutes
Cook Time:	18 minutes

Make Ahead:
Pan-cook chicken breasts early in the day, cover and refrigerate. Bake just before serving, adding 5 minutes to the baking time.

Serves 4

1. Preheat the oven to 425°F. Spray a baking sheet with cooking oil.

2. Working with one at a time, place the chicken breasts between sheets of waxed paper and pound to an even ¼-inch thickness.

3. Divide the prosciutto slices among the flattened chicken breasts. Sprinkle the grated cheese over top and finish with the roasted pepper strips. Starting at the short end, carefully roll the breasts up tightly. Secure the roll with a toothpick.

4. Whisk the egg with the water or milk in a small bowl. Put the breadcrumbs on a plate. Dip each chicken roll in the egg mixture, then in breadcrumbs.

5. Spray a non-stick skillet with cooking oil, add the vegetable oil and place over high heat. Brown the chicken on all sides, turning often, about 3 minutes.

6. Transfer to the prepared baking sheet and bake for 15 minutes, just until cooked through and no longer pink in the center. Remove the toothpicks before serving. Serve whole or sliced.

Chicken with Avocado Tomato Salsa

NUTRITIONAL ANALYSIS
PER SERVING

Calories	255
Protein	27.3 g
Fat	10.6 g
Saturated Fat	1.7 g
Carbohydrates	12.5 g
Cholesterol	65.8 mg
Sodium	96 mg
Fiber	2.7 g

Prep Time: 15 minutes

Cook Time: 5 minutes

Make Ahead:
Prepare salsa early in
the day and refrigerate,
covered closely to prevent
avocado from blackening.
Stir before serving.

Serves 4

I love to serve this chicken outdoors in the summer or at a Sunday brunch. The salsa is fresh tasting, and the contrasting colors are beautiful. For a more formal dinner, make this with chicken supreme, the breast with wing attached, removing the skin before eating. A student gave me a great tip to prevent avocados from going brown. Before cutting the avocado and without piercing it, heat on High in a microwave for 30 seconds. It truly works! Serve the chicken alongside grilled vegetables.

4 skinless boneless chicken breasts
   (about 1 lb)
3 Tbsp cornstarch
1 Tbsp vegetable oil

1 cup chopped plum tomatoes
½ cup diced avocado

3 Tbsp chopped cilantro
1 Tbsp olive oil
2 tsp freshly squeezed lime
   or lemon juice
1 tsp minced fresh garlic
½ tsp liquid honey
½ tsp hot sauce

1. Working with one at a time, place the chicken breasts between sheets of waxed paper and pound to an even ½-inch thickness. Dust with cornstarch.

2. Spray a non-stick skillet with cooking oil, add the vegetable oil and place over medium-high heat. Cook the chicken, turning once, for 5 to 8 minutes, or until no longer pink at the center. Place on a serving dish.

3. To make the salsa, combine the tomatoes, avocado, cilantro, olive oil, juice, garlic, honey and hot sauce.

4. Spoon the salsa over the chicken before serving.

Chicken with Avocado Tomato Salsa
Photo by Brian MacDonald

Phyllo Chicken and Spinach Bake

Calories	390
Protein	23 g
Fat	17 g
Saturated Fat	6 g
Carbohydrates	35 g
Cholesterol	88 mg
Sodium	350 mg
Fiber	2 g

Prep Time: 15 minutes

Cook Time: 31 minutes

Make Ahead:
Prepare to the baking
stage early in the day and
refrigerate. Bake just before
serving, adding 10 minutes
to the baking time.

Serves 6

To produce the ½ cup of spinach called for in this recipe, cook 3 cups of fresh spinach (or ½ package of frozen), drain and squeeze well to remove excess moisture. Ground beef or veal can replace the chicken.

2 Tbsp all-purpose flour

1 cup 2 percent evaporated milk

¾ cup chicken stock

1½ tsp Dijon mustard

⅔ cup grated light cheddar cheese

1 tsp vegetable oil

1 tsp minced fresh garlic

¾ cup finely chopped onion

¾ cup finely chopped mushrooms

12 oz lean ground chicken

1 egg

½ cup cooked, squeezed spinach, chopped

⅓ cup seasoned breadcrumbs

pinch salt and freshly ground black pepper

10 sheets phyllo pastry

1. Preheat the oven to 375°F. Spray a 13- by 9-inch baking dish with cooking oil.

2. Combine the flour, milk and stock in a saucepan and whisk until combined. Bring to a boil, then reduce the heat to a simmer. Cook until the sauce thickens, stirring constantly, approximately 3 minutes. Stir in the mustard and cheese and remove from the heat.

3. Spray a non-stick skillet with cooking oil, add the vegetable oil and place over medium heat. Add the garlic, onions and mushrooms; cook, stirring, for 3 minutes, or until softened. Add the chicken and cook for 5 minutes or until no longer pink, stirring to break it up. Drain off any excess liquid.

4. Whisk the egg in a medium bowl. Add the spinach, breadcrumbs, salt and pepper. Add the cheese sauce and mix well.

5. Place 2 sheets of phyllo pastry in the prepared baking dish, one on top of the other. Spray with cooking oil. Add 2 more sheets and spray again. Add one more sheet and spread the filling overtop. Continue adding phyllo, spraying every 2 sheets. Spray the top sheet and tuck in the edges. Bake for 20 to 25 minutes in the center of the oven, until the phyllo is nicely browned. Serve immediately.

Almond Chicken Breasts with Creamy Tarragon Mustard Sauce

Finely chopped almonds add delicious flavor and texture to these chicken breasts. The light mayonnaise and sour cream give the texture of a cream-based sauce without the excess calories and fat. Try other nuts, such as cashews or pecans, or substitute veal or turkey scaloppini for the chicken. Serve with steamed broccoli and Potato Wedge Fries (see page 268).

4 skinless boneless chicken breasts
  (about 1 lb)
⅓ cup finely chopped almonds
½ cup seasoned breadcrumbs
1 egg
2 Tbsp water or low-fat milk
2 tsp vegetable oil

¼ cup light mayonnaise
¼ cup low-fat sour cream
1 tsp Dijon mustard
1 tsp dried tarragon
3 Tbsp chopped fresh tarragon
  or parsley

1. Working with one at a time, place the chicken breasts between sheets of waxed paper and pound to an even ¼-inch thickness.

2. Finely grind the nuts and breadcrumbs in the bowl of a small food processor. (The finer the nuts the better they will adhere to the chicken.) Whisk the egg with the water in a shallow bowl.

3. Spray a non-stick skillet with cooking oil, add the vegetable oil and heat to medium. Dip the chicken in the egg mixture, then coat with the crumb mixture. Cook for 3 minutes on each side, or until browned and no longer pink at the center.

4. While the chicken is cooking, combine the mayonnaise, sour cream, mustard and tarragon in a small saucepan. Whisk over low heat until just warm.

5. To serve, drizzle the sauce over the chicken and garnish with tarragon.

NUTRITIONAL ANALYSIS
PER SERVING

Calories	304
Protein	32 g
Fat	12 g
Saturated Fat	2 g
Carbohydrates	16 g
Cholesterol	70 mg
Sodium	360 mg
Fiber	1 g

Prep Time:	15 minutes
Cook Time:	5 minutes

Make Ahead:
Bread chicken breasts
and prepare sauce early in
the day; refrigerate. Cook
chicken and reheat sauce
just before serving.

Serves 4

Chicken Breasts with Creamy Goat Cheese Sauce

NUTRITIONAL ANALYSIS
PER SERVING

Calories	347
Protein	41 g
Fat	14 g
Saturated Fat	4.3 g
Carbohydrates	12 g
Cholesterol	156 mg
Sodium	270 mg
Fiber	1.1 g

Prep Time: 15 minutes

Cook Time: 3 minutes

Make Ahead:
Prepare the sauce a day in advance and refrigerate; bring to room temperature before serving. Flatten and bread the chicken ahead of time, wrap well and refrigerate. Add an extra 10 minutes to baking time if chilled.

Serves 4

This has the taste and texture of a rich, cream-based sauce but without the fat and calories. Goat cheese is a lower fat cheese with intense flavor. Serve the chicken with Lemon Couscous with Cherry Totmatoes, Mint, Dill and Feta (page 252) and some steamed broccoli.

¼ cup goat cheese
2 Tbsp light cream cheese
2 Tbsp water
2 tsp olive oil
2 tsp freshly squeezed lemon juice
½ tsp crushed fresh garlic
3 Tbsp finely chopped fresh dill
  or parsley

4 large skinless boneless chicken breasts
  (about 1½ lb)
1 large egg
2 Tbsp milk
½ cup dry seasoned breadcrumbs
2 tsp vegetable oil

1. Place the goat cheese, cream cheese, water, olive oil, juice and garlic in the bowl of a small food processor and purée until smooth. Stir in 2 Tbsp of the chopped dill.

2. Working with one at a time, place the chicken breasts between sheets of waxed paper and pound to an even ½-inch thickness.

3. Whisk the egg and milk together in a small bowl. Spread the breadcrumbs on a plate. Dip the chicken in the egg mixture, then coat with the crumb mixture.

4. Spray a non-stick skillet with cooking oil, add the vegetable oil and place over high heat.

5. Sauté the chicken breasts, turning once, for approximately 3 to 5 minutes, until browned on both sides and no longer pink in the center.

6. Place on a serving platter and pour the goat cheese sauce over top. Garnish with the remaining 1 Tbsp chopped dill.

Chicken with Pistachio Pesto

Pistachio nuts instead of the traditional pine nuts give a great taste and color to this pesto. You can find shelled pistachios in the bulk food department, or you can shell them yourself. Serve this chicken alongside Couscous with Raisins and Dates (page 255). Grilled asparagus goes well with these flavors.

¼ cup shelled pistachios

½ cup fresh basil leaves, well packed

1 small clove garlic

2 Tbsp olive oil

1 Tbsp freshly squeezed lemon juice

4 skinless boneless chicken breasts (about 1 lb)

¼ cup all-purpose flour

2 tsp vegetable oil

1. Purée the pistachios, basil, garlic, olive oil and lemon juice in a small food processor until smooth. If the mixture is too thick, add a little water.

2. Working with one at a time, place the chicken breasts between sheets of waxed paper and pound to an even ½-inch thickness. Dust the chicken with flour.

3. Spray a large non-stick skillet with cooking oil, add the vegetable oil and place over high heat. Sauté the chicken for 3 to 5 minutes, or until it is lightly browned on both sides and no longer pink in the center.

4. Place on individual plates and serve with a dollop of pesto on top

NUTRITIONAL ANALYSIS PER SERVING

Calories	344
Protein	37 g
Fat	17 g
Saturated Fat	2.7 g
Carbohydrates	8.9 g
Cholesterol	94 mg
Sodium	84 mg
Fiber	1.3 g

Prep Time: 10 minutes

Cook Time: 3 minutes

Make Ahead:
Prepare pesto the day before, cover and refrigerate.

Serves 4

Chicken Morsels with Rice Noodles and Sesame Sauce

This stir-fry is outstanding with rice noodles, but it's also good over rice, couscous or linguini. Chicken thighs are more tender and flavorful than the breast, but you can use either. Dipping the chicken in the soy and cornstarch mixture keeps it very moist.

1 lb skinless boneless chicken thighs, diced
1 Tbsp low-sodium soy sauce
1 Tbsp cornstarch
2 tsp vegetable oil

½ cup chicken stock
2 Tbsp rice vinegar
3 Tbsp low-sodium soy sauce
2 Tbsp brown sugar
2 Tbsp molasses
1 Tbsp cornstarch

2 tsp sesame oil
1 tsp hot chili paste (or to taste)

6 oz medium rice noodles (¼ inch wide)
1½ cups thinly sliced red or yellow bell pepper
1½ cups thinly sliced snow or sugar snap peas
⅓ cup chopped cilantro or parsley
2 tsp sesame seeds, toasted
fresh bean sprouts and chopped red onion (optional)

NUTRITIONAL ANALYSIS PER SERVING

Calories	317
Protein	40 g
Fat	11 g
Saturated Fat	2 g
Carbohydrates	16 g
Cholesterol	148 mg
Sodium	506 mg
Fiber	1.9 g

Prep Time:	15 minutes
Cook Time:	11 minutes

Make Ahead:
Prepare the sauce up to a day in advance, cover and refrigerate.

Serves 4

1. For the chicken, place the diced chicken, soy sauce and cornstarch in a bowl; stir until well combined. Add oil to a large non-stick wok and place over medium heat. Sauté the chicken for 4 minutes, until almost cooked. Remove from the pan and set aside. Wipe out the pan.

2. For the sauce, combine the stock, vinegar, soy sauce, sugar, molasses, cornstarch, sesame oil and chili paste in a small bowl; stir until well combined.

3. Cook the noodles in boiling water for 2 minutes or just until tender. Drain and set aside.

4. Respray the wok with cooking oil and place over medium heat. When hot, add the bell peppers and peas. Sauté for 2 minutes, then stir in the sauce and chicken. Cook, stirring, for about 1 minute, until the sauce has thickened. Add the rice noodles and heat thoroughly, about 2 minutes. Serve on a large platter garnished with cilantro or parsley and sesame seeds. Scatter bean sprouts and onion overtop, if desired.

◄ Chicken Morsels with Rice Noodles and Sesame Sauce
Photo by Brian MacDonald

Chicken Thighs with Coconut Curry and Orange Sauce

NUTRITIONAL ANALYSIS PER SERVING

Calories	418
Protein	35 g
Fat	17 g
Saturated Fat	4 g
Carbohydrates	30 g
Cholesterol	113 mg
Sodium	267 mg
Fiber	2.7 g

Prep Time: 20 minutes

Cook Time: 31 minutes

Make Ahead:
Prepare the coconut sauce and yogurt topping a day in advance, cover and refrigerate.

Serves 4

The coconut milk and curry pair beautifully with the richer taste of chicken thighs, but you can also use boneless breast. This is a mild curry; if you prefer a more intense taste, increase the curry powder and/or pepper or chili paste. Serve alongside brown rice or rice noodles.

4 skinless boneless chicken thighs (about 1 lb)
¼ cup all-purpose flour
2 tsp vegetable oil
3 cups sliced onion
1½ cups sliced red bell pepper

1 cup light coconut milk
3 Tbsp orange juice concentrate
2 tsp brown sugar
2 tsp fish or oyster sauce

1 tsp curry powder
1½ tsp crushed fresh garlic
2 tsp minced fresh ginger
2 tsp minced, seeded jalapeño peppers
    or 1½ tsp chili paste (or to taste)

½ cup finely diced red onion
½ cup low-fat yogurt
3 Tbsp chopped cilantro or parsley
1 Tbsp freshly squeezed lemon juice

1. Dust the chicken with flour. Spray a large non-stick skillet with cooking oil, add the vegetable oil and place over medium heat. Sauté the chicken for 4 minutes per side, or until nicely browned. Add the sliced onion and sauté until lightly browned, about 8 minutes. Add the bell pepper and cook for 4 more minutes.

2. To make the sauce, combine the coconut milk, juice concentrate, sugar, fish sauce, curry, garlic, ginger and jalapeno in a bowl, mixing well. Add to the chicken mixture, reduce the heat to low and cover. Simmer for 15 minutes, until the chicken is cooked through, turning it halfway through the cooking time.

3. Combine the diced red onion, yogurt, cilantro and lemon juice in a small serving bowl. Place the chicken in a serving dish and serve the yogurt mixture alongside.

Chicken Breasts Stuffed with Portobello Mushrooms and Green Olives

Use any type of wild mushroom you like for this dish. The earthy mushrooms and intensely flavored green olives make a fantastic taste combination. I like to serve this with Smashed Potatoes (page 272) and steamed asparagus. The chicken also tastes great at room temperature and makes an attractive lunch or buffet item.

1½ lb chopped portobello mushrooms

⅓ cup sliced green olives

2 Tbsp seasoned breadcrumbs

1 Tbsp freshly squeezed lemon juice

1 tsp crushed fresh garlic

pinch freshly ground black pepper

4 large skinless boneless chicken breasts
  (approximately 1½ lb)

1 egg

2 Tbsp low-fat milk or water

½ cup seasoned breadcrumbs

2 tsp vegetable oil

¼ cup chopped cilantro or parsley

1. Preheat the oven to 425°F. Spray an 8-inch square baking dish with cooking oil.

2. Spray a non-stick skillet with cooking oil. Sauté the mushrooms over medium heat for 8 minutes, or until tender and browned.

3. Combine the mushrooms, olives, breadcrumbs, juice, garlic and pepper in the bowl of a food processor and finely chop (or chop by hand).

4. Working with one at a time, place the chicken breasts between sheets of waxed paper and pound to an even ¼-inch thickness.

5. Spread the mushroom mixture over the chicken breasts. Roll them up tightly and fasten with toothpicks.

6. Whisk the egg with the milk or water in a shallow bowl. Place the breadcrumbs on a plate. Dip the rolls in the egg mixture, then coat with the breadcrumbs.

7. Spray a large non-stick skillet with cooking oil, add the vegetable oil and place over medium heat. Add the chicken and brown on all sides, about 5 minutes. Place in the prepared baking dish and cook for 10 minutes, or until the chicken is no longer pink in the center.

8. Serve whole or slice into medallions. Garnish with the cilantro.

NUTRITIONAL ANALYSIS PER SERVING

Calories	317
Protein	40 g
Fat	9.5 g
Saturated Fat	2 g
Carbohydrates	16 g
Cholesterol	148 mg
Sodium	306 mg
Fiber	1.9 g

Prep Time: 15 minutes

Cook Time: 23 minutes

Make Ahead:
Prepare and bread the chicken rolls a day in advance and refrigerate; sauté and bake just before serving, adding 10 minutes to the baking time. If serving at room temperature, bake the day before, refrigerate and bring to room temperature before serving.

Serves 4

Turkey Scaloppini with Apricot and Dried Cherry Salsa

Most supermarkets now sell boneless turkey breast, which is leaner than chicken. A 3½-ounce serving of chicken has about 140 calories and 3 grams of fat, while the same amount of turkey breast has 120 calories and 1 gram of fat! If you can't find these thin cutlets, ask your grocer to slice boneless breast into scaloppini. Dusting it with flour keeps the turkey moist. The dried fruit salsa is a perfect accompaniment. Serve the scaloppini over Sweet Potato Mash (see page 279), with grilled vegetables alongside.

4 turkey scaloppini (about 1 lb)
¼ cup all-purpose flour
2 tsp vegetable oil

¼ cup chopped dried apricots
¼ cup dried cranberries
1 cup diced red bell pepper
⅓ cup diced green onions, white part only

1 tsp crushed fresh garlic
¼ cup chopped cilantro or parsley
3 Tbsp apricot jam
1 Tbsp pure maple syrup
1 tsp Dijon mustard
2 tsp apple cider vinegar or freshly squeezed lemon juice

3 Tbsp chopped cilantro or parsley

1. Dust the turkey with flour. Spray a non-stick grill pan or skillet with cooking oil, add the vegetable oil and heat to medium. Sauté the turkey just until browned on both sides and no longer pink, about 8 minutes in total. Remove from the heat and keep covered.

2. To make the salsa, combine the apricots, cranberries, bell pepper, green onion, garlic, cilantro, jam, maple syrup, mustard and vinegar or lemon juice.

3. Spoon the salsa over the turkey and garnish with cilantro or parsley.

Turkey Scaloppini with Apricot and Dried Cherry Salsa
Photo by Brian MacDonald

Turkey Scaloppini with Pesto Cream Sauce

NUTRITIONAL ANALYSIS
PER SERVING

Calories	283
Protein	31 g
Fat	15 g
Saturated Fat	3 g
Carbohydrates	7 g
Cholesterol	74 mg
Sodium	200 mg
Fiber	1 g

Prep Time: 6 minutes

Cook Time: 4 minutes

Make Ahead:
Prepare pesto sauce
up to a day in advance and
refrigerate, or freeze for
up to 3 weeks.

Serves 4

If you can't find turkey scaloppini, get your butcher to cut thin crosswise slices from a turkey breast for you. Otherwise, substitute chicken or veal scaloppini. (The scaloppini should be ¼ inch thick.) If you can, use homemade pesto (see page 342), which will be lower in calories and fat than the store-bought variety.

⅓ cup pesto
1½ Tbsp low-fat sour cream
1½ Tbsp grated Parmesan cheese
4 turkey scaloppini (about 1 lb)
¼ cup all-purpose flour
1 Tbsp vegetable oil

1. To make the cream sauce, combine the pesto, sour cream and Parmesan in a small bowl. Set aside.

2. Dust the turkey with the flour.

3. Spray a non-stick skillet with cooking oil, add the vegetable oil and heat to medium-high. Cook the scaloppini for 2 minutes per side, or until no longer pink at the center. Serve with a dollop of pesto cream sauce on top.

CHAPTER SEVEN

Meat

Flank Steak Pinwheels with Sun-Dried Tomatoes and Goat Cheese

NUTRITIONAL ANALYSIS
PER SERVING

Calories	397
Protein	51 g
Fat	19 g
Saturated Fat	8.1 g
Carbohydrates	4.4 g
Cholesterol	89 mg
Sodium	236 mg
Fiber	0.5 g

Prep Time: 10 minutes

Cook Time: 6 minutes

Make Ahead:
Marinate up to a day
in advance.

Serves 4

These decorative-looking beef pinwheels are great as an appetizer or main dish. The tip here is to have the flank steak as thin as possible so rolling and cooking is easier. Either ask your butcher to do it or slice it yourself and pound it until it's about ¼ inch thick. Butterflied meat is cut so it opens like a book; it's not cut all the way through. This technique is used when you want to make the meat as thin as possible for rolling purposes. Slice the steak across the grain and roll it along the grain, so when you slice the pinwheels, it will be across the grain.

1½ lb flank steak, butterflied

½ cup low-fat Italian dressing

2 Tbsp light smooth ricotta

⅓ cup goat cheese

2 Tbsp low-fat cream cheese

½ tsp crushed garlic

½ cup fresh spinach leaves

⅓ cup chopped rehydrated sun-dried
    tomatoes (see page 221)

3 Tbsp chopped fresh parsley

1. Place the steak and Italian dressing in a non-reactive container and marinate in the refrigerator for a minimum of 2 hours and preferably overnight.

2. Place the ricotta, goat and cream cheeses and garlic in the bowl of a small food processor and purée until smooth.

3. Remove the flank steak from the marinade, drain and lay flat on a work surface. Spread the cheese mixture evenly overtop. Arrange the spinach and sun-dried tomatoes over the cheese. Tightly roll the meat up along the grain. Slice into 1½-inch pinwheels and secure each with a toothpick.

4. Heat a non-stick grill pan or barbecue to medium-high and spray with cooking oil. Cook the pinwheels for approximately 3 minutes per side for medium-rare, longer for medium.

5. Garnish with chopped parsley before serving.

Black Bean Beef Tenderloin

Beef tenderloin is a delight to serve—cut the slices as thick or thin as you like. It has one of the lowest fat contents of any high-quality meat and a butter-like texture, which the black bean sauce complements beautifully. As an alternative to cooking the tenderloin in the oven, you can cut it into 4 serving pieces and barbecue it, brushing it with half the sauce as it cooks.

¼ cup packed brown sugar

¼ cup ketchup or sweet chili sauce

3 Tbsp black bean sauce

1 Tbsp rice vinegar

2 tsp sesame oil

1 tsp minced fresh garlic

1 tsp minced fresh ginger

1 lb beef tenderloin

1. Preheat the oven to 400°F.

2. Whisk the brown sugar, ketchup, black bean sauce, vinegar, sesame oil, garlic and ginger together in a bowl.

3. Spray a non-stick skillet with cooking oil and set over medium-high heat. Brown the tenderloin on all sides, about 4 minutes. Transfer to a shallow baking dish. Pour half the sauce over the beef.

4. Bake in the center of the oven for 15 to 20 minutes, or until it's done to your liking. (A meat thermometer inserted in the center of the meat will read 135°F for medium-rare.) While the meat cooks, heat the remaining sauce in a non-stick skillet over low heat. Serve on individual plates with some sauce drizzled over each serving.

NUTRITIONAL ANALYSIS PER SERVING

Calories	271
Protein	24 g
Fat	11 g
Saturated Fat	3.6 g
Carbohydrates	19 g
Cholesterol	70 mg
Sodium	321 mg
Fiber	0.4 g

Prep Time: 10 minutes

Cook Time: 23 minutes

Make Ahead:
Prepare sauce up to 2 days in advance, cover and refrigerate.

Serves 4

Marinated Flank Steak with Oyster Mushrooms
Photo by Brian MacDonald

Marinated Flank Steak with Oyster Mushrooms

Try a variety of mushrooms, such as portobello, cremini or button, in this dish. It's also delicious without the mushrooms. For the most tender meat, slice it across the grain. Serve alongside steamed rice and bok choy or other green vegetable.

¼ cup low-sodium soy sauce

¼ cup hoisin sauce

¼ cup rice vinegar

2 Tbsp brown sugar

2 Tbsp vegetable oil

1 tsp minced fresh ginger

2 tsp minced fresh garlic

1½ lb flank steak

1 tsp vegetable oil

4 cups sliced oyster mushrooms

2 tsp cornstarch

⅓ cup chopped green onion

⅓ cup chopped fresh cilantro or parsley

1. Whisk the soy sauce, hoisin sauce, vinegar, sugar, 2 Tbsp oil, ginger and 1 tsp of the garlic in a small bowl. Place the steak in a non-reactive container, add the marinade, cover and place in the refrigerator for at least 2 hours or overnight. Bring to room temperature before cooking.

2. Heat the 1 tsp oil in a large non-stick skillet over medium-high heat. Add the remaining 1 tsp. garlic and the mushrooms and cook for 6 to 8 minutes, or until the mushrooms are browned and the liquid has evaporated. Preheat the broiler or barbecue.

3. Remove the steak from the marinade and set the marinade aside. Barbecue or broil the steak until it's done to your liking, turning once. Depending on how thick it is, this can take anywhere from 8 to 15 minutes.

4. While the steak is cooking, whisk the cornstarch into the reserved marinade. Bring to a boil in a small skillet and simmer on medium-low heat for 5 minutes, until thickened. Add the mushrooms.

5. Slice the steak thinly across the grain and serve with the sauce. Garnish with a sprinkle of green onions and cilantro.

NUTRITIONAL ANALYSIS PER SERVING

Calories	266
Protein	26 g
Fat	13 g
Saturated Fat	4 g
Carbohydrates	11 g
Cholesterol	44 mg
Sodium	568 mg
Fiber	1 g

Prep Time: 10 minutes

Cook Time: 19 minutes

Make Ahead:
Marinate the meat and cook the mushrooms up to a day in advance.

Serves 6

Flank Steak

This is one of the leanest cuts of beef you can eat. It's low in fat, calories and cholesterol and it's very economical. It's flavorful, but because it's low in fat, you should tenderize it by marinating for at least 2 hours and preferably overnight. Slice it across the grain for tenderness. To make it even more economical, I buy flank steaks in bulk and freeze them.

Tex-Mex Flank Steak with Corn Salsa

**NUTRITIONAL ANALYSIS
PER SERVING**

Calories	286
Protein	26 g
Fat	9.6 g
Saturated Fat	3.9 g
Carbohydrates	16 g
Cholesterol	59 mg
Sodium	516 mg
Fiber	1.5 g

Prep Time: 10 minutes

Cook Time: 25 minutes

Make Ahead:
Prepare salsa up to a
day in advance, cover
and refrigerate.

Serves 6

With the sauce and corn salsa accompaniment, this is a great Southwestern dish. Sautéing the corn gives it a barbecued flavor. Be sure to allow time for marinating the steak (see page 203). Leftovers taste just as good the next day; either reheat gently or serve at room temperature.

1 cup barbecue sauce

⅓ cup cider vinegar

2 Tbsp molasses

¼ tsp hot pepper sauce

1½ lb flank steak

1 cup canned corn kernels, drained

1 cup diced red bell pepper

1 cup canned black beans, drained and rinsed

⅓ cup chopped green onion

¼ cup chopped cilantro or parsley

1. Whisk the barbecue sauce, vinegar, molasses and hot pepper sauce in a bowl. Place the flank steak in a shallow, non-reactive baking dish and pour the sauce over the steak. Cover with plastic wrap and refrigerate for 2 hours or overnight.

2. For the salsa, spray a non-stick skillet with cooking oil. Place over medium heat, and sauté the corn and red pepper until the corn begins to brown, about 5 minutes. Stir in the beans, onion and cilantro. Set aside.

3. Remove the steak from the marinade, and set the marinade aside in a small saucepan.

4. Preheat the barbecue or a non-stick grill pan to medium-high and spray with cooking oil. Cook the beef over medium-high heat for 5 to 8 minutes per side, or until it's done to your liking.

5. While the steak is cooking, bring the reserved marinade to a boil and boil for 5 minutes. Serve the steak with the sauce and salsa on the side.

Tex-Mex Flank Steak with Corn Salsa ▶
Photo by Lorella Zanetti

Grilled Steak over Split Pea and Orzo Pilaf

NUTRITIONAL ANALYSIS
PER SERVING

Calories	402
Protein	40 g
Fat	18 g
Saturated Fat	5.5 g
Carbohydrates	21 g
Cholesterol	55 mg
Sodium	399 mg
Fiber	1 g

Prep Time: 15 minutes

Cook Time: 35 minutes

Make Ahead:
Marinate the steak for up
to 2 days; grill just before
serving. Cook the pilaf
earlier in the day and serve
at room temperature.

Serves 6

The rice and orzo pilaf is a delicious and nutritious side dish on its own, but it goes beautifully with the steak. Remember to allow marinating time for the steak (see page 203).

1½ lb flank steak
⅓ cup low-fat Italian dressing
2 cups chicken or beef stock
½ cup green split peas
½ cup orzo
⅓ cup crumbled light feta cheese
⅓ cup sliced black olives
½ cup diced red bell pepper

⅓ cup chopped fresh basil or parsley
2 Tbsp olive oil
2 Tbsp freshly squeezed lemon juice
1½ tsp crushed fresh garlic
pinch freshly ground black pepper

2 Tbsp chopped fresh basil

1. Place the steak and Italian dressing in a non-reactive dish and marinate in the refrigerator for a minimum of 2 hours and preferably overnight.

2. Bring the stock and split peas to a boil in a medium saucepan. Cover, reduce the heat and simmer for 12 minutes. Add the orzo and simmer for 8 more minutes, just until the orzo is firm to the bite and the split peas are tender but not overcooked. Drain and set aside.

3. Remove the steak from the marinade and wipe it clean. Preheat a barbecue or non-stick grill pan to high and spray with cooking oil.

4. Grill the meat for approximately 5 minutes per side for medium-rare. Remove from the heat and let sit for 10 minutes.

5. Stir the cheese, olives, bell pepper, ⅓ cup basil, oil, juice, garlic and pepper into the split pea mixture. Place on a large serving dish.

6. Slice the flank steak across the grain into thin slices and place on top of the split pea mixture. Garnish with the remaining 2 Tbsp chopped basil.

Steak Kabobs with Honey Garlic Marinade

With non-stick indoor grill pans you can enjoy this dish all year round. Be sure to trim excess fat from your steaks. For a change, substitute chicken, turkey or pork for the beef in this recipe.

3 Tbsp low-sodium soy sauce

3 Tbsp rice vinegar

2 Tbsp honey

2 tsp crushed garlic

2 tsp sesame oil

4 tsp vegetable oil

2 Tbsp water

¾ lb lean steak, cut into cubes

1 tsp cornstarch

1 large green bell pepper, cut into sixteen 1-inch pieces

1 small white onion, cut into sixteen 1-inch pieces

16 small mushrooms

16 snow peas

1. Combine the soy sauce, vinegar, honey, garlic, sesame and vegetable oils and water in a non-reactive bowl. Add the steak and marinate for 30 minutes or overnight in the refrigerator.

2. Spray the barbecue with cooking oil and preheat to medium-high.

3. Remove the beef from the marinade. Place the marinade in a small saucepan and whisk in the cornstarch until dissolved. Cook over medium-low heat for 5 minutes until thick and syrupy. Set half of the sauce aside.

4. Thread the beef, green pepper, onion, mushrooms and snow peas alternately onto 8 metal skewers. Barbecue, turning and brushing with half of the marinade frequently, for 10 to 15 minutes, or until cooked to your liking. Serve with the remaining marinade on the side.

NUTRITIONAL ANALYSIS PER SERVING

Calories	228
Protein	20 g
Fat	9 g
Saturated Fat	4 g
Carbohydrates	16 g
Cholesterol	47 mg
Sodium	453 mg
Fiber	2 g

Prep Time: 12 minutes

Cook Time: 18 minutes

Make Ahead:
Prepare kabobs up to a day in advance. Cover and refrigerate.

Serves 4

Prime Veal Chop with Pesto and Feta Cheese

I created this recipe for The Pickle Barrel chain of restaurants in Toronto. The veal chop is beautifully lean and tender. The combination of pesto and feta complements it beautifully and gives the dish a Mediterranean twist. This goes well with grilled vegetables and Smashed Potatoes (see page 272)

four 6- to 8-oz prime veal chops with bone in (also known as the French cut)
2 Tbsp pesto (see page 342, or use store-bought)
2 Tbsp crumbled feta cheese

1. Preheat the oven to 425°F. Line a baking sheet with foil and spray with cooking oil.

2. Spray a non-stick skillet with cooking oil and place over medium-high heat. Cook the veal on both sides just until seared and browned, approximately 2 minutes per side. Place on the prepared baking sheet.

3. Spread both sides of the veal with pesto sauce and sprinkle with the feta, patting the cheese down firmly.

4. Bake for approximately 10 minutes, until the internal temperature registers about 135°F for medium- rare, or to desired doneness. Let rest 5 minutes before serving.

NUTRITIONAL ANALYSIS PER SERVING

Calories	204
Protein	26 g
Fat	10 g
Saturated Fat	3.7 g
Carbohydrates	0.8 g
Cholesterol	97 mg
Sodium	235 mg
Fiber	0.2 g

Prep Time: 10 minutes
Cook Time: 14 minutes

Make Ahead:
Prepare pesto up to 4 days in advance or freeze for 2 months.

Serves 4

Prime Veal Chop with Pesto and Feta Cheese
Photo by Brian MacDonald

Hoisin Garlic Meatloaf with Oyster Mushrooms and Bell Peppers

NUTRITIONAL ANALYSIS PER SERVING (1 SLICE)

Calories	248
Protein	19 g
Fat	12 g
Saturated Fat	3.6 g
Carbohydrates	13 g
Cholesterol	63 mg
Sodium	299 mg
Fiber	2.3 g

Prep Time: 15 minutes

Cook Time: 45 minutes

Make Ahead:
Prepare meatloaf to baking stage up to a day in advance, wrap well and refrigerate; bake just before serving.

Serves 8

The Sunday meatloaf may be a meal of the past, but this trendy rolled version will revive the tradition. If you don't feel like rolling the meatloaf, just spoon the vegetable filling over the glaze, cover with foil and bake.

2 tsp vegetable oil

½ cup chopped onion

1 cup chopped oyster mushrooms

½ cup chopped red bell pepper

1 Tbsp low-sodium soy sauce

1 Tbsp hoisin sauce

1 Tbsp water

2 tsp finely chopped garlic

2 tsp minced fresh ginger

2 tsp sesame oil

2 tsp rice vinegar

1 lb extra-lean ground beef

¼ cup dry seasoned breadcrumbs

¼ cup chopped green onion

3 Tbsp chopped cilantro or parsley

2 Tbsp hoisin sauce

1 tsp minced fresh ginger

1 tsp minced fresh garlic

1 large egg

2 Tbsp water

2 Tbsp hoisin sauce

1 tsp sesame oil

1. Preheat the oven to 375°F. Spray an 8½- × 4½-inch loaf pan with cooking oil.

2. For the filling, lightly spray a non-stick skillet with cooking oil, add the vegetable oil and place over medium heat. Sauté the onion for 3 minutes. Add the mushrooms and bell pepper and sauté for 5 minutes. Add the soy sauce, hoisin sauce, water, garlic, ginger, sesame oil and rice vinegar and cook for 1 minute. Set aside.

3. For the meat mixture, combine the ground beef, breadcrumbs, green onion, cilantro, hoisin sauce, ginger, garlic and egg. Mix well. Turn the mixture out onto waxed paper and pat into an approximate 10-inch square.

4. Spread the vegetable filling over the meatloaf and roll it up jelly-roll style with the help of the waxed paper. Place in the prepared loaf pan, seam side down.

5. For the glaze, whisk the water, hoisin sauce and sesame oil in a small bowl. Pour over the meatloaf and bake in the center of the oven for 35 minutes, or until a meat thermometer inserted in the center of the loaf registers 160°F. Let cool for at least 10 minutes before inverting the pan and slicing.

Beef Fajitas with Sweet Peppers, Coriander and Cheese

Fajitas are my favorite Tex-Mex food. These ones are creamy and rich tasting, but without the fat of regular fajitas loaded with too much cheese, sour cream, guacamole and beef. My version has plenty of vegetables, along with some light cheese and sour cream. Easy to make, and the whole family loves them.

8 oz boneless grilling steak, thinly sliced

2 tsp vegetable oil

1½ cups thinly sliced white onions

1½ tsp minced garlic

1½ cups red bell pepper cut into strips

¼ cup chopped cilantro or parsley

3 Tbsp chopped green onions

6 small flour tortillas

½ cup shredded light cheddar cheese

⅓ cup medium salsa

¼ cup low-fat sour cream

1. Preheat the oven to 425°F. Spray a baking sheet with cooking oil spray.

2. Spray a non-stick skillet with cooking oil and place over medium-high heat. Cook the beef for 5 minutes, or until cooked to your liking, turning once. Remove from the pan.

3. Add the oil to the pan and brown the onions and garlic, about 4 minutes. Reduce the heat to medium. Stir in the red pepper strips and cook until softened, about 5 minutes. Remove the pan from the heat. Stir in the cilantro, green onions and the cooked beef.

4. Divide the mixture among the tortillas. Top with the cheese, salsa and sour cream. Roll up.

5. Place on the prepared baking sheet. Bake in the center of the oven for 5 minutes, or until the fajitas are heated through and the cheese has melted. Cut in half and serve immediately.

NUTRITIONAL ANALYSIS
PER SERVING (1 ROLL)

Calories	231
Protein	15 g
Fat	7 g
Saturated Fat	2.3 g
Carbohydrates	26 g
Cholesterol	29 mg
Sodium	290 mg
Fiber	2.4 g

Prep Time: 20 minutes

Cook Time: 20 minutes

Make Ahead:
Prepare filling up to a day in advance and refrigerate. Add an extra 5 minutes to baking time.

Serves 6

Beef Cabbage Rolls with Orzo in Tomato Sauce

NUTRITIONAL ANALYSIS
PER SERVING

Calories	395
Protein	22 g
Fat	10 g
Saturated Fat	3.9 g
Carbohydrates	53 g
Cholesterol	35 mg
Sodium	331 mg
Fiber	9 g

Prep Time: 10 minutes

Cook Time: 110 minutes

Make Ahead:
Can be made up to 2 days
in advance, covered and
refrigerated. Reheat gently
before serving.

Serves 4

Nothing cooks up better than savoy cabbage. It's mild in flavor and doesn't lose its color or texture after being simmered. It's not always available, however, so you may have to make do with ordinary green cabbage.

1 head green savoy cabbage, core
  removed

½ cup orzo (or any small, shaped pasta)

1 cup chopped mushrooms

⅓ cup chopped onion

1 tsp minced fresh garlic

8 oz lean ground beef

3 Tbsp barbecue sauce

2 tsp dried basil

1 egg

Pinch salt and freshly ground black
  pepper

1 can (28 oz) tomatoes, with juice

3 Tbsp packed brown sugar

½ cup water

1 Tbsp freshly squeezed lemon juice

⅓ cup raisins (any variety)

3 Tbsp chopped fresh basil or parsley

1. Bring a large pot of water to a boil and cook the whole cabbage for 20 to 25 minutes; drain. When it's cool enough to handle, separate the leaves carefully. Set aside 8 leaves.

2. Cook the orzo in a pot of boiling water for 8 to 10 minutes, until the pasta is tender but firm. Drain and rinse under cold running water. Drain again and set aside.

3. Spray a non-stick skillet with cooking oil. Add the mushrooms, onion and garlic and cook over medium-high heat for 7 minutes, or until slightly browned. Transfer to a bowl. Add the orzo, ground beef, barbecue sauce, 1 tsp of the dried basil, egg, salt and pepper; mix well.

4. Place about ⅓ cup of the beef-orzo mixture in the center of a cabbage leaf. Fold in the sides and roll it up. Repeat with the remaining filling.

5. Combine the tomatoes and juice, brown sugar, remaining 1 tsp dried basil, water and lemon juice in a food processor; purée. Add the raisins, and pour the mixture into a large non-stick saucepan over medium-high heat. Bring to a boil, then reduce the heat to low.

6. Add the cabbage rolls and cook, covered, for 1 hour and 15 minutes, turning the rolls over at the halfway point through the cooking. Serve hot, garnished with the fresh basil.

Beef Cabbage Rolls with Orzo in Tomato Sauce ▶
Photo by Mark Shapiro

Asian Beef Lettuce Wraps with Peanut Sauce

I love the mu shiu served in Chinese restaurants. Minced pork, chicken or beef with hoisin sauce and vegetables is served in lettuce leaves or flour wraps. They're high in calories and fat due to extra oil and the fattier quality of the beef. These home-made ones taste great and they're leaner. The peanut sauce is made with light coconut milk.

NUTRITIONAL ANALYSIS PER SERVING

Calories	276
Protein	21 g
Fat	16 g
Saturated Fat	4.2 g
Carbohydrates	12 g
Cholesterol	31 mg
Sodium	274 mg
Fiber	2.8 g

Prep Time: 15 minutes
Cook Time: 20 minutes

Make Ahead:
Prepare filling up to a day in advance and reheat in a skillet over low heat.

Serves 4

2 tsp vegetable oil

1 cup chopped onion

½ cup diced carrot

¾ cup diced red bell pepper

12 oz extra-lean ground beef

1½ tsp minced garlic

1 tsp honey

1 tsp sesame seeds

1 tsp minced fresh ginger

½ tsp hot Asian chili sauce

¼ cup light coconut milk

2 Tbsp natural peanut butter

4 tsp low-sodium soy sauce

4 tsp rice wine vinegar

2 tsp sesame oil

¼ cup chopped cilantro or parsley

¼ cup chopped green onions

8 large Boston or butter lettuce leaves

1. Spray a large non-stick skillet with cooking oil, add the vegetable oil and place over medium-high heat. Sauté the onion until browned, about 5 minutes. Add the carrot and bell pepper and sauté for another 8 minutes, until the vegetables are tender-crisp. Add the beef and sauté until no longer pink, about 4 minutes.

2. Combine the coconut milk, peanut butter, soy sauce, vinegar, sesame oil, garlic, honey, sesame seeds, ginger and chili sauce. Add to the beef mixture and simmer for 3 minutes.

3. Stir in the cilantro and green onions. Divide among lettuce leaves and roll up or allow your guests to roll their own.

Asian Beef Lettuce Wraps with Peanut Sauce
Photo by Brian MacDonald

Beef Pizza with Aged Cheddar and Feta

NUTRITIONAL ANALYSIS
PER SERVING

Calories	190
Protein	17 g
Fat	8.6 g
Saturated Fat	3.6 g
Carbohydrates	11 g
Cholesterol	77 mg
Sodium	189 mg
Fiber	1.6 g

Prep Time: 15 minutes

Cook Time: 33 minutes

Make Ahead:
Prepare to baking stage, refrigerate and bake just before serving.

Serves 6

This is a great recipe for children, teens and adults young at heart! I even serve it as an appetizer. The lean beef that replaces the bread in standard pizzas is a great source of nutrition and protein.

2 tsp vegetable oil
2 cups chopped onion
2 tsp crushed fresh garlic
12 oz extra-lean ground beef
3 Tbsp seasoned breadcrumbs
1 egg
¼ cup finely diced onion
¼ cup tomato sauce
1 tsp dried basil
½ tsp dried oregano

2 Tbsp grated Parmesan cheese
Pinch salt and freshly ground black
   pepper

⅓ cup tomato sauce
⅓ cup shredded aged light cheddar
   cheese
¼ cup chopped green onion
3 Tbsp chopped fresh basil

1. Preheat the oven to 400°F. Spray a 9-inch springform pan with cooking oil.

2. Heat the oil in a non-stick saucepan. Add the 2 cups chopped onion and garlic and sauté for 8 minutes, or just until the onions begin to brown.

3. Place the cooked onion mixture in a large bowl and add the beef, breadcrumbs, egg, ¼ cup finely diced onion, tomato sauce, dried basil, oregano, Parmesan cheese, salt and pepper; mix well. Pat the mixture into the prepared springform pan. Bake in the center of the oven for 20 minutes. Remove from the oven.

4. Spread the tomato sauce overtop and sprinkle with the cheese and green onion. Bake for a further 5 minutes, or until the cheese melts. Remove the sides of the pan and garnish with a sprinkling of fresh basil.

Calf's Liver with Caramelized Onions

Calf's liver melts in your mouth. More delicate and milder in flavor than beef liver, this liver is outstanding with the caramelized onions.

2 tsp vegetable oil

4 cups sliced sweet onions (2 large onions)

2 Tbsp packed brown sugar

1½ tsp minced garlic

1½ lb calf's liver

¼ cup chopped fresh parsley

1. Spray a large non-stick skillet with cooking oil, add the vegetable oil and place over medium heat. Add the onions and cook until softened, about 8 minutes. Stir in the sugar and garlic and reduce the heat to low. Cook until the onions are browned, stirring occasionally, about 15 minutes.

2. While the onions are cooking, preheat the barbecue or a non-stick grill pan and spray with cooking oil. Cook the liver to medium, about 5 minutes, or to your liking.

3. Place on a serving platter and spoon the onions overtop. Serve garnished with parsley.

NUTRITIONAL ANALYSIS PER SERVING

Calories	220
Protein	21.7 g
Fat	6.7 g
Saturated Fat	2 g
Carbohydrates	18.2 g
Cholesterol	350 mg
Sodium	76 mg
Fiber	2.2 g

Prep Time: 5 minutes

Cook Time: 28 minutes

Make Ahead:
Prepare the onions up to 2 days in advance and refrigerate. Reheat in a skillet over low heat.

Serves 6

Pork Tenderloin with Orange-Balsamic Glaze

Calories	206
Protein	24 g
Fat	5.5 g
Saturated Fat	1.6 g
Carbohydrates	14 g
Cholesterol	74 mg
Sodium	80 mg
Fiber	0.7 g

Prep Time: 5 minutes

Cook Time: 25 minutes

Make Ahead:
Prepare glaze up to
2 days in advance, cover
and refrigerate. Dish can
be cooked the day before
and reheated in a 300°F
oven just until warm,
being careful not to
overcook. Add garnish
just before serving.

Serves 6

Pork tenderloins are usually sold in packages of two, each package averaging 1½ pounds. If you buy them from your butcher the tenderloins may be larger and you'll have to increase the cooking time. Today's improved agricultural methods mean that pork can safely be eaten medium or medium-rare.

1½ lb pork tenderloin (2 small loins)
¼ cup orange juice concentrate
¼ cup apricot jam
1 Tbsp balsamic vinegar
1 Tbsp olive oil
2 tsp grated orange zest

1 tsp minced garlic
pinch salt and freshly ground black
    pepper
3 Tbsp chopped fresh parsley or cilantro
¼ cup diced dried apricots

1. Preheat the oven to 425°F. Line a 13- by 9-inch baking dish with parchment paper.

2. Lightly spray a non-stick grill pan or skillet with cooking oil and place over high heat.

3. Sear the tenderloins for about 2 minutes per side, or just until browned. Place in the prepared baking pan.

4. To make the glaze, combine the juice concentrate, jam, vinegar, oil, orange zest, garlic, salt and pepper until smooth. Spoon ¼ cup of the glaze over the tenderloins and bake for about 20 minutes or until the internal temperature reaches 145°F for medium.

5. Reheat the remaining glaze. Slice the tenderloin and serve with the glaze overtop. Garnish with chopped parsley and diced apricots.

Pork Tenderloin with Orange-Balsamic Glaze ▶
Photo by Lorella Zanetti

Oriental Sesame Pork Tenderloin

Calories	344
Protein	38 g
Fat	12 g
Saturated Fat	4.1 g
Carbohydrates	15 g
Cholesterol	117 mg
Sodium	326 mg
Fiber	0.6 g

Prep Time: 10 minutes

Cook Time: 19 minutes

Make Ahead:
Prepare sauce up to 3 days in advance and refrigerate.

Serves 4

Pork tenderloin goes beautifully with this sweet Asian hoisin sauce. Serve alongside rice noodles or rice.

1½ lb pork tenderloin

¼ cup hoisin sauce

2 Tbsp sweet chili sauce or barbecue
 sauce

2 Tbsp brown sugar

2 tsp sesame oil

1½ tsp crushed fresh garlic

1½ tsp crushed fresh ginger

1 tsp low-sodium soy sauce

1 tsp sesame seeds, toasted

¼ cup chopped fresh cilantro or parsley

1. Preheat the oven to 425°F. Line a baking sheet with parchment paper.

2. Spray a non-stick skillet with cooking oil and heat to medium-high. Sear the tenderloin for approximately 2 minutes per side, or just until browned. Place on the prepared baking sheet.

3. Combine the hoisin, chili sauce, sugar, oil, garlic, ginger and soy sauce in a small bowl.

4. Brush approximately 2 Tbsp of the mixture over the tenderloin and sprinkle with sesame seeds. Bake for approximately 15 minutes, or until a meat thermometer reads 145°F for medium. Let rest for 10 minutes before slicing.

5. Slice and serve with the remaining sauce on the side. Garnish with fresh cilantro.

Leg of Lamb Stuffed with Sun-Dried Tomatoes

One of my favorite cuts of meat, leg of lamb has only 7 grams of fat per 3½-ounce serving. Be sure to trim any extra fat. The stuffing is out of this world.

2 lb boneless leg of lamb, butterflied

3 tsp crushed garlic

⅔ cup beef or low-sodium chicken stock

⅔ cup red wine

1¼ cups sun-dried tomatoes, rehydrated
   (see below)

⅓ cup sliced black olives

⅓ cup goat cheese

2 tsp olive oil

½ tsp dried basil

¼ cup chopped fresh basil or parsley

1. Preheat the oven to 425°F. Spray a roasting pan with cooking oil.

2. Place the lamb on a rack in the roasting pan. Spray the lamb with cooking oil and rub with 2 tsp. of the garlic. Pour the stock and wine in the bottom of the pan.

3. Purée the tomatoes, olives, cheese, oil, remaining 1 tsp. garlic and basil in a food processor. Spread half the mixture over one side of the lamb and fold the lamb in half to enclose the filling. Place the remaining mixture in a bowl to serve later.

4. Roast the lamb for 15 to 20 minutes per pound or until done to your liking. A meat thermometer should register 135°F for medium-rare. If the pan liquid evaporates, add more wine or stock.

5. Let the lamb rest for 10 minutes before carving. Slice thinly and pour the pan juices over the lamb. Garnish with fresh basil. Serve the extra sun-dried tomato stuffing on the side.

Sun-Dried Tomatoes

Always purchase the dry-packed version of sun-dried tomatoes since those packed in oil have excess fat and calories. To rehydrate them, either add boiling water to cover and let them sit for 15 minutes until softened, or bring water and the sun-dried tomatoes to a boil and cook for 2 minutes. You can also microwave them with a little water for 1 minute. Drain before using.

NUTRITIONAL ANALYSIS
PER SERVING

Calories	460
Protein	40 g
Fat	18 g
Saturated Fat	5 g
Carbohydrates	9 g
Cholesterol	220 mg
Sodium	260 mg
Fiber	2 g

Prep Time: 15 minutes

Cook Time: 30 minutes

Make Ahead:
Prepare stuffing up
to 3 days in advance
and refrigerate.

Serves 6

Curried Lamb Casserole with Sweet Potatoes

NUTRITIONAL ANALYSIS
PER SERVING

Calories	296
Protein	22 g
Fat	8 g
Saturated Fat	3 g
Carbohydrates	30 g
Cholesterol	47 mg
Sodium	296 mg
Fiber	5 g

Prep Time: 15 minutes

Cook Time: 41 minutes

Make Ahead:
Make a day in advance,
cover and refrigerate.
Reheat over low heat. This
dish can also be frozen.

Serves 4

This is a dish you can easily tailor to your preferences or what's in your pantry. Use different vegetables, adjust the curry powder to your taste, and if you don't want lamb, substitute beef or pork. Serve this over rice, linguini or couscous.

1 lb lamb, cut into ¾-inch cubes

3 Tbsp all-purpose flour

1 Tbsp vegetable oil

2 tsp crushed fresh garlic

1 cup finely chopped onion

1 cup finely chopped carrot

1 cup finely chopped green bell pepper

1 cup peeled, cubed sweet potato

4 cups sliced mushrooms (about ½ lb)

2 ¼ cups beef or chicken stock

⅓ cup red wine

3 Tbsp tomato paste

2 tsp curry powder

1½ tsp brown sugar

½ tsp hot chili paste

pinch salt and freshly ground black
   pepper

⅓ cup chopped cilantro or parsley

1. Dust the lamb with the flour.

2. Spray a large non-stick Dutch oven with cooking oil. Heat 2 tsp of the vegetable oil over medium-high heat and sauté the lamb for 3 minutes or just until seared and browned all over, stirring frequently. Remove the lamb and set aside. Wipe out the pan.

3. Respray the pan, heat the remaining 1 tsp oil over medium-high heat and add the garlic and onion. Sauté for 3 minutes until softened. Add the carrots, green pepper, sweet potatoes and mushrooms; cook, stirring often, for 10 minutes, or until the vegetables are tender and the moisture has evaporated.

4. Stir in the stock, wine, tomato paste, curry powder, sugar, chili paste, salt, pepper and lamb. Cover and bring to a boil, then simmer for 25 to 30 minutes, until the lamb is tender and the sauce thickens. Garnish with cilantro just before serving.

Roasted Leg of Lamb with Tahini Sauce, Feta and Pine Nuts

My first choice for the tenderest cut of meat is a boneless leg of lamb. This Middle Eastern–style sauce is outstanding with lamb, but I use it over fish, chicken and vegetables as well.

2 lb boneless leg of lamb, butterflied
¼ cup beef or chicken stock
¼ cup smooth light ricotta cheese
2 Tbsp tahini (sesame seed paste)
2 Tbsp freshly squeezed lemon juice
1½ Tbsp light mayonnaise
1 Tbsp olive oil
2 tsp low-sodium soy sauce

1½ tsp crushed fresh garlic
½ tsp dried oregano

⅓ cup crumbled light feta cheese
⅓ cup sliced black olives
2 Tbsp pine nuts, toasted
⅓ cup chopped cilantro or parsley

1. Preheat the oven to 400°F. Line a baking sheet with foil and spray with cooking oil.

2. Spray a non-stick grill pan or skillet with cooking oil and place over medium-high heat.

3. Sear the lamb for approximately 3 minutes per side until browned. Place on the baking sheet and roast for approximately 12 minutes per side or until the internal temperature reaches 145°F for medium-rare. Let rest for 10 minutes before slicing.

4. While the meat is resting, make the sauce. Combine the stock, ricotta, tahini, juice, mayonnaise, oil, soy sauce, garlic and oregano in the bowl of a small food processor and process until smooth.

5. Cut the steak across the grain into ½-inch slices and place on a serving platter. Drizzle some sauce overtop. Garnish with the feta cheese, olives, pine nuts and cilantro. Serve with the remaining sauce on the side.

NUTRITIONAL ANALYSIS PER SERVING

Calories	418
Protein	45 g
Fat	21 g
Saturated Fat	5 g
Carbohydrates	3.3 g
Cholesterol	163 mg
Sodium	312 mg
Fiber	0.8 g

Prep Time:	10 minutes
Cook Time:	30 minutes

Make Ahead:
Prepare sauce up to 2 days in advance and refrigerate.

Serves 6

Pasta and Grains

Creamy Baked Beefaroni

This is a recipe I created for *Rose Reisman's Enlightened Home Cooking* back in the late '90s. I find it even more delicious today and I've simplified it so it takes less time. It has become a weekly staple in our home, and lately I've been substituting ground soy for the ground beef, which adds to the soy protein in our diet. The soy version is also great for vegetarians or for people who keep kosher. I freeze portions for future meals.

1 lb penne

1 tsp vegetable oil
1 cup chopped onions
2 tsp minced fresh garlic
12 oz extra-lean ground beef
1¾ cups tomato-based pasta sauce
½ cup beef or chicken stock

¼ cup all-purpose flour
2 cups low-fat milk
1¾ cups beef or chicken stock
1 cup shredded light cheddar cheese

½ cup shredded part-skim mozzarella cheese
2 Tbsp grated Parmesan cheese

1. Preheat the oven to 450°F. Spray a 13- by 9-inch glass baking dish with cooking oil.

2. Bring a large pot of water to a boil and cook the penne for 8 to 10 minutes, or until tender but firm. Drain.

3. Heat the oil in a non-stick saucepan over medium heat. Add the onions and garlic and sauté until softened, about 4 minutes. Stir in the beef and cook, stirring to break up the meat, until no longer pink, about 4 minutes. Stir in the tomato sauce and stock. Cover and cook for 10 minutes, or until thickened. Set aside.

4. Whisk the flour, milk, and stock in a non-stick saucepan until smooth. Place over medium heat and cook until the mixture begins to boil. Reduce the heat to low and continue to cook, stirring occasionally, for 5 minutes or until thickened. Stir in the cheddar cheese. Remove from the heat. Stir the cheese sauce into the meat sauce.

5. Toss the pasta with the sauce. Pour into the prepared baking dish. Sprinkle with the mozzarella and Parmesan cheeses.

6. Bake in the center of the oven for 10 minutes, until bubbly.

NUTRITIONAL ANALYSIS
PER SERVING

Calories	326
Protein	21 g
Fat	7.2 g
Saturated Fat	3.3 g
Carbohydrates	44 g
Cholesterol	21 mg
Sodium	507 mg
Fiber	2.5 g

Prep Time:	15 minutes
Cook Time:	25 minutes

Make Ahead:
Prepare to the baking stage and freeze for up to 2 months; thaw before baking. Or bake and freeze for up to 1 month.

Serves 10

Beef Manicotti with Wild Mushrooms and Three Cheeses

NUTRITIONAL ANALYSIS PER SERVING

Calories	285
Protein	17 g
Fat	9 g
Saturated Fat	4 g
Carbohydrates	35 g
Cholesterol	61 mg
Sodium	300 mg
Fiber	3 g

Prep Time: 20 minutes

Cook Time: 39 minutes

Make Ahead:
Prepare up to 2 days in advance and refrigerate. Reheat in a 300°F oven, covered, for 25 minutes.

Serves 6

This pasta dish can be served as an appetizer or main course. I like to use oyster or portobello mushrooms, but regular cultivated mushrooms work too.

12 manicotti shells

3 cups chopped wild mushrooms (about ½ lb)

1½ tsp minced fresh garlic

2 cups washed, chopped leeks, white and pale green parts only

6 oz lean ground beef

¼ cup beef or chicken stock

2 Tbsp tomato paste

1½ tsp dried basil

½ cup smooth light ricotta

⅓ cup shredded part-skim mozzarella cheese

3 Tbsp grated Parmesan cheese

1 large egg

pinch salt and freshly ground black pepper

1½ cup tomato-based pasta sauce

¼ cup low-fat milk

¼ cup chopped fresh basil or parsley

1. Preheat the oven to 400°F. Spray a 13- by 9-inch baking dish with cooking oil.

2. Bring a large pot of water to a boil and cook the manicotti shells for 14 minutes, or until tender. Drain and rinse under cold running water. Drain thoroughly and set aside.

3. Spray a large non-stick skillet with cooking oil and place over medium-high heat. Add the mushrooms and garlic; cook until browned, about 3 minutes. Add the leeks and sauté for 2 minutes. Add the beef and cook, stirring to break up the chunks, for 3 minutes or until no longer pink. Add the stock, tomato paste and dried basil. Cook for 2 minutes. Remove from the heat.

4. Place the ricotta, mozzarella, 2 Tbsp of the Parmesan cheese, egg, salt and pepper in a food processor or blender. Pulse until well mixed. Add to meat mixture and combine well.

5. Combine the tomato sauce and milk in a small bowl. Spread half the sauce over the bottom of the prepared baking dish. Slit manicotti and open like a book, stuff each manicotti shell with about 3 Tbsp of the filling and enclose. Place the stuffed shells in the baking dish. Cover with the remaining sauce and sprinkle with the remaining 1 Tbsp Parmesan cheese.

6. Cover the dish with foil and bake for 15 minutes, or until heated through. Garnish with the fresh basil before serving.

Shell Pasta with Creamy Italian Sausage

If you like spicy food, use hot Italian sausages instead of the mild ones. Look for lean sausage. You can use regular 2 percent milk, but evaporated milk gives the dish a creamier, richer texture and flavor.

8 oz small shell pasta

1 tsp vegetable oil

6 oz mild Italian sausages, casings removed and meat chopped

1 cup beef or chicken stock

¾ cup 2 percent evaporated milk

5 tsp all-purpose flour

¼ cup grated Parmesan cheese

¼ cup chopped fresh parsley or basil

1. Cook the pasta in boiling water according to package directions, or until firm to the bite. Drain and place in a serving bowl.

2. Heat the oil in a non-stick skillet over medium heat. Sauté the sausages, breaking the meat up with a wooden spoon, just until cooked, approximately 5 minutes.

3. Meanwhile, combine the stock, milk and flour in a small bowl and whisk until smooth. Add to the sausage mixture and simmer just until slightly thickened, approximately 3 minutes, stirring constantly.

4. Pour the sauce over the pasta. Toss with the cheese and parsley, and serve immediately.

NUTRITIONAL ANALYSIS PER SERVING

Calories	445
Protein	18 g
Fat	16 g
Saturated Fat	7 g
Carbohydrates	52 g
Cholesterol	36 mg
Sodium	505 mg
Fiber	2 g

Prep Time: 10 minutes

Cook Time: 8 minutes

Make Ahead:
Prepare sauce in advance and refrigerate. Bring to a simmer over low heat, adding more stock if too thick.

Serves 4

Manicotti Stuffed with Smoked Salmon and Cheese in a Creamy Tomato Sauce

NUTRITIONAL ANALYSIS
PER SERVING

Calories	295
Protein	18 g
Fat	10 g
Saturated Fat	7 g
Carbohydrates	32 g
Cholesterol	32 mg
Sodium	442 mg
Fiber	2 g

Prep Time: 15 minutes
Cook Time: 25 minutes

Make Ahead:
Stuff the shells and make the sauce up to a day in advance and refrigerate. Bake just before serving, adding an extra 10 minutes to the baking time.

Serves 6

Manicotti Stuffed with
Smoked Salmon and
Cheese in a Creamy
Tomato Sauce
Photo by Mark Shapiro

This can be served as a main meal with a side salad or soup, or it can accompany a main dish. The smoked salmon gives it a sophisticated flair that makes it a good company dish as well as a nutritious family dinner. You can substitute jumbo pasta shells (8 ounces will yield about 24 shells) for the manicotti, or stuff approximately 12 cannelloni shells.

10 manicotti
1¼ cups smooth light ricotta
½ cup shredded light cheddar cheese
¼ cup grated Parmesan cheese
2 oz smoked salmon, chopped
¼ cup finely chopped chives or green onion
3 Tbsp 2 percent milk

1 egg
pinch salt and freshly ground black pepper
1½ cups tomato-based pasta sauce
½ cup 2 percent evaporated milk
1 tsp dried basil
2 Tbsp grated mozzarella cheese
¼ cup chopped fresh basil or parsley

1. Preheat the oven to 400°F. Spray a 13- by 9-inch baking dish with cooking oil.

2. Cook the manicotti in boiling water according to package instructions, or until firm to the bite, approximately 10 minutes. Drain, cover and set aside.

3. Combine the ricotta, cheddar and Parmesan cheeses in a medium mixing bowl. Add the smoked salmon, chives, 3 Tbsp milk, egg, salt and pepper. Mix until well combined. Slit the manicotti along one side and open like a book. Divide the cheese mixture among the manicotti. Close the manicotti around the stuffing.

4. Combine the tomato sauce, basil and ½ cup milk in a small bowl and mix until smooth. Pour half the mixture in the bottom of the prepared baking dish. Place the stuffed manicotti in the baking dish and pour the remaining sauce over the pasta. Sprinkle with the mozzarella cheese.

5. Cover and bake for 15 minutes, or until hot through. Garnish with the chopped fresh basil before serving.

Seafood Macaroni and Three-Cheese Casserole

Calories	537
Protein	36 g
Fat	14 g
Saturated Fat	7.5 g
Carbohydrates	65 g
Cholesterol	103 mg
Sodium	545 mg
Fiber	3 g

Prep Time: 20 minutes

Cook Time: 20 minutes

Make Ahead:
Prepare up to a day in advance and refrigerate. Bring to room temperature before reheating in a 425°F oven for 15 minutes.

Serves 4

This is an upscale version of good old mac and cheese with a real twist. Play around with your choice of seafood or fresh fish and the various cheeses.

16 mussels in the shell, scrubbed
1 cup diced red bell pepper
½ cup chopped onion
1½ tsp minced fresh garlic
2 Tbsp all-purpose flour
¾ cup seafood or chicken stock
1 cup 2 percent evaporated milk
1 tsp Dijon mustard
6 oz raw shrimp, peeled, deveined and chopped
4 oz scallops, chopped
½ cup shredded light cheddar cheese

½ cup shredded light Swiss cheese
2 Tbsp grated Parmesan cheese
¼ cup chopped fresh dill or parsley
freshly ground black pepper to taste
8 oz macaroni

3 Tbsp dry breadcrumbs
1 Tbsp chopped fresh dill or parsley
½ tsp minced fresh garlic
1 tsp olive oil
1 tsp water

1. Preheat the oven to 425°F. Spray a 13- by 9-inch baking dish with cooking oil.

2. Bring ½ cup water to a boil in a saucepan over medium-high heat. Add the mussels and cover the pot. Cook, shaking the pot occasionally, for 3 minutes or until the mussels open. Discard the liquid, any unopened mussels and the shells and set aside.

3. Spray a non-stick saucepan with cooking oil and place over medium heat. Cook the red pepper, onion and garlic until softened, about 5 minutes. Add the flour and cook, stirring, for 1 minute. Add the stock, milk and mustard and stir until it comes to a boil. Add the shelled mussels, shrimp and scallops. Reduce the heat to medium. Cook, stirring occasionally, for 2 minutes, or until the shrimp turn pink, the scallops are cooked through, and the sauce thickens.

4. Add the cheddar cheese, Swiss cheese, Parmesan cheese and dill. Cook, stirring, for 1 minute or until the cheese melts. Season with pepper and set aside.

5. Bring a large pot of water to a boil and cook the macaroni for 6 to 8 minutes, until tender but firm. Drain. Add the pasta to the seafood sauce and pour into the prepared baking dish.

6. For the topping, combine all the ingredients in a bowl. Sprinkle over the pasta mixture. Bake for 8 minutes, or just until the casserole is hot through and the topping is browned or crunchy.

Shrimp, Crab, Pasta and Cheese Casserole

This is my updated version of macaroni and cheese. Every so often we want to serve this type of comfort food, but in a more sophisticated way. Use any variety of seafood or substitute chicken or firm tofu.

8 oz medium-sized shell pasta

¾ cup chicken or fish stock

1 cup 2 percent evaporated milk

2 Tbsp all-purpose flour

½ tsp Dijon mustard

⅔ cup shredded light aged cheddar cheese

3 Tbsp grated Parmesan cheese

1 cup frozen green peas or edamame

¼ tsp freshly ground black pepper

12 oz raw shrimp, peeled and chopped

4 oz crabmeat or surimi (imitation crabmeat, see page 155), diced

¼ cup chopped fresh dill or parsley

¼ cup seasoned breadcrumbs

1 tsp vegetable oil

2 tsp water

1 Tbsp chopped fresh dill or parsley

1. Preheat the oven to broil. Spray a 13- by 9-inch baking dish with cooking oil.

2. Bring a large pot of water to a boil and cook the pasta according to package directions until firm to the bite, about 10 minutes. Drain and set aside.

3. Combine the stock, milk, flour and mustard in a small pot. Whisk until the flour is completely incorporated and the mixture is smooth. Place over low heat and simmer, stirring constantly, until slightly thickened, about 3 minutes. Add the cheddar and Parmesan cheese, peas and pepper. Add the shrimp and cook until pink, about 2 minutes. Add the crabmeat and dill or parsley and mix well. Combine the pasta and sauce, mixing well. Pour into the prepared baking dish.

4. Mix the breadcrumbs, oil, water and the 1 Tbsp dill. Crumble over the casserole. Place under the broiler for 2 minutes. Serve immediately.

NUTRITIONAL ANALYSIS
PER SERVING:

Calories	256
Protein	19 g
Fat	5.8 g
Saturated Fat	2.7 g
Carbohydrates	31 g
Cholesterol	67 mg
Sodium	275 mg
Fiber	1.5 g

Prep Time: 15 minutes

Cook Time: 16 minutes

Make Ahead:

Prepare casserole early in the day and refrigerate. Reheat in a 350°F oven for 20 minutes, or until hot throughout.

Serves 8

Seafood Pasta Pizza with Dill and Goat Cheese

NUTRITIONAL ANALYSIS
PER SERVING

Calories	306
Protein	22 g
Fat	8 g
Saturated Fat	4 g
Carbohydrates	33 g
Cholesterol	80 mg
Sodium	382 mg
Fiber	1 g

Prep Time: 20 minutes

Cook Time: 25 minutes

Make Ahead:
Make crust a day in advance, cover and refrigerate. Make filling a day in advance and refrigerate; add more stock if too thick.

Serves 6

Small shell pasta or broken spaghetti can be substituted for the linguini. Breaking up the pasta makes the pizza base easier to mix and eat. Instead of seafood, any firm white fish fillets can be used, such as orange roughy, swordfish or grouper. Try adding a few tablespoons of sliced olives for color and texture.

6 oz linguini, broken into pieces
1 egg
⅓ cup 2 percent milk
3 Tbsp grated Parmesan cheese

1 tsp vegetable oil
1½ tsp crushed fresh garlic
¾ cup diced red bell pepper
⅓ cup sliced red onion
8 oz seafood, cut in pieces or left whole (shrimp, scallops, squid)

1 cup cold seafood or chicken stock
1 cup 2 percent evaporated milk
3 Tbsp all-purpose flour
1½ tsp Dijon mustard
⅓ cup chopped fresh dill
⅓ cup shredded part-skim mozzarella cheese
⅓ cup crumbled goat cheese
¼ cup chopped green onion

1. Preheat the oven to 450°F. Spray a 10- to 11-inch springform pan with cooking oil.

2. Cook the pasta in boiling water according to package directions, or until firm to the bite. Drain and place in a mixing bowl. Add the egg, milk and Parmesan cheese. Mix well. Pour into the pan and bake for 15 minutes.

3. Spray a large skillet with cooking oil, add the vegetable oil and place over medium heat. Add the garlic, red pepper and red onion; sauté for 4 minutes. Add the seafood and sauté for 3 minutes, or just until cooked.

4. Meanwhile, combine the stock, milk, flour and mustard in a small bowl and whisk until smooth. Add to the skillet and simmer on low heat, stirring constantly, until thickened, approximately 3 minutes. Stir in the dill. Pour over the baked pasta crust. Sprinkle with the mozzarella and goat cheese.

5. Bake for 10 minutes. Remove the sides of the pan and serve, garnished with green onions.

Linguini with Baby Clams and Goat Cheese in Marinara Sauce

Try fresh, coarsely chopped tomatoes instead of canned if you have extra tomatoes on hand. You can use whole canned tomatoes with the juice—just break up the tomatoes during cooking with the back of a spoon.

12 oz linguini	2 tsp dried basil
2 tsp vegetable oil	2 tsp dried oregano
2 tsp crushed fresh garlic	1 Tbsp capers
1½ cups chopped onion	1 tsp hot chili sauce (or to taste)
1 cup chopped green bell pepper	½ cup crumbled goat cheese
3 cups canned crushed tomatoes	⅓ cup chopped fresh basil or parsley
1 can (5 oz) baby clams, drained	

1. Cook the pasta in boiling water according to package instructions. Spray some cooking oil into the water to prevent sticking.

2. While the pasta cooks, heat the oil in a non-stick skillet over medium heat. Sauté the garlic and onion until soft, approximately 4 minutes. Add the green pepper and sauté until tender, another 2 minutes. Add the tomatoes, clams, basil, oregano, capers and chili sauce. Bring to a boil, then simmer on medium heat, stirring occasionally, for 15 minutes or until thickened. Add the cheese and cook for 1 minute.

3. When the pasta is done, drain and place in a serving bowl. Pour the sauce over the pasta and toss with the fresh basil.

NUTRITIONAL ANALYSIS
PER SERVING

Calories	368
Protein	18 g
Fat	6 g
Saturated Fat	2 g
Carbohydrates	61 g
Cholesterol	21 mg
Sodium	296 mg
Fiber	4 g

Prep Time:	10 minutes
Cook Time:	22 minutes

Make Ahead:
Prepare sauce up to a day in advance but don't add cheese. Simmer until hot, add cheese, and cook 1 minute.

Serves 6

Roasted Seafood over Linguini with Lemon Olive Oil
Photo by Brian MacDonald

Roasted Seafood over Linguini with Lemon Olive Oil

This dish tastes heavenly, presents beautifully and is quick to prepare. Feel free to substitute the seafood of your choice. Buy cleaned squid and use tentacles if desired. For some extra spice sprinkle with dried chili flakes.

12oz raw shrimp, peeled and deveined (tail left on)

8 oz cleaned squid cut into rings

12 mussels, scrubbed

8 oz linguini

2 tsp vegetable oil

1 cup thinly sliced red onion

½ cup thinly sliced red bell pepper

½ cup thinly sliced zucchini

3 Tbsp olive oil

3 Tbsp freshly squeezed lemon juice

2 tsp crushed fresh garlic

1 tsp hot chili sauce, or to taste

⅓ cup chopped cilantro or basil

pinch salt and freshly ground black pepper

NUTRITIONAL ANALYSIS PER SERVING

Calories	491
Protein	32 g
Fat	17 g
Saturated Fat	2.5 g
Carbohydrates	52 g
Cholesterol	230 mg
Sodium	379 mg
Fiber	3.4 g

Prep Time:	10 minutes
Cook Time:	12 minutes

Serves 4

1. Preheat the oven to 425°F. Line a baking sheet with foil and spray with cooking oil.

2. Place the shrimp, squid and mussels on the prepared baking sheet. Roast for 8 minutes, or until the mussels open. Remove from the oven and keep covered.

3. While the seafood roasts, cook the linguini in boiling water until al dente, about 8 minutes. Drain, reserving 2 Tbsp of the pasta water for the sauce. Set aside.

4. While the pasta cooks, spray a large non-stick skillet with cooking oil, add the vegetable oil and place over medium heat. Add the onion, bell pepper and zucchini; stir-fry for 4 minutes, just until the vegetables begin to soften. Add the seafood, pasta, reserved pasta water, olive oil, lemon juice, garlic, chili sauce, cilantro, salt and pepper. Toss well and serve.

Spaghetti with Sun-Dried Tomatoes and Broccoli

Make Ahead:
Prepare pasta dish early
in the day and refrigerate.
Bring to room temperature
and toss just before serving.

Serves 4

I like to break my spaghetti before cooking—it makes the dish easier to mix and eat—but leave the strands whole if you prefer. Choose firm yet ripe tomatoes, preferably plum tomatoes, which are meatier.

8 oz spaghetti, broken into thirds

3 cups finely chopped broccoli

⅔ cup sun-dried tomatoes, rehydrated (see page 221)

3 cups diced fresh tomatoes, seeded

3 Tbsp olive oil

1½ tsp crushed fresh garlic

1 tsp hot chili sauce or to taste

½ cup chopped fresh basil or cilantro

pinch salt and freshly ground black pepper

3 Tbsp grated Parmesan cheese

1. Cook the pasta in boiling water according to the package directions, or until still firm to the bite. During the last minute of cooking add the broccoli. Drain, rinse with cold water and place in a serving bowl.

2. Chop the sun-dried tomatoes and add to the pasta, along with the tomatoes, oil, garlic, chili sauce, basil, salt, pepper and cheese. Toss and serve immediately.

Smoked Salmon Fettuccine Alfredo

Everyone seems to love fettuccine Alfredo, also known as "heart attack on a plate"! My recipe is delicious and rich tasting but has a fraction of the fat and calories in the conventional version. The evaporated milk gives the sauce the creaminess and texture that butter and cream would traditionally provide.

12 oz fettuccine

1 cup cold fish or chicken stock

1 cup 2 percent evaporated milk

3 Tbsp all-purpose flour

1 tsp Dijon mustard

1 tsp minced fresh garlic

pinch freshly ground black pepper

½ cup frozen green peas

⅓ cup grated Parmesan cheese

⅓ cup chopped fresh dill

6 oz smoked salmon, chopped

1. Bring a large pot of water to a boil and cook the fettuccine for 8 to 10 minutes, until tender but firm. Drain.

2. While the pasta cooks, prepare the sauce. Combine the stock, milk, flour, mustard, garlic and pepper in a large skillet, whisking until the flour is incorporated. Stirring constantly, cook over medium heat until thickened, about 3 minutes.

3. Stir in the peas, half the Parmesan cheese and half the dill. Add the sauce to the drained pasta and toss.

4. Place on a serving platter. Garnish with the remaining Parmesan and dill, and scatter the smoked salmon overtop.

NUTRITIONAL ANALYSIS PER SERVING

Calories	339
Protein	21 g
Fat	5.7 g
Saturated Fat	2.4 g
Carbohydrates	51.5 g
Sodium	498 mg
Cholesterol	16 mg
Fiber	2.7 g

Prep Time: 10 minutes

Cook Time: 10 minutes

Make Ahead:

Make sauce up to a day in avance and refrigerate. Add extra stock when reheating if too thick.

Serves 6

Creamy Seafood Lasagna with Leeks and Bell Peppers

NUTRITIONAL ANALYSIS
PER SERVING

Calories	345
Protein	27 g
Fat	12 g
Saturated Fat	7 g
Carbohydrates	32 g
Cholesterol	82 mg
Sodium	426 mg
Fiber	0.9 g

Prep Time: 20 minutes

Cook Time: 42 minutes

Make Ahead:
Bake up to a day in advance and refrigerate; reheat in a 300°F oven for 15 minutes, or until warmed through.

Serves 10

Creamy Seafood
Lasagna with Leeks and
Bell Peppers
Photo by Mark Shapiro

You can use any combination of fish you like in this creamy lasagna, but I like shrimp for its sweet flavor and firm texture. Don't use a fish that's too delicate or it will fall apart.

9 cooked lasagna noodles

1 tsp vegetable oil
2 tsp crushed fresh garlic
⅔ cup diced red or green bell pepper
⅔ cup diced leeks or red onion
1 lb seafood, cut into small pieces
¼ cup all-purpose flour
1 cup seafood or chicken stock

1¼ cups 2 percent evaporated milk
1 tsp Dijon mustard
⅓ cup chopped fresh dill or 1 Tbsp dried
Pinch freshly ground black pepper

1¼ cups smooth light ricotta
1 cup shredded cheddar cheese
½ cup shredded Swiss cheese
¼ cup grated Parmesan cheese

1. Preheat the oven to 375°F. Spray a 13- by 9-inch baking dish with cooking oil.

2. To make the seafood mixture, heat the oil in a non-stick skillet over medium heat. Sauté the garlic, bell pepper and leeks for 5 minutes or just until tender.

3. Add the seafood and sauté until the fish is opaque, approximately 3 minutes. Pour off any excess liquid. Set aside.

4. Combine the flour, stock, milk and mustard in a non-stick saucepan and stir until smooth. Simmer over medium heat until just thickened, approximately 4 minutes, stirring often. Stir in the dill, pepper and the seafood mixture. Remove from the heat.

5. For the cheese mixture, combine the ricotta, ¾ cup of the cheddar cheese, Swiss and Parmesan cheese in a small bowl, mixing well.

6. To assemble, place 3 lasagna noodles in the prepared baking dish. Spread ⅓ of the seafood mixture over top, then ½ of the cheese mixture. Repeat for second layer. Top with the remaining 3 lasagna noodles and the remaining seafood mixture. Sprinkle the remaining ¼ cup cheddar cheese over the top. Cover with foil and bake approximately 30 minutes, removing the foil for the last 10 minutes of baking time. Allow to rest for 5 minutes before cutting and serving.

Pasta with Goat Cheese and Fresh Basil

NUTRITIONAL ANALYSIS
PER SERVING

Calories	262
Protein	9.7 g
Fat	9.7 g
Saturated Fat	2.8 g
Carbohydrates	34 g
Cholesterol	9.1 mg
Sodium	269 mg
Fiber	2.2 g

Prep Time: 10 minutes

Cook Time: 8 minutes

Make Ahead:
Prepare a day in advance
and refrigerate. Bring
to room temperature
before serving.

Serves 6

This is a wonderfully fresh tasting light pasta that's good hot or at room temperature. Tomatoes contain lycopene, a powerful antioxidant that is showing promise in the fight against prostate and breast cancer, as well as lowering cholesterol levels. If you prefer, substitute feta or a milder cheese, such as mozzarella, for the goat cheese.

3 cups chopped plum tomatoes

½ cup diced sweet onion

¼ cup sliced black olives

3 Tbsp grated Parmesan cheese

2 Tbsp olive oil

1½ Tbsp balsamic vinegar

1½ tsp minced fresh garlic

1 tsp Dijon mustard

1 tsp hot chili paste, or to taste

⅓ cup crumbled goat cheese

4 anchovy fillets, diced

8 oz rigatoni

½ cup chopped fresh basil or parsley

1. Stir the tomato, onion, olives, Parmesan, oil, vinegar, garlic, mustard, chili paste, goat cheese and anchovies in a large bowl.

2. Bring a large pot of water to a boil. Cook the rigatoni 6 to 8 minutes, until tender but firm. Drain and place in a serving bowl.

3. Add the tomato mixture and toss to coat. Add the fresh basil and toss again.

Linguini with Tomatoes and Three Cheeses

The hot pasta melts the cheese and warms the tomatoes just enough to soften them slightly—delicious! The variety of cheese is what makes this an outstanding pasta dish. If you ever need to cook your pasta early in the day, rinse it with cold water and drain. When ready to serve, run it under hot water for 30 seconds and then add the rest of your ingredients.

8 oz linguini

2 cups diced plum tomatoes

⅓ cup crumbled goat cheese

¾ cup shredded part-skim mozzarella cheese

½ cup chopped green onion

½ cup chopped fresh basil or parsley

¼ cup grated Parmesan or Asiago cheese

2 Tbsp olive oil

2 tsp minced fresh garlic

pinch salt and freshly ground black pepper

1. Bring a large pot of water to a boil and cook the linguini according to the package directions, approximately 8 to 10 minutes, until tender but firm. Drain and place in a serving bowl.

2. Add the remaining ingredients. Toss until well combined and serve immediately.

NUTRITIONAL ANALYSIS PER SERVING

Calories	381
Protein	17.8 g
Fat	14 g
Saturated Fat	6 g
Carbohydrates	37.9 g
Cholesterol	26.4 mg
Sodium	510 mg
Fiber	3.4 g

Prep Time: 15 minutes

Cook Time: 10 minutes

Make Ahead:
Mix all ingredients except pasta early in the day. When ready to serve, toss with just-cooked or reheated pasta.

Serves 4

Chicken Tetrazzini

NUTRITIONAL ANALYSIS
PER SERVING

Calories	330
Protein	17 g
Fat	9 g
Saturated Fat	1 g
Carbohydrates	40 g
Cholesterol	29 mg
Sodium	350 mg
Fiber	2 g

Prep Time: 20 minutes

Cook Time: 24 minutes

Make Ahead:
Prepare up to baking stage
a day in advance and
refrigerate. Bring to room
temperature, then bake
until hot, approximately
15 minutes.

Serves 6

Try this dish with macaroni or penne instead of spaghetti. I like to break the spaghetti into thirds before cooking for ease of mixing and eating, but leave it long if you prefer. Use any mushrooms you like, but wild mushrooms give the dish an earthy robust flavor. You can use leftover chicken in this dish, or grill or sauté it fresh.

8 oz spaghetti	1 cup 2 percent evaporated milk
2 tsp vegetable oil	1½ tsp Dijon mustard
1½ tsp crushed fresh garlic	2 tsp dried basil
1 cup chopped onion	4 oz diced cooked skinless boneless
1 cup chopped red bell pepper	chicken breast (about 1 breast)
1 cup chopped mushrooms	¾ cup shredded light cheddar cheese
3 Tbsp all-purpose flour	2 Tbsp grated Parmesan cheese
1½ cups chicken stock	2 Tbsp chopped fresh parsley or basil

1. Preheat the oven to 450°F. Spray a 13- by 9-inch baking dish with cooking oil.

2. Bring a saucepan of water to a boil and cook the spaghetti according to package directions, or until firm to the bite. Drain.

3. Meanwhile, spray a non-stick saucepan with cooking oil, add the vegetable oil and place over medium heat. Sauté the garlic, onion and red pepper for 6 minutes. Add mushrooms and sauté another 6 minutes. Add the flour and cook for 1 minute.

4. Stir in the stock, milk, mustard and dried basil. Cook, stirring constantly, until thickened, about 3 minutes. Add the chicken, ½ cup of the cheddar cheese and 1 Tbsp of the Parmesan cheese. Cook until the cheese has melted.

5. Combine the sauce with the spaghetti and toss to mix well. Place in the prepared baking dish. Sprinkle the remaining ¼ cup cheddar and 1 Tbsp Parmesan cheese overtop. Bake for 8 minutes or just until topping is lightly browned. Garnish with parsley and serve immediately.

Old-Fashioned Baked Macaroni and Cheese Casserole

Enjoy this classic comfort food without the fat and calories. I often make it and freeze individual servings in plastic containers—they're perfect for the children's lunches. It's their favorite pasta dish, and when they prefer it to any of the boxed versions, you know their taste buds are healthier! Feel free to add some vegetables, such as green peas, diced bell peppers or carrots.

3 Tbsp all-purpose flour

1⅓ cups chicken or vegetable stock

1¼ cups low-fat milk

1¼ cups shredded light cheddar cheese

6 Tbsp grated Parmesan cheese

1 tsp Dijon mustard

3¾ cups elbow macaroni

⅓ cup dry seasoned breadcrumbs

1½ tsp vegetable oil

2 tsp water

3 Tbsp chopped fresh parsley

NUTRITIONAL ANALYSIS PER SERVING

Calories	257
Protein	14 g
Fat	4.5 g
Saturated Fat	2 g
Carbohydrates	40 g
Cholesterol	8.4 mg
Sodium	380 mg
Fiber	1.3 g

Prep Time:	10 minutes
Cook Time:	24 minutes

Make Ahead:
Make sauce up to 2 days in advance and refrigerate. Dilute with a little water before adding to cooked pasta and baking.

Serves 8

1. Preheat the oven to 450°F. Spray an 8-cup casserole dish with cooking oil.

2. Whisk the flour, stock and milk in a saucepan until smooth. Place over medium heat and cook, whisking constantly, for 3 minutes or until hot and thickened. Stir in the cheddar cheese, 3 Tbsp of the Parmesan cheese and the mustard. Cook until the cheese melts, about 1 minute. Remove from the heat.

3. Bring a large pot of water to a boil. Cook the macaroni until tender but firm, 8 to 10 minutes. Drain. Toss with the cheese sauce. Pour into the prepared casserole dish.

4. Combine the breadcrumbs, the remaining 3 Tbsp Parmesan cheese, oil and water in a small bowl and stir until well mixed. Sprinkle evenly over the casserole.

5. Bake in the center of the oven for 10 minutes, until the filling is hot and the top is golden. Garnish with the parsley.

Rice Cakes with Tomato Purée

Serve these with soup and salad for a delicious lighter meal, or serve them as a side dish. The cakes can also be sautéed in a non-stick skillet sprayed with cooking oil. Try brown rice for a change, adding more stock if necessary.

4 cups vegetable or chicken stock

½ cup wild rice

½ cup white rice

1 tsp minced fresh garlic

½ cup shredded part-skim mozzarella cheese

¼ cup shredded Swiss cheese

¼ cup chopped green onion

2 Tbsp grated Parmesan cheese

1 tsp dried basil

2 eggs

½ cup tomato-based pasta sauce

2 Tbsp 2 percent evaporated milk

¼ tsp dried basil

1. Preheat the oven to 400°F. Spray a baking sheet with cooking oil.

2. For the rice cakes, bring the stock to a boil in a saucepan. Stir in the wild rice and simmer for 25 minutes. Add white rice, cover, reduce the heat to medium-low and cook for 10 more minutes, or until the rice is tender. Let the rice cool slightly. Drain off any liquid. Rinse with cold water.

3. Combine the cooled rice, garlic, mozzarella and Swiss cheese, green onion, Parmesan cheese, basil and eggs in a bowl. Stir until well mixed. Using a ⅓-cup measure, form the mixture into approximately 10 patties and place on the prepared baking sheet. Bake approximately 12 minutes per side, until browned.

4. For the sauce, heat the tomato sauce, milk and basil in a small saucepan.

5. Serve the rice cakes with the sauce on the side.

NUTRITIONAL ANALYSIS PER SERVING (1 RICE CAKE)

Calories	114
Protein	6 g
Fat	3 g
Saturated Fat	1 g
Carbohydrates	16 g
Cholesterol	27 mg
Sodium	149 mg
Fiber	1 g

Prep Time: 15 minutes

Cook Time: 45 minutes

Make Ahead:
Prepare up to the baking stage a day in advance and refrigerate. Bake just before serving. Or bake ahead and reheat in a 300°F oven for 10 minutes.

Makes 10 rice cakes

Rice Cakes with Tomato Purée
Photo by Mark Shapiro

Vidalia Onion Risotto

NUTRITIONAL ANALYSIS
PER SERVING

Calories	320
Protein	14 g
Fat	7.5 g
Saturated Fat	2.8 g
Carbohydrates	49 g
Cholesterol	8.8 mg
Sodium	390 mg
Fiber	3.1 g

Prep Time: 10 minutes

Cook Time: 30 minutes

Serves 4

Once you've tried a Vidalia onion, you'll never want a regular onion again. It's so sweet you can enjoy it raw—I don't even cry when I chop them! This risotto beats all others in flavor and texture, without the use of butter or excess fat. Risotto is a dish that must be served immediately for the best flavor. If you do reheat it, add more stock and simmer for a few minutes until the extra stock is absorbed.

3 to 3 ½ cups chicken or vegetable stock

2 tsp vegetable oil

2 cups diced Vidalia onion or other sweet onion

1 ½ tsp minced fresh garlic

1 tsp dried oregano

1 cup arborio rice

⅓ cup light feta cheese, crumbled

3 Tbsp grated Parmesan cheese

1 ⅓ cups chopped fresh basil or parsley

1. Bring the stock to a boil in a saucepan. Reduce the heat to a simmer.

2. Heat the oil in a non-stick saucepan over medium heat. Add the onion, garlic and oregano. Cook, stirring frequently, until golden and soft, about 10 minutes.

3. Stir in the rice. Cook and stir for 1 minute. Add ½ cup of the simmering stock. Cook, stirring constantly, until the liquid is absorbed. Continue adding stock ½ cup at a time, stirring constantly and making sure all the liquid is absorbed before adding more, for about 18 minutes. The rice should be tender but slightly firm at the center. Adjust the heat as necessary to maintain a slow simmer.

4. Remove from the heat. Stir in the feta cheese, Parmesan cheese and basil. Serve immediately.

Chicken Teriyaki over Rotini

My family could eat this dish every night of the week. Bottled teriyaki sauces contain excess sodium and preservatives and never taste as good as the sauce in this recipe. Double the teriyaki sauce recipe; it will keep for two weeks in the refrigerator and is great in pasta dishes or with cooked fish or chicken. You can use other vegetables, such as broccoli, mushrooms or sugar snap peas, or substitute leftover beef or pork for the chicken. Make this a vegetarian dish by using firm tofu instead of chicken.

12 oz rotini	12 oz skinless boneless chicken breast (about 3 breasts), cubed
3 Tbsp packed brown sugar	3 Tbsp cornstarch
¼ cup rice vinegar	2 tsp vegetable oil
¼ cup water	1 cup thinly sliced red bell peppers
¼ cup low-sodium soy sauce	1 cup thinly sliced yellow bell peppers
1 Tbsp sesame oil	1 cup halved snow peas
1 Tbsp cornstarch	2 tsp sesame seeds, toasted
1½ tsp minced fresh garlic	
1½ tsp minced fresh ginger	⅓ cup fresh chopped cilantro or parsley

1. Bring a large pot of water to a boil and cook the rotini for 8 to 10 minutes, until tender but firm. Drain.

2. Combine the sugar, vinegar, water, soy sauce, sesame oil, cornstarch, garlic and ginger together in a bowl and whisk until smooth. Set aside.

3. Dust the chicken cubes with the cornstarch. Spray a wok or large non-stick skillet with cooking oil, add the vegetable oil and place over medium-high heat. Cook the chicken for 3 minutes or until browned but not yet cooked through. Add the red and yellow bell pepper, snow peas and sesame seeds. Cook for 3 minutes, until the chicken is just cooked through and the vegetables are tender-crisp. Add the sauce and cook for 2 minutes or until thickened and bubbly.

4. Toss the pasta with the chicken-vegetable mixture in a large serving bowl. Serve immediately garnished with cilantro.

NUTRITIONAL ANALYSIS PER SERVING

Calories	375
Protein	22 g
Fat	5.5 g
Saturated Fat	0.7 g
Carbohydrates	59 g
Cholesterol	33 mg
Sodium	403 mg
Fiber	2.3 g

Prep Time: 15 minutes
Cook Time: 8 minutes

Make Ahead:
Prepare sauce up to
4 days in advance and
refrigerate.

Serves 6

Chicken and Hoisin Fried Rice

NUTRITIONAL ANALYSIS
PER SERVING

Calories	254
Protein	18 g
Fat	5.1 g
Saturated Fat	0.6 g
Carbohydrates	34 g
Cholesterol	33 mg
Sodium	500 mg
Fiber	3.1 g

Prep Time: 10 minutes

Cook Time: 20 minutes

Make Ahead:
Prepare up to a day in
advance and refrigerate.
Reheat in a skillet over
low heat until just
warmed through.

Serves 4

My children rate this better than any restaurant fried rice they've had. Traditional fried rice is often made with lard or large amounts of oil, adding greatly to the fat and calories. This version calls for only a single tablespoon of vegetable oil; the hoisin sauce provides the flavor and moisture. Substitute cooked beef, pork, shrimp or firm tofu for the chicken and add other vegetables of your choice. I freeze remainders of this rice in small containers for the kids' lunches.

1 cup long-grain rice

2 skinless boneless chicken breasts

⅓ cup chicken stock

3 Tbsp low-sodium soy sauce

3 Tbsp hoisin sauce

⅔ cup chopped carrots

1 Tbsp vegetable oil

1 cup diced red bell pepper

1 cup diced snow peas

1½ tsp minced fresh garlic

1 tsp minced fresh ginger

2 green onions, chopped

1. Bring 1¼ cups of water to a boil in a saucepan. Stir in the rice. Cover, reduce the heat to low and cook for 12 minutes. Remove from the heat. Let stand, covered, for 10 minutes. Transfer to a bowl. Cool.

2. While the rice is cooking, preheat the barbecue or a non-stick grill pan to medium-high and spray with cooking oil. Cook the chicken for 6 minutes per side, or until cooked through and no longer pink in the center. Dice and set aside.

3. Whisk the stock, soy sauce and hoisin sauce in a small bowl. Set aside.

4. Cook the carrots in a pot of boiling water until tender-crisp, about 4 minutes. Drain.

5. Spray a non-stick wok or large skillet with cooking oil, add the vegetable oil and place over high heat. Add the red peppers, snow peas, garlic, ginger and carrots; cook for 2 minutes, stirring constantly. Add the cooled rice and cook, stirring, for 2 minutes longer. Stir in the stock mixture and the chicken. Cook for 1 minute longer, until heated through.

6. Serve immediately, garnished with green onions.

Pesto Shrimp Paella

If you're short on time, you can substitute about ¼ cup store-bought pesto for this recipe, but the fat and calories are considerably higher. Stretch the pesto and lessen the calories by adding 2 tablespoons of low-fat sour cream. If basil is unavailable, substitute parsley or use a combination.

1 tsp vegetable oil

2 tsp minced fresh garlic

1 cup chopped onion

1 cup chopped red bell pepper

¾ cup wild rice

¾ cup brown rice

2 ½ cups chicken stock

1 ¼ lb peeled and deveined raw shrimp, chopped

1 ½ cups packed fresh basil leaves

2 ½ Tbsp grated Parmesan cheese

2 ½ Tbsp olive oil

2 ½ Tbsp pine nuts, toasted

1 ½ tsp minced garlic

5 Tbsp chicken stock or water

3 Tbsp chopped fresh basil or parsley

NUTRITIONAL ANALYSIS PER SERVING

Calories	346
Protein	20 g
Fat	11 g
Saturated Fat	2 g
Carbohydrates	43 g
Cholesterol	103 mg
Sodium	364 mg
Fiber	3 g

Prep Time: 15 minutes

Cook Time: 37 minutes

Make Ahead:
Prepare pesto up to a day in advance and refrigerate, or freeze for up to 2 weeks. Prepare rice mixture earlier in the day and refrigerate; reheat before mixing with pesto.

Serves 6

1. For the paella, spray a saucepan with cooking oil, add the vegetable oil and place over medium heat. Add the 2 tsp garlic, onion and red pepper; cook for 4 minutes or until softened.

2. Add the wild rice, brown rice and 2 ½ cups stock. Bring to a boil. Cover, reduce the heat to medium-low and simmer for 30 minutes, or until the rice is tender and the liquid absorbed.

3. Add the shrimp and cook until no longer pink, about 2 minutes. Remove the paella from the heat, cover and let sit for 10 minutes.

4. For the pesto, combine the basil, cheese, olive oil, pine nuts and 1 ½ tsp garlic in a food processor. Process until finely chopped, scraping down the sides of the bowl once. With the machine running, gradually add the 5 Tbsp stock through the feed tube. Process until smooth.

5. Add the pesto to the rice and shrimp, mixing well. Place in a serving dish and garnish with the chopped basil.

Couscous, Chickpea and Cranberry Salad

NUTRITIONAL ANALYSIS
PER SERVING

Calories	235
Protein	6.2 g
Fat	3.2 g
Saturated Fat	0.7 g
Carbohydrates	45 g
Cholesterol	0 mg
Sodium	204 mg
Fiber	3.7 g

Prep Time: 15 minutes

Cook Time: 5 minutes

Make Ahead:
Prepare up to a day
in advance and refrigerate.
Bring to room temperature
before serving.

Serves 6

This is a beautiful salad to serve as part of a buffet meal. The sweet orange dressing goes so well with the dried cranberries, chickpeas and basil. Always have a container of orange juice concentrate on hand in the freezer for cooking and baking purposes; you can remove the amount needed while still frozen.

1 cup chicken stock
1 cup couscous
¾ cup canned chickpeas, rinsed and
    drained
⅓ cup dried cranberries
¼ cup chopped green onion
¼ cup diced red bell pepper
¼ cup chopped fresh basil or parsley

1 Tbsp olive oil
2 Tbsp orange juice concentrate
2 Tbsp freshly squeezed lemon juice
2 tsp grated orange rind
3 Tbsp liquid honey
1 tsp minced fresh garlic

1. Bring the stock to a boil in a small saucepan. Remove from the heat. Stir in the couscous, cover and let stand for 5 minutes. Transfer to a large bowl, fluff with a fork and cool.

2. Stir the chickpeas, cranberries, green onions, red peppers and basil or parsley into the cooled couscous.

3. To make the dressing, whisk the olive oil, orange juice concentrate, lemon juice, orange rind, honey and garlic in a small bowl. Pour over the couscous mixture and toss to coat.

Couscous, Chickpea and Cranberry Salad ▶
Photo by Lorella Zanetti

Lemon Couscous with Cherry Tomatoes, Mint, Dill and Feta

**NUTRITIONAL ANALYSIS
PER SERVING:**

Calories	189
Protein	7.3 g
Fat	6.1 g
Saturated Fat	1.5 g
Carbohydrates	27 g
Cholesterol	3 mg
Sodium	230 mg
Fiber	2.8 g

Prep Time: 10 minutes

Cook Time: 5 minutes

Serves 6

This is a wonderful, light-tasting couscous that can be served as a side dish or main dish if some protein is added. To prevent the couscous from lumping, add a spray of cooking oil to the stock. Feel free to substitute whatever herbs you have on hand.

1 cup couscous

1 cup chicken or vegetable stock

1 cup halved cherry tomatoes

½ cup diced cucumber

¼ cup chopped green onion

¼ cup freshly squeezed lemon juice

1 Tbsp olive oil

2 tsp grated lemon rind

1 tsp crushed fresh garlic

¼ cup chopped fresh mint

¼ cup chopped fresh dill

⅓ cup crumbled light feta cheese

pinch freshly ground black pepper

1. Bring the couscous and stock to a boil. Remove from the heat, cover and let sit for 5 minutes. Transfer to a large bowl and fluff with a fork. Cool.

2. Add the remaining ingredients and toss to combine. Serve at room temperature.

Caesar Corn and Red Pepper Risotto

This is an outstanding and unusual risotto dish. People always think risotto is difficult and time-consuming to make. On the contrary, it takes about 20 minutes more than regular rice. Instead of the butter and cheese in many restaurant risottos, my version uses heart-healthy olive oil and a small amount of Parmesan cheese for flavor.

1¾ cups canned corn kernels, drained (or use frozen)

1 egg
¼ cup grated Parmesan cheese
3 Tbsp olive oil
1 Tbsp freshly squeezed lemon juice
1 tsp minced fresh garlic
½ tsp Dijon mustard

4¼ cups chicken or vegetable stock
2 tsp vegetable oil
¾ cup chopped onion
1½ tsp minced fresh garlic
1½ cups arborio rice
½ cup chopped fresh parsley
1 large red bell pepper, roasted and chopped (see page 122)

1. Spray a non-stick skillet with cooking oil and place over medium heat. Sauté the corn, stirring often, until slightly charred, about 8 minutes. Set aside.

2. Combine the egg, cheese, olive oil, lemon juice, 1 tsp garlic and mustard in a food processor. Purée until smooth.

3. Bring the stock to a boil in a large saucepan. Reduce the heat to a simmer.

4. Spray a non-stick saucepan with cooking oil, add the vegetable oil and place over medium-high heat. Add the onion and 1 ½ tsp garlic and sauté until softened, about 5 minutes. Stir in the rice and cook, stirring, for 1 minute.

5. Reduce the heat to medium. Add ½ cup of the simmering stock and cook, stirring constantly, until the liquid is absorbed. Continue to add stock, ½ cup at a time, stirring constantly and making sure all the liquid is absorbed before making the next addition. It will take about 18 minutes. The rice should be tender but slightly firm at the center. Adjust the heat as necessary to maintain a slow, bubbling simmer.

6. When the rice is done, stir in the parsley, red pepper and corn. Stir in the sauce and serve immediately.

NUTRITIONAL ANALYSIS
PER SERVING

Calories	385
Protein	13 g
Fat	13 g
Saturated Fat	2.6 g
Carbohydrates	54 g
Cholesterol	39 mg
Sodium	467 mg
Fiber	3.5 g

Prep Time: 15 minutes
Cook Time: 32 minutes

Make Ahead:
Roast pepper and sauté corn up to 2 days in advance and refrigerate. Roasted peppers can be frozen for up to 4 months. Prepare the sauce and refrigerate for up to 2 days or freeze for up to 1 month.

Serves 6

Citrus Risotto with Shrimp

NUTRITIONAL ANALYSIS PER SERVING

Calories	222
Protein	18 g
Fat	5.6 g
Saturated Fat	0.8 g
Carbohydrates	23 g
Cholesterol	126 mg
Sodium	320 mg
Fiber	1 g

Prep Time: 10 minutes

Cook Time: 27 minutes

Make Ahead:
Sauté onions early in the day.

Serves 4

This light risotto requires no butter or cream, yet the flavor is outstanding. You can substitute lemon or orange for the lime or use any firm seafood or chicken in place of the shrimp.

3 ¼ cups vegetable or chicken stock
1 tsp vegetable oil
¾ cup chopped onion
1½ tsp crushed fresh garlic
1 cup arborio rice

1 lb raw shrimp, peeled and deveined
3 Tbsp freshly squeezed lemon juice
2 tsp grated lemon zest

¼ cup chopped dill or parsley

1. Bring the stock to a boil, then lower the heat to keep it at a simmer.

2. Heat the oil over medium heat in a medium non-stick saucepan. Add the onion and garlic; sauté for 5 minutes, or until the onion begins to brown. Add the rice and sauté for 1 minute.

3. Add the stock ½ cup at a time, stirring constantly and making sure all the liquid is absorbed before adding more. It will take about 18 minutes. The rice should be tender but slightly firm at the center. Adjust the heat as necessary to maintain a slow simmer.

4. When adding the last portion of stock, add the shrimp and cook until pink, approximately 2 minutes. Stir in the lemon juice and zest; simmer for 1 minute.

5. Garnish with the dill and serve immediately.

Couscous with Raisins and Dates

This dish is delicious served at room temperature, which makes it perfect for a pot-luck or buffet. The key to perfect couscous is the one-to-one ratio of the stock and couscous. Try spraying a little vegetable oil into the stock to prevent the couscous from clumping.

1 cup chicken or vegetable stock

1 cup couscous

2 tsp vegetable oil

¾ cup finely chopped onion

1 cup finely chopped red bell pepper

¼ cup raisins

1 Tbsp olive oil

2 Tbsp freshly squeezed lemon juice

2 tsp honey

1 tsp crushed fresh garlic

¼ cup diced dried dates or apricots

¼ cup chopped cilantro or parsley

1. Bring the stock to a boil in a small saucepan. Stir in the couscous and remove from the heat. Cover and let stand until the liquid is absorbed, approximately 5 minutes. Place in a large serving bowl and fluff with a fork.

2. Spray a non-stick saucepan with cooking oil, add the vegetable oil and place over medium heat. Add the onion and red pepper and sauté until softened, approximately 5 minutes. Add the raisins, olive oil, lemon juice, honey, garlic and dates; mix until combined. Add to the couscous and mix well. Garnish with the cilantro.

NUTRITIONAL ANALYSIS PER SERVING

Calories	162
Protein	4 g
Fat	2 g
Saturated fat	0 g
Carbohydrates	31 g
Cholesterol	0 mg
Sodium	159 mg
Fiber	2 g

Prep Time: 10 minutes

Cook Time: 10 minutes

Make Ahead:
Prepare up to a day in advance and refrigerate. Reheat over low heat or warm to room temperature before serving.

Serves 6

Quinoa with Charred Corn, Bell Pepper and Spinach

Quinoa is a "super" food—low glycemic, with an abundance of nutrients. Containing eight essential amino acids, it's the only grain that's considered a complete protein, making this recipe a vegetarian's delight. Instead of fresh spinach you can use half a 10-ounce package of frozen spinach—cooked and squeezed dry.

1 cup quinoa

2 cups vegetable or chicken stock

1 ½ cups canned corn kernels, drained

1 tsp vegetable oil

1 cup diced onion

½ cup diced red bell pepper

2 tsp crushed fresh garlic

½ tsp ground cumin

1 tsp seeded minced jalapeño pepper (or
   1 tsp hot chili sauce or paste)

4 cups chopped fresh spinach

1 Tbsp water

⅓ cup chopped green onion

⅓ cup chopped cilantro or parsley

⅓ cup crumbled light feta cheese

2 Tbsp olive oil

2 Tbsp freshly squeezed lemon juice

NUTRITIONAL ANALYSIS PER SERVING

Calories	379
Protein	14 g
Fat	13 g
Saturated Fat	2.4 g
Carbohydrates	53 g
Cholesterol	5 mg
Sodium	436 mg
Fiber	7.0 g

Prep Time:	15 minutes
Cook Time:	30 minutes

Make Ahead:
Prepare early in the day and refrigerate. Bring to room temperature before serving.

Serves 4

1. Bring the quinoa and stock to a boil. Cover and simmer for 15 minutes, just until the stock is absorbed and the quinoa tender. Remove from the heat and place in a serving bowl.

2. Spray a small non-stick skillet with cooking oil and place over medium heat. Sauté the corn for approximately 8 minutes, just until browned, stirring constantly. Set aside.

3. Spray a medium non-stick skillet with cooking oil, add the vegetable oil and place over medium heat. Add the diced onion, bell pepper, garlic, cumin and jalapeño pepper and sauté until the onion begins to brown, about 5 minutes.

4. Add the spinach and water. Cook until the spinach wilts, approximately 2 minutes.

5. Remove from the heat. Stir in the green onion, cilantro, cheese, olive oil, lemon juice and sautéed corn. Add the mixture to the quinoa and mix well.

Quinoa with Charred Corn, Bell Pepper and Spinach
Photo by Lorella Zanetti

Brown Rice, Black Bean and Avocado Pilaf

NUTRITIONAL ANALYSIS
PER SERVING

Calories	325
Protein	11 g
Fat	8 g
Saturated Fat	1.1 g
Carbohydrates	53 g
Cholesterol	0 mg
Sodium	309 mg
Fiber	6.7 g

Prep Time: 10 minutes

Cook Time: 30 minutes

Make Ahead:
Prepare up to 2 hours in advance, omitting the avocado, and refrigerate. Reheat in a skillet over low heat until just warmed through; mix in the avocado just before serving.

Serves 4

This pilaf is both sensational and simple, not to mention healthy: brown rice is a low-glycemic food that keeps you full for a long time, and rice and beans make a complete protein when combined. If you cut the avocado ahead of time, sprinkle it with lemon juice to help prevent browning.

1 cup brown rice
2 cups chicken or vegetable stock

1½ cups canned black beans, drained and rinsed
1½ cups sliced cherry tomatoes
½ cup diced ripe avocado

⅓ cup diced green onion
pinch freshly ground black pepper
1 Tbsp olive oil
3 Tbsp freshly squeezed lime or lemon juice
⅓ cup chopped cilantro or parsley

1. Combine the rice and stock in a medium saucepan, cover and bring to a boil. Lower the heat and simmer for approximately 30 minutes, or until the rice is still slightly tender.

2. Cool for 10 minutes.

3. Combine the remaining ingredients in a bowl, mixing well. Stir into the rice mixture and serve immediately.

Asparagus Bundles Wrapped with Goat Cheese and Prosciutto

NUTRITIONAL ANALYSIS
PER SERVING

Calories	142
Protein	5.6 g
Fat	11.7 g
Saturated Fat	5.3 g
Carbohydrates	1.5 g
Cholesterol	17 mg
Sodium	163 mg
Fiber	1.7 g

Prep Time: 10 minutes

Cook Time: 10 minutes

Make Ahead:
Assemble asparagus
bundles up to a day in
advance and refrigerate.
Bake just before serving.

Serves 6

This substantial vegetable dish with its colorful and elegant presentation is a great way to complete the dinner entrée. Prosciutto and goat cheese bring out the subtle flavor of asparagus. You can substitute thinly sliced roast turkey in place of the prosciutto.

6 slices prosciutto (about 4 oz)
½ cup goat cheese, softened
1 lb trimmed asparagus
2 Tbsp finely diced red bell pepper

1. Preheat the oven to 400°F. Spray a baking sheet with cooking oil.

2. Place the prosciutto flat on a clean work surface. Divide the goat cheese among the prosciutto slices, spreading it thinly down the center. Place 3 to 4 asparagus spears crosswise on top of each slice of prosciutto. Wrap the prosciutto tightly around the asparagus and transfer to the prepared baking sheet. Spray the bundles with cooking oil.

3. Bake in the centre of the oven for 10 minutes or just until the asparagus turns bright green and is slightly tender. Garnish with red pepper.

Green Beans with Coconut Sauce

The combination of light coconut milk, peanut butter, sautéed vegetables and cilantro brings a whole new dimension to green beans, which are high in vitamin C and folate. Be sure not to overcook the beans or they'll lose their bright green color and crisp texture. If you want to cook them earlier in the day, rinse with cold water after cooking until they are no longer warm. When you're ready to serve, rinse them with boiling water, then pour the sauce over them.

⅓ cup light coconut milk

1½ Tbsp natural peanut butter

1 Tbsp freshly squeezed lemon juice

2 tsp low-sodium soy sauce

1 tsp sesame oil

1 tsp honey

½ tsp minced fresh ginger

1½ lb green beans

2 tsp vegetable oil

1 cup chopped onion

⅓ cup diced red bell pepper

1 tsp minced fresh garlic

3 Tbsp chopped cilantro

1. Whisk the coconut milk, peanut butter, lemon juice, soy sauce, sesame oil, honey and ginger together in a bowl. Set aside.

2. Blanch or steam the green beans for 2 minutes or until tender-crisp. Drain.

3. Spray a non-stick skillet with cooking oil, and heat the vegetable oil over medium-high heat. Add the onion, red pepper and garlic and sauté for 5 minutes, stirring occasionally.

4. Add the green beans to the pan. Stir in the coconut milk mixture and cook for 1 minute, or until heated through. Serve garnished with cilantro.

NUTRITIONAL ANALYSIS PER SERVING

Calories	118
Protein	3.6 g
Fat	5.3 g
Saturated Fat	1.2 g
Carbohydrates	14 g
Cholesterol	0 mg
Sodium	74 mg
Fiber	4.6 g

Prep Time: 10 minutes

Cook Time: 8 minutes

Make Ahead:
Prepare sauce up to 2 days in advance and refrigerate.

Serves 6

Roasted Asparagus with Tahini Sauce and Toasted Pine Nuts

NUTRITIONAL ANALYSIS PER SERVING

Calories	70
Protein	2.3 g
Fat	5.3 g
Saturated Fat	0.5 g
Carbohydrates	4.6 g
Cholesterol	1 mg
Sodium	140 mg
Fiber	1.8 g

Prep Time: 5 minutes

Cook Time: 15 minutes

Serves 6

I always steamed asparagus until I had roasted asparagus in a restaurant. Now I take the time to roast—it brings out a totally different flavor. Serve this either warm or at room temperature.

1 lb trimmed asparagus

1½ Tbsp light mayonnaise

1 Tbsp tahini (sesame seed paste)

1 Tbsp olive oil

1 Tbsp freshly squeezed lemon juice

1 Tbsp water

2 tsp low-sodium soy sauce

½ tsp crushed fresh garlic

2 Tbsp chopped cilantro or parsley

2 Tbsp pine nuts, toasted (see page 75)

1. Preheat the oven to 425°F. Line a baking sheet with foil and spray with cooking oil.

2. Place the asparagus on the prepared baking sheet and spray with vegetable oil. Roast for 15 minutes, turning after 10 minutes. Place on a serving dish.

3. While the asparagus is roasting, whisk the mayonnaise, tahini, oil, lemon juice, water, soy sauce and garlic in a small bowl. Pour over the asparagus, and garnish with cilantro and pine nuts.

Asparagus, Roasted Bell Pepper and Cheese Strudel

Phyllo is a great way to enjoy pastry without having the excess calories and fat of regular pastry. I spray each sheet with cooking oil instead of the commonly used butter. This dish is so versatile that it can be served as an appetizer, side dish or main course with a side salad. It's perfect for the vegetarian. For tips on working with phyllo pastry, see page 71.

½ cup smooth light ricotta

½ cup shredded light mozzarella cheese

⅓ cup crumbled goat cheese

1 Tbsp low-fat milk

1 tsp dried basil

½ tsp crushed fresh garlic

¼ tsp freshly ground black pepper

¼ lb trimmed asparagus

1 medium roasted bell pepper, diced (see page 122)

¼ cup rehydrated sun-dried tomato, chopped (see page 221)

6 sheets phyllo pastry

1. Preheat the oven to 375°F. Line a baking sheet with foil and spray with cooking oil.

2. Combine the ricotta, mozzarella and goat cheeses, milk, basil, garlic and pepper and process in a food processor or with a hand beater until smooth and well mixed.

3. Steam the asparagus for 3 minutes, or just until bright green. Rinse with cold water until no longer warm to prevent discoloration.

4. Place one sheet of phyllo pastry on your work surface, with the long side facing you, and spray with cooking oil. Repeat with the other 5 sheets. Spread the cheese mixture evenly overtop, leaving a 1-inch margin on all sides. Place the asparagus over the cheese, laying it parallel to the long side of the phyllo. Dot with bell pepper and sun-dried tomato.

5. Fold in the sides of the phyllo pastry and roll it up. Place on a baking sheet and spray with cooking oil. Bake for 25 minutes, or just until lightly browned. It's best if served immediately.

NUTRITIONAL ANALYSIS PER SERVING

Calories	112
Protein	6.9 g
Fat	4.6 g
Saturated Fat	2.4 g
Carbohydrates	11 g
Cholesterol	12 mg
Sodium	259 mg
Fiber	1.3 g

Prep Time: 10 minutes

Cook Time: 28 minutes

Make Ahead:
Prepare filling a day in advance and refrigerate. Roll the strudel early in the day and refrigerate, keeping it well covered. Bake just before serving.

Serves 8

Sliced Tomato Stacks

**NUTRITIONAL ANALYSIS
PER SERVING**

Calories	92
Protein	5.2 g
Fat	4.8 g
Saturated Fat	2.4 g
Carbohydrates	6.9 g
Cholesterol	8.6 mg
Sodium	173 mg
Fiber	1.6 g

Prep Time: 10 minutes

Cook Time: 5 minutes

Make Ahead:
Prepare the stacks early
in the day and refrigerate.
Bake just before serving.

Serves 4

What a way to liven up the basic field tomato! These "sandwiches" are filled with a delicious cheese and sun-dried tomato filling and topped with toasted pine nuts.

2 large field tomatoes

¼ cup crumbled goat cheese

¼ cup light cream cheese, softened

¼ cup rehydrated chopped sun-dried
   tomatoes (see page 221)

½ tsp dried basil

2 tsp grated Parmesan cheese

1½ tsp toasted pine nuts

1. Preheat the oven to 400°F. Spray a baking sheet with vegetable oil.

2. Slice each tomato into 4 thick slices.

3. Stir the goat cheese, cream cheese, sun-dried tomatoes, basil and half the Parmesan cheese together in a bowl. Place 4 slices of tomato on a baking sheet. Spread the goat cheese mixture evenly over the slices. Top with the remaining slices of tomato. Sprinkle with the pine nuts and the remaining Parmesan.

4. Bake in the center of the oven for 5 minutes or until just warmed through.

Teriyaki Sesame Vegetables

This flavorful dish is the easiest way to get your children to enjoy vegetables. Make extra sauce and serve it over fish or chicken.

1 tsp crushed fresh garlic

4 tsp soy sauce

4 tsp rice vinegar

½ tsp minced fresh ginger

1 tsp sesame oil

4 tsp water

4 tsp brown sugar

1½ tsp vegetable oil

1 tsp vegetable oil

1 cup thinly sliced carrot

1 tsp crushed fresh garlic

½ large red or yellow bell pepper, thinly sliced

½ large green bell pepper, thinly sliced

1½ cups snow peas

1 tsp toasted sesame seeds

2 Tbsp chopped cilantro or parsley

1. To make the sauce, combine 1 tsp garlic, soy sauce, vinegar, ginger, sesame oil, water, sugar and 1 ½ tsp vegetable oil in a small saucepan. Bring it to a boil and cook for 3 minutes or until thickened and syrupy. Set aside.

2. To make the vegetables, heat 1 tsp vegetable oil in a large non-stick skillet. Add the carrot and sauté over medium-high heat for 2 minutes, until just barely tender. Add 1 tsp garlic, bell pepper and snow peas; sauté, stirring constantly, for 2 minutes.

3. Add the sauce to the pan and simmer for 1 minute, or until the vegetables are just tender-crisp. Place in a serving dish and sprinkle with sesame seeds and cilantro.

NUTRITIONAL ANALYSIS PER SERVING

Calories	96
Protein	2 g
Fat	4 g
Saturated Fat	0.7 g
Carbohydrates	12 g
Cholesterol	0 mg
Sodium	271 mg
Fiber	2 g

Prep Time: 15 minutes

Cook Time: 8 minutes

Make Ahead:

The sauce keeps for over a week in the refrigerator and for up to 2 months frozen.

Serves 4

Broccoli, Carrot and Dill Vegetable Strudel

NUTRITIONAL ANALYSIS
PER SERVING

Calories	112
Protein	6 g
Fat	6 g
Saturated Fat	2 g
Carbohydrates	34 mg
Cholesterol	40 mg
Sodium	490 mg
Fiber	2.2 g

Prep Time: 10 minutes

Cook Time: 35 minutes

Make Ahead:
Prepare the filling up to
a day in advance, cover and
refrigerate. Roll the strudel
early in the day and keep
it well covered. Bake just
before serving.

Serves 6

This strudel is filled with great nutrients and beautiful colors. Sweet potatoes can replace the carrots, but pre-cook them in boiling water for 3 minutes to soften them slightly. You can use parsley or basil instead of dill, and cheddar or mozzarella instead of the Swiss cheese, though a stronger cheese tastes best. For tips on working with phyllo, see page 71.

2 tsp vegetable oil
1½ tsp minced fresh garlic
1½ cups chopped onion
3 cups finely chopped broccoli
2 cups finely chopped carrots
⅓ cup chopped fresh dill

1 egg
¼ cup dry seasoned breadcrumbs
⅔ cup shredded light Swiss cheese
pinch salt and freshly ground black
   pepper
6 sheets phyllo pastry

1. Preheat the oven to 375°F. Spray a baking sheet with cooking oil.

2. Spray a large non-stick skillet with cooking oil and heat the vegetable oil over medium heat. Cook the garlic, onion, broccoli and carrots for 10 minutes or until tender-crisp, stirring occasionally. Remove from the heat and stir in the dill, egg, breadcrumbs, cheese, salt and pepper.

3. Lay one sheet of phyllo on your work surface, with the long side facing you, and spray with cooking oil. Repeat with the remaining phyllo sheets, but do not spray the last sheet. Spread the vegetable mixture over the surface, leaving a 1-inch border on all sides.

4. Roll up tightly, jelly-roll style, and tuck the ends under. Spray with cooking oil. Place on the prepared baking sheet and bake for 25 minutes or until golden brown.

Mushroom and Cheese Phyllo Strudel

If you love mushrooms, you'll get your fill in this strudel—6 cups of meaty oyster mushrooms. You can use any variety of mushrooms you like; just be sure to sauté them on high heat to get rid of the moisture. Regular field mushrooms have more moisture than wild ones and especially need to be cooked over high heat.

2 tsp vegetable oil

1 cup chopped onion

2 tsp minced fresh garlic

6 cups sliced oyster mushrooms
     (about 1 lb)

¼ cup vegetable stock

¾ cup light smooth ricotta

⅓ cup goat cheese

⅓ cup low-fat milk

⅓ cup chopped fresh dill

¼ cup sliced black olives

2 Tbsp grated Parmesan cheese

pinch salt and freshly ground black
     pepper

6 sheets phyllo pastry

NUTRITIONAL ANALYSIS PER SERVING

Calories	159
Protein	8.6 g
Fat	7.2 g
Saturated Fat	2.8 g
Carbohydrates	15 g
Cholesterol	12 mg
Sodium	256 mg
Fiber	2.1 g

Prep Time: 15 minutes

Cook Time: 37 minutes

Make Ahead:
Prepare strudel up to the point of baking a day in advance. Refrigerate, keeping the phyllo well covered. Bake just before serving.

Serves 8

1. Preheat the oven to 375°F. Spray a baking sheet with cooking oil.

2. Spray a large non-stick skillet with cooking oil, add the vegetable oil and place over medium-high heat. Add the onions and garlic; sauté, stirring occasionally, for 4 minutes or until softened.

3. Stir in the mushrooms and stock. Continue to cook, stirring frequently, for 8 to 10 minutes, or until the mushrooms are browned and there is no liquid left in the skillet. Transfer to a bowl. Cool for 5 minutes.

4. Stir the ricotta, goat cheese, milk, dill, olives, Parmesan cheese, salt and pepper into the cooled mushroom mixture.

5. Keep the phyllo covered with a cloth to prevent drying (see page 71). Remove 2 sheets of phyllo and place in a single layer on your work surface, with the long side facing you. Spray with cooking oil. Layer 2 more sheets of phyllo on top and spray with cooking oil. Place the remaining 2 sheets of phyllo on the stack. Spread the filling over the surface of the phyllo, leaving a 2-inch border along the edges. Roll the strudel up, jelly-roll style.

6. After several rolls, tuck in the ends and continue to roll to the end. Place on the prepared baking sheet. Spray with cooking oil. Bake in the center of the oven for 25 to 30 minutes, or until golden. Cool for 5 minutes before slicing.

Potato Wedge Fries

**NUTRITIONAL ANALYSIS
PER SERVING (4 WEDGES)**

Calories	156
Protein	3 g
Fat	5.3 g
Saturated Fat	1 g
Carbohydrates	24 g
Cholesterol	1.6 mg
Sodium	47 mg
Fiber	2.3 g

Prep Time: 5 minutes

Cook Time: 40 minutes

Serves 6

These are the best and healthiest French fries you'll ever eat—forget deep-fried fast-food fries that can contain over 20 grams of fat for a small serving. Experiment and use any seasonings you like. You can cut the potatoes early in the day, as long as you keep them in cold water so they won't brown.

3 large baking potatoes, scrubbed

2 Tbsp olive oil

1 tsp minced fresh garlic

2 Tbsp grated Parmesan cheese

¼ tsp chili powder

3 Tbsp chopped fresh parsley

1. Preheat the oven to 375°F. Spray a rimmed baking sheet with cooking oil.

2. Cut each potato lengthwise into 8 wedges. Place on the prepared baking sheet. Combine the oil and garlic in a small bowl. Combine the cheese and chili powder in another small bowl. Brush the potato wedges with half the oil mixture, then sprinkle with half the cheese mixture.

3. Bake for 20 minutes. Turn the wedges; brush with the remaining oil mixture and sprinkle with the remaining cheese mixture. Bake for another 20 minutes, or just until potatoes are tender-crisp.

Potato Wedge Fries
Photo by Mark Shapiro

Portobello Pizzas

NUTRITIONAL ANALYSIS
PER SERVING

Calories	179
Protein	11 g
Fat	7.1 g
Saturated Fat	3.6 g
Carbohydrates	19 g
Cholesterol	71 mg
Sodium	309 mg
Fiber	2.9 g

Prep Time: 10 minutes

Cook Time: 11 minutes

Serves 4

This is a great use for this wonderful mushroom. Serve it as a side dish or a whole meal for the vegetarian. Use any cheese you like and flavor the tomato sauce with herbs or vegetables of your choice.

4 large portobello mushrooms, cleaned and stems removed
1 egg
2 Tbsp water or milk
½ cup dry seasoned breadcrumbs
½ cup tomato sauce

½ tsp dried basil
¼ cup finely chopped rehydrated sun-dried tomatoes (see page 221)
⅔ cup shredded light fontina or havarti cheese
1 Tbsp grated Parmesan cheese

1. Preheat the oven to 425°F. Line a small baking sheet with foil and spray with cooking oil.

2. Combine the egg and water in a shallow bowl. Place the breadcrumbs in a separate shallow bowl. Dip each mushroom cap in the egg mixture and then the breadcrumbs. Place on the prepared baking sheet. Bake for 10 minutes, turning the mushrooms over halfway through or until the mushrooms are soft. Remove from the oven and set aside.

3. Set the oven to broil.

4. Combine the tomato sauce, basil and sun-dried tomatoes. Divide the mixture evenly among the mushroom caps. Sprinkle with the fontina cheese and top with the Parmesan cheese. Broil for 1 minute. Serve immediately.

Asparagus with Caesar Dressing

Asparagus is always an elegant addition to a meal and this Caesar dressing is sensational. To make it even more elegant, use a cheese slicer or a vegetable paring knife to garnish with thin curls of fresh Parmesan overtop. As an alternative to steaming, roast the asparagus for 15 minutes in a 425°F oven, turning it after 10 minutes. Asparagus is a source of vitamin C, vitamin A and iron, and is an excellent source of folate.

1 lb asparagus, trimmed	2 tsp water
1 Tbsp grated Parmesan cheese	2 anchovy fillets, chopped
1 Tbsp olive oil	1 tsp crushed fresh garlic
2 tsp freshly squeezed lemon juice	½ tsp Dijon mustard

1. Steam the asparagus until tender, approximately 4 minutes. Place on a serving dish.

2. Combine ½ Tbsp of the Parmesan, olive oil, lemon juice, water, anchovies, garlic, and mustard in a bowl. Pour over the asparagus. Sprinkle with the remaining ½ Tbsp Parmesan.

NUTRITIONAL ANALYSIS PER SERVING

Calories	76
Protein	4.1 g
Fat	4.4 g
Saturated Fat	0.9 g
Carbohydrates	5 g
Cholesterol	2.9 mg
Sodium	130 mg
Fiber	1.7 g

Prep Time: 10 minutes

Cook Time: 4 minutes

Make Ahead:
This dish can be made ahead and served at room temperature.

Serves 4

Smashed Potatoes

NUTRITIONAL ANALYSIS
PER SERVING

Calories	145
Protein	3.1 g
Fat	7.9 g
Saturated Fat	1.4 g
Carbohydrates	15 g
Cholesterol	2.5 mg
Sodium	82 mg
Fiber	1.5 g

Prep Time: 5 minutes

Cook Time: 45 minutes

Make Ahead:
Boil and flatten potatoes
up to a day ahead
and refrigerate.

Serves 4

We all love mashed potatoes, but if you've never had a "smashed" potato, you're in for a treat. Seasoning and baking turns these flattened potatoes into a crispy, delicious dish.

8 small red or white potatoes

2 Tbsp olive oil

2 Tbsp grated Parmesan cheese

¼ tsp garlic powder

pinch paprika

pinch salt

3 Tbsp finely chopped fresh parsley

1. Preheat the oven to 400°F. Line a baking sheet with foil and spray with cooking oil.

2. Place the potatoes in a saucepan, cover with water and bring to a boil. Boil for 15 minutes, or just until fork-tender. Drain and place on the prepared baking sheet. With the palm of your hand, press the potatoes flat, trying not to break them (cracks are normal).

3. Brush with 1 Tbsp of the olive oil.

4. Combine the cheese, garlic powder, paprika and salt in a small bowl. Sprinkle half the mixture over the potatoes. Bake for 15 minutes. Turn them over, brush with the remaining olive oil and sprinkle with the remaining cheese mixture. Bake for another 15 minutes. Garnish with the parsley.

Bean, Roasted Garlic and Potato Purée

These are the healthiest "mashed potatoes" ever. Potatoes are an excellent source of potassium and fiber, and they're high in vitamin C, iron and folate. Combined with beans, which are an excellent source of fiber and plant protein, the dish becomes a nutritional powerhouse. Roasting garlic brings out its sweet flavor—it's wonderful as a side vegetable or as a spread with bread or crackers. Never mash potatoes in a food processor; it makes them sticky.

1 head garlic
1 lb Yukon gold potatoes, peeled and
    quartered
1 tsp vegetable oil
1 cup chopped onion
1 cup canned white kidney beans,
    drained and rinsed

¼ cup 2 percent evaporated milk
1 Tbsp olive oil
¼ tsp salt
¼ tsp freshly ground black pepper
3 Tbsp chopped fresh parsley

NUTRITIONAL ANALYSIS PER SERVING

Calories	155
Protein	4.8 g
Fat	3.6 g
Saturated Fat	0.6 g
Carbohydrates	26 g
Cholesterol	1.6 mg
Sodium	114 mg
Fiber	1.8 g

Prep Time: 10 minutes
Cook Time: 20 minutes

Make Ahead:
Prepare the day before and reheat in a skillet over low heat, adding a little evaporated milk if too dry.

Serves 6

1. Preheat the oven to 450°F. Cut the top ½ inch from the head of garlic to slightly expose the cloves. Wrap in foil. Bake for 20 minutes.

2. Place the potatoes in a large pot and add cold water to cover. Bring to a boil; cover and cook for 15 minutes or until tender.

3. Meanwhile, heat the oil in a non-stick skillet over medium-high heat. Add the onion and sauté, stirring occasionally, for 5 minutes or until golden.

4. Drain the potatoes and return them to the saucepan. Add the garlic, squeezing the cloves out of the skins into the pot. Add the onions. Mash well.

5. Combine the beans, milk, oil, salt and pepper in the bowl of a food processor and purée. Stir into the mashed potatoes. If desired, return to the stovetop and reheat gently. Garnish with parsley.

Cheddar Cheese Potato Skins

NUTRITIONAL ANALYSIS
PER SERVING

Calories	156
Protein	4.9 g
Fat	6.3 g
Saturated Fat	1.4 g
Carbohydrates	20 g
Sodium	70 mg
Cholesterol	2 mg
Fiber	3.5 g

Prep Time: 5 minutes

Cook Time: 75 minutes

Make Ahead:
Bake whole potatoes
a day in advance and
refrigerate. Bake skins
just before serving.

Serves 4

Every time you eat these in restaurants, keep in mind they are usually fried and contain loads of fat and calories. My baked version is crispy and light, using a small amount of light cheese. I love these as a side vegetable dish, appetizer or light lunch. Try different cheeses and seasonings if you like. Save the pulp for mashed potatoes at another meal.

2 large baking potatoes
1½ Tbsp olive oil
1½ tsp minced fresh garlic
pinch chili powder
pinch salt and freshly ground black
     pepper

⅓ cup shredded light cheddar cheese
1 Tbsp grated Parmesan cheese
1 Tbsp chopped parsley

1. Preheat the oven to 450°F. Bake potatoes for 1 hour or until tender. (Or pierce the skins and microwave on High for 8 to 10 minutes.) Cool. Slice in half lengthwise. Carefully remove the pulp, leaving the skin intact. Reserve the pulp for another use. Place the skins on a baking sheet. Spray both sides with cooking oil.

2. Combine the oil, garlic, chili powder, salt and pepper in a small bowl and stir well. Spread or brush the mixture over the inner surface of the potato skins. Sprinkle with the cheddar and Parmesan.

3. Bake in the center of the oven for 15 minutes or until crisp. Garnish with parsley.

Baked Potatoes Stuffed with Smoked Salmon and Broccoli

If you like, substitute red onions or sweet Vidalia onions for the green onions in these potatoes. If you're in a hurry, microwave the potatoes; pierce the skin with a fork and microwave for 8 to 10 minutes on the High setting.

4 medium baking potatoes

1 cup finely chopped broccoli florets

⅔ cup low-fat sour cream

¼ cup low-fat milk

1 tsp crushed fresh garlic

2 Tbsp olive oil

¼ cup grated Parmesan cheese

¼ cup chopped fresh dill

¼ cup chopped green onion

4 oz smoked salmon, chopped

1. Preheat the oven to 425°F.

2. Spray the potatoes with cooking oil. Bake them until easily pierced with a fork, about 1 hour. Set aside to cool slightly.

3. While the potatoes are cooling, cook the broccoli in a saucepan of boiling water until tender-crisp, about 4 minutes (or microwave for 2 minutes). Drain, rinse with cold water and set aside.

4. Cut the potatoes in half lengthwise and carefully scoop the flesh into a bowl, leaving the skins intact. Mash the pulp with the sour cream, milk, garlic and oil. Stir in half the cheese, half the dill, half the green onions, half the smoked salmon and all of the broccoli.

5. Spoon the mixture back into the potato shell and sprinkle with the remaining 2 Tbsp Parmesan. Bake for 10 to 15 minutes, or until heated through.

6. Garnish with the remaining dill, green onion and smoked salmon.

NUTRITIONAL ANALYSIS PER SERVING (½ POTATO)

Calories	125
Protein	7 g
Fat	5 g
Saturated Fat	1 g
Carbohydrates	16 g
Cholesterol	12 mg
Sodium	168 mg
Fiber	1 g

Prep Time: 15 minutes

Cook Time: 75 minutes

Make Ahead:
Prepare filling up to a day in advance and fill potatoes. Bake and garnish just before serving.

Serves 8

Sweet Potato and Carrot Casserole with Molasses and Pecans

I adapted this recipe from my first low-fat cookbook, *Rose Reisman's Light Cooking*. It's not only a great side dish, but also perfect for serving during the Jewish holiday of Passover. If you can find fresh sweet pineapple, use it instead of canned. You're getting a double blast of beta carotene from the sweet potatoes and carrots.

1 lb sweet potatoes, peeled and cut in
 ½-inch rounds

1 lb carrots, thinly sliced into rounds

1¼ cups fresh or drained canned pineapple chunks or diced apples

½ cup dried cranberries or raisins

⅓ cup packed brown sugar

3 Tbsp orange juice concentrate

1 Tbsp vegetable oil

2 Tbsp molasses

1½ tsp ground cinnamon

3 Tbsp chopped toasted pecans
 (see page 75)

¼ cup chopped fresh parsley or cilantro

6 thin slices apple or pineapple

1. Preheat the oven to 350°F. Spray a 13- by 9-inch baking dish with cooking oil.

2. Place the sweet potatoes and carrots in a saucepan and cover with cold water. Bring to a boil. Cook for 7 minutes at a boil, or until tender. Drain.

3. Toss the sweet potatoes and carrots with the pineapple and cranberries. Place in the prepared baking dish.

4. Combine the brown sugar, juice concentrate, oil, molasses and cinnamon in a small saucepan. Cook over medium heat, stirring frequently, for 1 minute or until melted and smooth.

5. Pour the sauce over the vegetables. Cover and bake for 15 minutes, or until heated through. Remove from the oven and toss the vegetables. Sprinkle the pecans overtop. Garnish with parsley and sliced apple.

**NUTRITIONAL ANALYSIS
PER SERVING**

Calories	233
Protein	2.2 g
Fat	4.9 g
Saturated Fat	0.6 g
Carbohydrates	45 g
Cholesterol	0 mg
Sodium	62 mg
Fiber	5.3 g

Prep Time: 15 minutes

Cook Time: 23 minutes

Make Ahead:
Prepare a day in advance and refrigerate. Reheat in a 350°F oven for 10 minutes, until warmed through.

Serves 6

Sweet Potato and Carrot Casserole
with Molasses and Pecans
Photo by Mark Shapiro

Sweet Potato Fries with Cinnamon and Maple Syrup

NUTRITIONAL ANALYSIS
PER SERVING

Calories	160
Protein	2.1 g
Fat	3.5 g
Saturated Fat	0.2 g
Carbohydrates	30 g
Sodium	12 mg
Cholesterol	0 mg
Fiber	3.9 g

Prep Time: 10 minutes

Cook Time: 35 minutes

Make Ahead:
Prepare early in the day
and reheat in a 350°F
oven for 10 minutes,
or just until hot.

Serves 6

Sweet potatoes are the newest craze. They are more nutritious than regular potatoes and contain antioxidants that may help in the fight against cancer.

2 large sweet potatoes (about 1½ lb), unpeeled and scrubbed
1½ Tbsp vegetable oil
4 tsp maple syrup
¾ tsp ground cinnamon
¼ tsp ground ginger
Pinch nutmeg
3 Tbsp chopped fresh parsley

1. Preheat the oven to 425°F. Spray a rimmed baking sheet with cooking oil.

2. Cut the sweet potatoes in half lengthwise and then cut each half into 4 wedges. Spray with cooking oil. Place on the prepared baking sheet.

3. Combine the remaining ingredients except parsley in a small bowl; brush half the mixture over the sweet potatoes.

4. Bake in the center of the oven for 20 minutes. Turn and brush with the remaining maple syrup mixture. Bake another 15 minutes or until tender. Sprinkle with parsley.

Sweet Potato Mash

In these days of reducing intake of simple carbohydrates and avoiding foods with a higher glycemic index, we're enjoying a lot more sweet potatoes. A sweet potato mash goes well with any entrée. I like to enhance its natural sweetness by adding some maple syrup and brown sugar.

1½ lb sweet potatoes	1 tsp balsamic vinegar
¼ cup low-fat sour cream	½ tsp ground cinnamon
2 Tbsp pure maple syrup	pinch salt
1 Tbsp olive oil	3 Tbsp chopped fresh parsley
1 Tbsp brown sugar, packed	

1. Pierce the sweet potatoes several times with a fork. Microwave on high until tender, about 8 minutes. Peel. (Alternatively, peel and dice the potatoes, and cook in a large pot of boiling water until tender, about 10 minutes. Drain well.)

2. Mash the sweet potatoes. Stir in the sour cream, maple syrup, oil, sugar, vinegar, cinnamon and salt. Place in a serving bowl and garnish with parsley before serving.

NUTRITIONAL ANALYSIS PER SERVING

Calories	184
Protein	2.8 g
Fat	3.7 g
Saturated Fat	1.3 g
Carbohydrates	31 g
Cholesterol	4.4 mg
Sodium	75 mg
Fiber	3.6 g

Prep Time: 10 minutes
Cook Time: 10 minutes

Make Ahead:
Prepare a day in advance and refrigerate; reheat in a non-stick skillet over low heat until warmed through.

Serves 6

Snow Peas with Sesame Sauce

Calories	100
Protein	2.8 g
Fat	5.3 g
Saturated Fat	0.8 g
Carbohydrates	10 g
Cholesterol	0 mg
Sodium	93 mg
Fiber	2.2 g

Prep Time: 10 minutes

Cook Time: 3 minutes

Serves 6

This is a simple Asian-style recipe that can be used to accompany any main course. Substitute sugar snap peas for an upscale change. Green beans are also good.

1 Tbsp honey

1 Tbsp rice vinegar

1 Tbsp sesame oil

1 Tbsp low-sodium soy sauce

½ tsp minced fresh garlic

1 tsp vegetable oil

1 lb snow peas, trimmed

2 Tbsp chopped toasted cashews

1 Tbsp sesame seeds, toasted
   (see page 75)

1. Combine the honey, vinegar, sesame oil, soy sauce and garlic in a small bowl. Set aside.

2. Heat the vegetable oil in a large non-stick skillet over medium-high heat. Add the snow peas and cook until tender-crisp, about 3 minutes. Pour the sauce over the peas and cook until heated through. Serve immediately, sprinkled with cashews and sesame seeds.

Peppers with Barley Stuffing and Tuna-Caper Dressing

These stuffed peppers look fabulous on the plate, but if you haven't time to prepare the peppers, the barley makes a delicious side dish on its own. You can use more nutritious pot barley instead of the pearl barley, but it takes longer to cook (see page 89).

3 cups vegetable or chicken stock

¾ cup pearl barley

4 medium red, yellow or green bell peppers

½ can (6 oz) water-packed tuna, drained

¼ cup water

2 Tbsp light mayonnaise

1 Tbsp olive oil

4 tsp freshly squeezed lemon juice

1 Tbsp drained capers

1½ tsp minced fresh garlic

Pinch freshly ground black pepper

⅔ cup diced ripe plum tomatoes

⅓ cup diced red onion

¼ cup chopped green onion

¼ cup chopped dill or parsley

¼ cup diced black olives

1. Preheat the oven to broil. Line a baking sheet with foil.

2. Bring the stock to a boil in a saucepan over medium-high heat. Add the barley and reduce the heat to medium-low. Cook, covered, for 25 to 30 minutes, or until the barley is tender. Drain off any excess liquid.

3. While the barley is cooking, prepare the peppers. Slice off the top 1 inch of each pepper and remove the ribs and seeds. Place the peppers and their tops 6 inches from the broiler element and broil for 8–10 minutes, turning periodically until all sides are charred.

4. To make the dressing, combine the tuna, water, mayonnaise, oil, lemon juice, capers, garlic and black pepper in a food processor or blender and purée.

5. Combine the barley, tomatoes, red and green onion, dill or parsley and olives in a bowl. Add the dressing and toss to coat well. Spoon the mixture into the peppers, replace the tops and serve.

NUTRITIONAL ANALYSIS PER SERVING

Calories	307
Protein	17 g
Fat	10 g
Saturated Fat	1.3 g
Carbohydrates	41 g
Cholesterol	19 mg
Sodium	345 mg
Fiber	8 g

Prep Time: 15 minutes

Cook Time: 30 minutes

Make Ahead:
Prepare the peppers a day in advance, cover and refrigerate. Bring to room temperature before serving.

Serves 4

Carrot Salad with Orange Honey Dressing

NUTRITIONAL ANALYSIS
PER SERVING

Calories	112
Protein	2.2 g
Fat	2.6 g
Saturated Fat	0.4 g
Carbohydrates	21 g
Sodium	114 mg
Cholesterol	0 mg
Fiber	5.1 g

Prep Time: 10 minutes

Cook Time: 5 minutes

Make Ahead:
Prepare up to a day
in advance, cover
and refrigerate.

Serves 6

This salad is perfect for a buffet—it can be served warm, at room temperature or chilled. Remember: the sweeter your carrots, the tastier the salad. The mint and cilantro bring out the flavor of the carrots, but you can always substitute parsley or basil.

2 lb peeled carrots, sliced diagonally into ¼-inch slices

2 Tbsp orange juice concentrate

1 Tbsp freshly squeezed lemon juice

1 Tbsp honey

2 tsp sesame oil

1 tsp crushed fresh garlic

¼ tsp ground cinnamon

¼ cup chopped green onion

¼ cup chopped cilantro or parsley

¼ cup chopped fresh mint or basil

2 tsp sesame seeds, toasted (see page 75)

1. Boil the carrots for 5 minutes, until just fork-tender. Drain.

2. Whisk the juice concentrate, lemon juice, honey, oil, garlic and cinnamon in a small bowl. Pour over the carrots. Add the onion, cilantro, mint and sesame seeds. Toss and serve.

Rösti Potatoes with Caramelized Onions

This recipe was inspired by the Mövenpick Swiss restaurant chain, where "rösti" means "grated potatoes sautéed in oil." I took the idea, made a filling of cheese and sautéed onions, and used only 2 tsp of butter to brown the potatoes. They are amazing. When sautéing, be sure not to use too high a heat or the potatoes will burn before they're thoroughly cooked.

2 tsp vegetable oil
1½ cups finely diced sweet onion
1 tsp minced fresh garlic
¼ cup shredded light cheddar cheese

1 Tbsp grated Parmesan cheese
3 medium Yukon Gold potatoes
½ tsp salt
pinch freshly ground black pepper
2 tsp butter or margarine
⅓ cup low-fat sour cream

NUTRITIONAL ANALYSIS PER SERVING

Calories	146
Protein	4.4 g
Carbohydrates	22 g
Fat	4.5 g
Saturated Fat	2 g
Cholesterol	9.7 mg
Sodium	275 mg
Fiber	2.2 g

Prep Time: 10 minutes
Cook Time: 20 minutes

Make Ahead:
Make early in the day, refrigerate and reheat in a skillet over low heat until warm.

Serves 6

1. Spray a non-stick skillet with cooking oil, add the vegetable oil and place over high heat. Add the onion and garlic and cook for 2 minutes. Reduce the heat to medium-low and cook for 10 minutes, or until soft and golden. Transfer to a bowl. Stir in the cheddar and Parmesan.

2. Peel the potatoes. Coarsely grate them into a bowl. Toss with the salt and pepper.

3. Melt the butter in a 9- or 10-inch non-stick skillet over medium-low heat. Add half the potatoes, spreading them over the bottom of the pan and pressing them flat. Top with the onion mixture. Sprinkle evenly with the remaining potatoes, pressing them down firmly. Cook for 8 minutes, until golden brown underneath. Slide the potatoes out onto a dinner plate and flip them back into the pan. Cook for another 8 minutes, until the other side is golden. Cut into 6 wedges. Serve with sour cream on the side.

Roasted Sweet Pepper Salad with Pine Nuts, Goat Cheese and Basil

**NUTRITIONAL ANALYSIS
PER SERVING**

Calories	88
Protein	2.7 g
Fat	4.9 g
Saturated Fat	1.3 g
Carbohydrates	8.3 g
Sodium	20 mg
Cholesterol	2.2 mg
Fiber	2.5 g

Prep Time: 10 minutes

Make Ahead:
Prepare up to 2 days in advance, cover with plastic wrap and refrigerate.

Serves 6

I can never make enough of this simple salad. In restaurants roasted peppers are often marinated in oil, which adds calories and fat. Here I use only 1 tablespoon of olive oil—and the results are outstanding. Red, yellow, and orange bell peppers contain an abundance of beta carotene and antioxidants, which help in the fight against cancer.

6 bell peppers of various colors, roasted (see page 122)

1 Tbsp olive oil

1 tsp balsamic vinegar

¼ cup crumbled goat cheese

3 Tbsp chopped fresh basil or parsley

2 Tbsp pine nuts, toasted (see page 75)

1. Slice the roasted peppers in thick slices and arrange on a platter.

2. Whisk the oil and vinegar together in a small bowl. Drizzle over the peppers.

3. Sprinkle with goat cheese, basil and pine nuts.

Roasted Sweet Pepper Salad with
Pine Nuts, Goat Cheese and Basil
Photo by Lorella Zanetti

Broiled Baby Spinach with Three Cheeses

NUTRITIONAL ANALYSIS
PER SERVING

Calories	196
Protein	11 g
Fat	8.7 g
Saturated Fat	2.9 g
Carbohydrates	21 g
Cholesterol	14 mg
Sodium	350 mg
Fiber	7.4 g

Prep Time: 10 minutes

Cook Time: 7 minutes

Make Ahead:
Prepare dish up to the
broiling point early in the
day, cover and refrigerate.
Bake at 450°F for 5 minutes
or until warm.

Serves 4

It's so easy to serve baby spinach today since most of it comes pre-washed. This is a tempting way to serve spinach for those who resist including it in their diet. Substitute any cheeses of your choice. I love to use blue cheese—it really intensifies the flavor.

two 10-oz packages fresh baby spinach,
   chopped
1 tsp vegetable oil
1 cup diced red onion
1½ tsp crushed fresh garlic

1 tsp dried basil
⅓ cup grated Parmesan cheese
⅓ cup smooth light ricotta
¼ cup grated light Swiss cheese

1. Preheat the oven to broil. Place the oven rack no closer than 6 inches from the broiler.

2. Spray an 8-inch baking dish with cooking oil.

3. Place the spinach in a large pot with ¼ cup water. Cover and steam just until the spinach wilts. Drain well.

4. Spray a small non-stick skillet with cooking oil, heat the vegetable oil and sauté the onion, garlic and basil for 4 minutes, or until the onions are soft. Add the spinach and mix well. Place in the baking dish.

5. Combine the three cheeses and sprinkle over the spinach mixture. Broil for 2 minutes, until the cheese is lightly browned.

Tofu Parmesan

Forget eggplant or chicken Parmesan! This dish is a terrific, healthy alternative to those old favorites. It's important to buy firm tofu, as softer tofu will fall apart, but don't get the extra-firm product, which is too tough.

½ cup dry seasoned breadcrumbs

1 Tbsp grated Parmesan cheese

1 egg

2 Tbsp water

1 lb firm tofu, sliced horizontally into
    1-inch slices

2 tsp vegetable oil

¾ cup tomato-based pasta sauce

½ tsp dried basil

½ cup shredded light mozzarella cheese

1. Preheat the oven to 425°F.

2. Stir the breadcrumbs and Parmesan together on a plate. Whisk the egg and water in a shallow bowl. Dip the tofu slices into the egg mixture, then coat with the breadcrumb mixture.

3. Spray a large non-stick skillet with cooking oil, add the vegetable oil and place over medium heat. Brown the tofu on both sides, turning once, about 5 minutes.

4. Mix the tomato sauce with the basil. Spread half over the bottom of a 9-inch square baking dish. Lay the tofu slices overtop, and pour the remaining sauce over the tofu. Sprinkle with the mozzarella.

5. Bake in the center of the oven for 5 to 8 minutes, or just until the cheese melts and the sauce is warm.

NUTRITIONAL ANALYSIS PER SERVING

Calories	260
Protein	15 g
Fat	10 g
Saturated Fat	3.1 g
Carbohydrates	12 g
Cholesterol	64 mg
Sodium	370 mg
Fiber	1.5 g

Prep Time: 10 minutes

Cook Time: 10 minutes

Make Ahead:

Prepare up to the point of baking a day in advance, cover and refrigerate. Bake just before serving.

Serves 4

Three-Cheese Ground Soy Lasagna

This lasagna is so fabulous that nobody will ever suspect there's no meat in it. The ground soy tastes like ground beef or chicken with all the healthy components of soy, which is known to help in the fight against heart disease and cancer. If you want a spicier flavor, try the Mexican flavored ground soy or add a teaspoon of hot sauce.

9 lasagna noodles

1 tsp vegetable oil

1 cup diced onion

2 tsp minced fresh garlic

3 cups tomato-based pasta sauce

1 tsp dried basil

12 oz soy-based ground beef substitute

2 cups light smooth ricotta

1 cup shredded part-skim mozzarella

⅓ cup low-fat milk

¼ cup grated Parmesan cheese

3 Tbsp chopped fresh basil or parsley

1. Preheat the oven to 350°F.

2. Bring a large pot of water to a boil, add the lasagna noodles and cook 12 to 14 minutes or until tender. Drain. Rinse under cold running water and drain again. Set aside.

3. For the sauce, spray a non-stick saucepan with cooking oil, add the vegetable oil and place over medium-high heat. Add the onion and garlic and cook, stirring frequently, until browned, about 5 minutes. Stir in the tomato sauce and basil. Bring to a boil, then reduce the heat to simmer. Cover and cook for 12 to 15 minutes, or until slightly thickened. Stir in the ground soy and simmer for 3 more minutes. Set aside.

4. For the cheese mixture, stir the ricotta, mozzarella, milk and 3 Tbsp of the Parmesan together in a bowl.

5. Spread ¼ cup of the tomato sauce over the bottom of a 13- by 9-inch glass baking dish. Top with three noodles. Spread half the cheese mixture over the noodles. Top with one-third of the tomato sauce. Top with three noodles. Spread the remaining cheese mixture over the noodles. Top with one-third of the tomato sauce. Top with the last 3 noodles.

6. Spread the remaining tomato sauce overtop. Sprinkle with the remaining 1 Tbsp Parmesan cheese. Cover the pan tightly with foil.

7. Bake in the center of the oven for 20 minutes or until hot. Garnish with the basil or parsley.

Tofu Satays with Hoisin Sesame Sauce

I love chicken, beef and shrimp satays, but if you're a vegetarian or you just want a healthy alternative, try these tofu satays. Tofu absorbs whatever flavors it's cooked with. Be sure to buy firm tofu: the medium tofu is too soft and the extra-firm is too tough. Once opened, cover unused tofu with water in a container and refrigerate for up to 3 days.

1 large green bell pepper, cut into 16 squares

1 large red bell pepper, cut into 16 squares

½ sweet onion, cut into 16 pieces

12 oz firm tofu, cut into 16 cubes 2 inches square

¼ cup hoisin sauce

¼ cup packed brown sugar

5 tsp black bean sauce

5 tsp low-sodium soy sauce

1 Tbsp sesame oil

1½ tsp minced fresh garlic

1½ tsp minced fresh ginger

¼ cup chopped cilantro or parsley

1. Thread the pepper, onion, and tofu alternately on 4 long or 8 short wooden or metal skewers, dividing the vegetables evenly among them. (If using wooden skewers, soak for at least 20 minutes in water prior to using them.)

2. To make the sauce, whisk the hoisin, sugar, bean sauce, soy sauce, oil, garlic and ginger in a bowl until smooth.

3. Spray a barbecue or a non-stick grill pan with cooking oil and heat to medium. Grill the satays, turning occasionally, for 10 minutes or until browned on all sides. Brush half the sauce over the satays and continue cooking, turning occasionally, for another 10 minutes or just until the vegetables are soft. Garnish with the cilantro and serve with the remaining sauce on the side.

NUTRITIONAL ANALYSIS PER SERVING

Calories	240
Protein	9.9 g
Fat	7 g
Saturated Fat	1 g
Carbohydrates	38.7 g
Cholesterol	0.5 mg
Sodium	501 mg
Fiber	5.3 g

Prep Time:	15 miutes
Cook Time:	20 minutes

Serves 4

Black Bean Marinated Tofu Cakes with Steamed Bok Choy

NUTRITIONAL ANALYSIS PER SERVING

Calories	239
Protein	14 g
Fat	10 g
Saturated Fat	2 g
Carbohydrates	29 g
Cholesterol	0 mg
Sodium	229 mg
Fiber	2.3 g

Prep Time: 10 minutes

Cook Time: 11 minutes

Make Ahead:
Prepare the sauce
and marinate tofu in the
refrigerator up to a day
in advance.

Serves 4

This is a complete meal for the vegetarian or anyone who wants a change from meat or poultry. The tofu takes on the black bean flavor and goes wonderfully with the bok choy. I like to buy baby bok choy, but the larger variety is fine. If you don't have time, you don't have to marinate the tofu, but the flavor is enhanced when you do.

3 Tbsp honey

2 Tbsp sweet chili sauce or ketchup

1 ½ Tbsp black bean sauce

1 tsp sesame oil

1 tsp crushed fresh garlic

1 tsp crushed fresh ginger

12 oz extra-firm tofu, cut into squares 2 ½ inches wide × ½ inch deep (about 3 cups)

4 bunches baby bok choy

1 tsp sesame seeds, toasted

¼ cup chopped cilantro or parsley

1. For the sauce, whisk the honey, chili sauce, black bean sauce, oil, garlic and ginger in a 9-inch baking dish until combined. Add the tofu and marinate for at least 10 minutes, or longer for a more intense flavor. Remove the tofu and scrape the marinade off. Reserve the marinade.

2. Spray a non-stick skillet with cooking oil and brown the tofu on both sides, approximately 3 minutes per side. Brush some sauce over the tofu, turn again and brush once more, cooking for 1 more minute. Set aside.

3. Warm the remaining sauce in a small skillet over low heat.

4. Steam the bok choy just until bright green, approximately 2 minutes. Do not overcook. Place the bok choy on individual serving plates.

5. Top the bok choy with the tofu and drizzle with the sauce. Garnish with sesame seeds and chopped cilantro.

Butternut Squash with Caramelized Onions and Dried Cranberries

I enjoy this rich-tasting vegetable dish on its own or alongside fish, chicken or beef. This combination—smooth, creamy squash, dried cranberries, cinnamon and maple syrup—is like candy food!

1½ lb butternut squash, peeled and cut in 1-inch cubes (about ½ squash)

2 tsp vegetable oil

3 cups sliced sweet onion

2 Tbsp brown sugar, packed

1 tsp ground cinnamon

⅓ cup dried cranberries

2 Tbsp pure maple syrup

2 tsp olive oil

pinch salt and freshly ground black pepper

3 Tbsp almonds, toasted (see page 75)

2 Tbsp chopped fresh parsley

1. Cook the squash in a large pot of boiling water just until tender, about 15 minutes.

2. While it cooks, heat the vegetable oil in a large non-stick skillet over medium-high heat. Add the onion and sauté for 5 minutes, stirring frequently. Stir in the sugar and cinnamon. Reduce the heat to medium-low and cook until the onions are golden, about 8 minutes, stirring often so as not to burn them. Toss in the cranberries.

3. Drain the squash. Add the maple syrup, olive oil, salt and pepper; mash thoroughly. Transfer to a serving dish and sprinkle with the onion mixture. Garnish with almonds and parsley.

NUTRITIONAL ANALYSIS PER SERVING

Calories	210
Protein	3.4 g
Fat	6.7 g
Saturated Fat	0.7 g
Carbohydrates	27 g
Cholesterol	0 mg
Sodium	59 mg
Fiber	6.9 g

Prep Time: 15 minutes
Cook Time: 15 minutes

Make Ahead:
Prepare a day in advance, omitting the garnish, cover and refrigerate. Reheat in a non-stick skillet over low heat until warmed through, garnish and serve.

Serves 6

Tuna Stir-Fry with Coconut Thai Sauce

There's nothing like the texture and taste of fresh grilled or seared tuna. The key is not to overcook it. In fact, serving it slightly rare is the only way to go! You can substitute another firm fish, chicken, pork or tofu for the tuna in this dish. The light coconut milk and hoisin makes for a creamy, Asian-style sauce.

¾ cup light coconut milk

¼ cup hoisin sauce

1½ Tbsp honey

1½ tsp sesame oil

1½ Tbsp low-sodium soy sauce

2 tsp rice vinegar

2 tsp cornstarch

1½ tsp minced fresh garlic

1 tsp minced fresh ginger

12 oz fresh tuna steak

1½ cups sliced red bell pepper

1½ cups sugar snap peas or snow peas

⅓ cup chopped green onion

¼ cup chopped fresh cilantro or parsley

2 tsp sesame seeds, toasted

NUTRITIONAL ANALYSIS PER SERVING

Calories	250
Protein	22 g
Fat	8 g
Saturated Fat	2.5 g
Carbohydrates	34 g
Cholesterol	35 mg
Sodium	360 mg
Fiber	2 g

Prep Time: 15 minutes

Cook Time: 8 minutes

Make Ahead:
Prepare sauce up to 3 days in advance and refrigerate.

Serves 4

1. To make the sauce, whisk the coconut milk, hoisin sauce, honey, oil, soy sauce, rice vinegar, cornstarch, garlic and ginger in a bowl until smooth. Set aside.

2. Spray a non-stick skillet or grill pan with cooking oil and heat to high. Cook the tuna just until seared on both sides but still rare on the inside, about 3 minutes. Immediately remove from the skillet. Cut into 1-inch cubes and set aside.

3. Spray a non-stick skillet or wok with cooking oil and place over high heat. Add the red pepper and peas and stir-fry for 3 minutes. Add the sauce and stir-fry for 2 minutes, or until slightly thickened. Add the tuna at the last minute and toss, being careful not to overcook the tuna.

4. Transfer to a serving platter. Sprinkle with green onion, cilantro and sesame seeds.

Seafood Stir-Fry with Plum and Sweet Chili Sauce

NUTRITIONAL ANALYSIS
PER SERVING

Calories	130
Protein	7.6 g
Fat	4 g
Saturated Fat	0.3 g
Carbohydrates	20 g
Cholesterol	43 mg
Sodium	490 mg
Fiber	1.5 g

Prep Time: 15 minutes

Cook Time: 10 minutes

Make Ahead:
Prepare the sauce up
to 3 days in advance
and refrigerate.

Serves 4

The secret to this delicious stir-fry is the contrasting texture of the asparagus, baby corn and water chestnuts. Substitute scallops for the shrimp if you like; cut into bite-sized pieces. The sweet-sour sauce works equally as well with chicken, pork or tofu. Serve over rice or noodles.

⅓ cup corn syrup

⅓ cup plum sauce

3 Tbsp rice vinegar

2 Tbsp sweet chili sauce or ketchup

2 Tbsp low-sodium soy sauce

1½ tsp minced fresh garlic

1 tsp minced fresh ginger

1½ tsp cornstarch

2 tsp vegetable oil

1 cup coarsely chopped onion

2 cups asparagus cut into ½-inch pieces

1 cup canned baby corn, drained and chopped

½ cup sliced water chestnuts

16 oz raw shrimp, peeled and deveined

¼ cup chopped fresh cilantro or parsley

1 Tbsp chopped toasted cashews

1. To make the sauce, combine the corn syrup, plum sauce, vinegar, chili sauce, soy sauce, garlic, ginger and cornstarch in a bowl. Whisk until the cornstarch is dissolved. Set aside.

2. Spray a non-stick wok with cooking oil, add the vegetable oil and place over medium heat. Add the onion and stir-fry for 5 minutes. Add the asparagus, corn, and water chestnuts and stir-fry for 2 minutes or until the asparagus begins to turn bright green. Add the shrimp and stir-fry just until it turns pink, approximately 2 minutes.

3. Add the sauce and cook until it thickens, about 1 minute. Transfer to a serving platter and sprinkle with cilantro and toasted cashews.

Chinese Beef with Crisp Vegetables

The colors and textures of this dish give it great eye appeal. Be sure not to overcook the vegetables and use the best quality steak, such as rib-eye, sirloin, filet or New York. For a change, replace the beef with chicken, pork or firm tofu and use any vegetables of your choice. Serve it over steamed rice, noodles or couscous.

¾ cup beef or chicken stock

¼ cup packed brown sugar

2 Tbsp low-sodium soy sauce

2 Tbsp rice vinegar

2 tsp sesame oil

1 Tbsp cornstarch

2 tsp minced fresh garlic

1½ tsp minced fresh ginger

12 oz boneless grilling steak

2 tsp vegetable oil

1½ cups chopped broccoli

1½ cups thinly sliced red bell pepper

1½ cups snow peas

¼ cup chopped cilantro or parsley

¼ cup chopped green onion

2 Tbsp chopped toasted cashews (optional)

1. To make the sauce, whisk the stock, sugar, soy sauce, vinegar, sesame oil, cornstarch, garlic and ginger in a bowl. Set aside.

2. Spray a large non-stick skillet with cooking oil and place over high heat. When it's hot, brown the beef for 3 minutes, or until it's browned but still rare. Remove from the pan, let it rest for 5 minutes, then slice thinly.

3. Respray the pan. Heat the vegetable oil, then add the broccoli, red pepper and snow peas. Cook for 3 minutes. Return the beef to the pan. Stir the sauce and add it to the pan. Stir-fry for 2 minutes, or until the sauce is thickened and bubbly and the beef is done to your liking. Be careful not to overcook it.

4. Place on a serving platter and garnish with cilantro, green onion and cashews (if using).

NUTRITIONAL ANALYSIS PER SERVING

Calories	161
Protein	10 g
Fat	10 g
Saturated Fat	2.5 g
Carbohydrates	25 g
Cholesterol	15 mg
Sodium	375 mg
Fiber	3 g

Prep Time: 15 minutes

Cook Time: 8 minutes

Make Ahead:
Prepare sauce up to 4 days in advance and refrigerate.

Serves 4

Chicken, Red Pepper and Snow Pea Stir-Fry

NUTRITIONAL ANALYSIS
PER SERVING

Calories	277
Protein	17 g
Fat	5 g
Saturated Fat	0.6 g
Carbohydrates	20 g
Cholesterol	37 mg
Sodium	503 mg
Fiber	2.8 g

Prep Time: 15 minutes

Cook Time: 9 minutes

Make Ahead:
Prepare sauce up to 3 days
in advance and refrigerate.

Serves 4

My family prefers this standard, yet delicious, stir-fry to all the others. Dusting the chicken with flour keeps it moist. Substitute any protein you like, such as steak, pork or firm tofu. Serve it over rice or rice noodles.

1 cup chicken stock

2 Tbsp low-sodium soy sauce

3 Tbsp hoisin sauce

4 tsp cornstarch

1 Tbsp brown sugar

1 tsp sesame oil

1½ tsp crushed fresh garlic

1 tsp minced fresh ginger

8 oz skinless boneless chicken breast, cut in 1-inch cubes (about 2 breasts)

2 Tbsp all-purpose flour

2 tsp vegetable oil

1½ cups thinly sliced red bell pepper

1½ cups snow peas cut in half

½ cup sliced water chestnuts

¼ cup coarsely chopped cashews

1 large green onion, chopped

1. To make the sauce, place the stock, soy sauce, hoisin sauce, cornstarch, brown sugar, sesame oil, garlic and ginger in a small bowl and whisk to combine. Set aside.

2. Dust the chicken with the flour. Spray a non-stick wok or skillet with cooking oil and place over medium heat. Brown the chicken on all sides for 3 minutes, or until browned but not cooked through. Remove from the pan.

3. Respray the pan and heat the oil over medium heat. Add the red pepper and snow peas; stir-fry for 2 minutes or until the vegetables are tender-crisp. Stir the sauce and add it to the pan along with the chicken and water chestnuts. Cook for 2 minutes, until the chicken is cooked through and the sauce has thickened.

4. Serve immediately, garnished with cashews and green onion.

Tofu Stir-Fry with Sweet and Sour Sauce, Snow Peas and Red Peppers

I adapted this recipe from one that used chicken or pork. Extra-firm tofu is great with a sweet and sour sauce. I like to serve this over a pilaf of rice, a bed of couscous or a plate of thick rice noodles. Be sure to use the sweet chili sauce, not the hot! You can substitute ketchup, but you may have to add some extra brown sugar; taste and adjust. It's best not to cook a stir-fry until you're actually ready to eat, or you'll overcook the vegetables.

1 cup vegetable or chicken stock

⅓ cup packed brown sugar

⅓ cup sweet chili sauce

2 Tbsp rice vinegar

4 tsp cornstarch

1 Tbsp low-sodium soy sauce

2 tsp sesame oil

2 tsp minced fresh garlic

1½ tsp minced fresh ginger

12 oz extra-firm tofu, cubed

1 tsp vegetable oil

1½ cups snow peas or sugar snap peas, diced

1¼ cups red bell pepper strips

¾ cup green bell pepper strips

½ cup chopped green onion

⅓ cup chopped cilantro or parsley

1. To make the sauce, whisk the stock, brown sugar, chili sauce, vinegar, cornstarch, soy sauce, sesame oil, garlic and ginger together in a small bowl. Set aside.

2. Spray a non-stick wok or skillet with cooking oil and place over medium-high heat. Add the tofu and brown on all sides, about 5 minutes. Remove from the pan.

3. Add the vegetable oil to the wok. When it's hot, stir-fry the peas and red and green pepper until tender-crisp, about 3 minutes. Stir the sauce again and add to the wok along with the cooked tofu. Cook for 1 minute or until thickened. Serve garnished with the green onions and cilantro or parsley.

NUTRITIONAL ANALYSIS
PER SERVING

Calories	311
Protein	16 g
Fat	6 g
Saturated Fat	0.6 g
Carbohydrates	37 g
Cholesterol	0 mg
Sodium	391 mg
Fiber	3.9 g

Prep Time:	20 minutes
Cook Time:	9 minutes

Make Ahead:
Prepare sauce and vegetables a day in advance and refrigerate. Stir-fry just before serving.

Serves 4

Tofu Stir-Fry with Light Coconut Sauce

NUTRITIONAL ANALYSIS
PER SERVING

Calories	250
Protein	22 g
Fat	5 g
Saturated Fat	2 g
Carbohydrates	34 g
Cholesterol	35 mg
Sodium	360 mg
Fiber	2 g

Prep Time: 10 minutes

Cook Time: 13 minutes

Make Ahead:
Prepare the sauce a day in
advance and refrigerate.
Marinate and stir-fry just
before serving.

Serves 4

The tofu absorbs the taste of the coconut sauce to make a rich-tasting dish that's low in fat and calories. Serve this with basmati rice or rice noodles.

⅔ cup light coconut milk

3 Tbsp hoisin sauce

1 Tbsp honey

1 Tbsp low-sodium soy sauce

1 tsp sesame oil

1 tsp rice vinegar

1 tsp crushed fresh garlic

1 tsp crushed fresh ginger

12 oz firm tofu, cut into 1-inch cubes

1 cup sliced snow peas

1 cup sliced red bell pepper

6 oz rice noodles (½ inch wide)

⅓ cup chopped cilantro or parsley

2 tsp sesame seeds, toasted

1. To make the sauce, whisk the coconut milk, hoisin sauce, honey, soy sauce, sesame oil, vinegar, garlic and ginger in a large bowl. Add the tofu and marinate for 10 to 30 minutes. Drain well, reserving the sauce.

2. Spray a large non-stick wok or skillet with cooking oil and place over medium heat. Add the tofu and stir-fry for 5 minutes, just until it's browned. Add the snow peas and bell pepper; sauté for 2 minutes. Add the reserved sauce and heat for 2 minutes, just until the mixture is hot.

3. Cook the noodles in boiling water for 4 minutes, until they're barely tender. Do not overcook. Drain well and stir into the tofu mixture. Toss with the cilantro and sesame seeds and serve immediately.

Beef and Sautéed Corn Chili

Browning the corn is what gives this chili its deliciously distinctive taste. Feel free to make it vegetarian by substituting ground soy for the beef. Use fresh minced jalapeño peppers for a hot flavor. For a beautiful presentation, serve the chili in kaiser rolls or any large firm roll. Cut the top off the roll and remove the soft bread, leaving the outer crust intact. Fill with chili.

2 tsp vegetable oil	1 cup diced potato
1½ cups chopped onion	½ cup chicken or beef stock
1 cup canned corn kernels, drained	2 tsp chili powder
2 tsp minced fresh garlic	1½ tsp dried basil
8 oz extra-lean ground beef	1 tsp brown sugar
1 can (19 oz) red kidney beans, drained and rinsed	½ tsp cumin
2½ cups tomato sauce	¼ cup chopped fresh parsley

1. Spray a non-stick skillet with cooking oil, add the vegetable oil and place over medium heat. Add the onions and cook until soft, stirring frequently, about 5 minutes. Stir in the corn and garlic. Cook and stir for 8 minutes, or until the corn is browned. Stir in the beef and cook for 5 minutes, until the beef is browned.

2. Stir in the beans, tomato sauce, potato, stock, chili powder, basil, sugar and cumin. Bring to a boil, reduce the heat and cover. Simmer for 25 to 30 minutes, or just until the potatoes are tender. Serve immediately, garnished with parsley.

NUTRITIONAL ANALYSIS PER SERVING

Calories	320
Protein	18 g
Fat	6 g
Saturated Fat	2 g
Carbohydrates	40 g
Cholesterol	16 mg
Sodium	430 mg
Fiber	7 g

Prep Time: 15 minutes
Cook Time: 48 minutes

Make Ahead:
Prepare up to a day in advance and refrigerate, or freeze for up to 2 months. Defrost and reheat over low heat.

Serves 6

Mango Beef Stir-Fry

NUTRITIONAL ANALYSIS
PER SERVING

Calories	290
Protein	18 g
Fat	10 g
Saturated Fat	4 g
Carbohydrates	28 g
Cholesterol	48 mg
Sodium	460 mg
Fiber	3 g

Prep Time: 15 minutes
Cook Time: 15 minutes

Make Ahead:
Prepare sauce up to 3 days in advance and refrigerate.

Serves 4

Don't be put off fish sauce by its strong aroma—the flavor is much more mellow once it's cooked. If you can't find fish sauce, use either soy sauce or oyster sauce. The steaks I like to use are sirloin, rib-eye, filet or New York strip, but chicken, pork or tofu make good substitutes for the beef. The most delicious mangos are from Indonesia—they're sweet and tender.

½ cup light coconut milk
¼ cup hoisin sauce
3 Tbsp brown sugar
2 Tbsp fish sauce
1 Tbsp natural peanut butter
1 Tbsp water
2 tsp cornstarch
1½ tsp minced fresh garlic
1 tsp minced fresh ginger

12 oz boneless grilling steak
2 tsp vegetable oil
1½ cups sliced onion
2 cups sliced red bell pepper

½ cup diced mango
¼ cup chopped cilantro or parsley
3 Tbsp chopped green onion

1. For the sauce, whisk the coconut milk, hoisin sauce, sugar, fish sauce, peanut butter, water, cornstarch, garlic and ginger in a bowl until smooth. Set aside.

2. Spray a barbecue or a non-stick grill pan with cooking oil and heat to high. Grill the beef until medium-rare, about 5 to 8 minutes. Let it rest 5 minutes. Slice the steak thinly and keep covered.

3. Spray a non-stick skillet with cooking oil, add the vegetable oil and place over medium heat. Stir-fry the onions until softened, about 5 minutes. Add the red pepper and stir-fry for 3 minutes.

4. Add the sauce and beef. Stir-fry until the sauce thickens, about 2 minutes, being careful not to overcook the beef.

5. Transfer to a serving platter. Scatter mango, cilantro and green onion overtop and serve immediately.

Southwest Bean and Chicken Chili

This chili is easy enough for a weekday meal and impressive enough for an upscale weekend dinner. I love to serve it with homemade cornbread (see page 305), polenta or warm crusty Italian bread. It can be frozen and reheats beautifully.

2 tsp vegetable oil

1½ cups chopped onion

1 cup canned corn kernels, drained

2 tsp minced fresh garlic

8 oz ground chicken

1½ cups canned black beans, drained and rinsed

¾ cup diced rehydrated sun-dried tomatoes (see page 221)

2½ cups tomato-based pasta sauce

¾ cup chicken or beef stock

4 tsp chili powder

2½ tsp dried basil

1½ tsp dried oregano

1½ tsp brown sugar

1 tsp minced seeded jalapeño pepper or ½ tsp hot chili paste

¼ cup chopped cilantro or parsley

¼ cup shredded light old cheddar cheese

¼ cup low-fat sour cream

1. Spray a non-stick skillet with cooking oil, add the vegetable oil and place over medium heat. Add the onion and cook until soft, stirring frequently, about 5 minutes. Stir in the corn and garlic; continue to cook and stir for 8 minutes, or until the corn is browned. Add the chicken and cook for 5 minutes, or just until browned and cooked.

2. Stir in the beans, sun-dried tomatoes, tomato sauce, stock, chili powder, basil, oregano, sugar and jalapeño. Bring to a boil, reduce the heat and cover. Simmer for 20 minutes.

3. Serve in individual bowls, garnished with cilantro, cheese and sour cream.

NUTRITIONAL ANALYSIS
PER SERVING

Calories	254
Protein	16 g
Fat	5 g
Saturated Fat	2 g
Carbohydrates	33 g
Cholesterol	33 mg
Sodium	401 mg
Fiber	5.8 g

Prep Time: 10 minutes

Cook Time: 38 minutes

Make Ahead:
Prepare a day in advance and refrigerate, or freeze for up to 2 months. Reheat on low, adding more stock if too thick.

Serves 6

Miniature Hoisin Garlic Burgers
Photo by Brian MacDonald

Miniature Hoisin Garlic Burgers

These burgers are extremely moist and flavorful due to the hoisin sauce. Instead of meat, use ground chicken, veal or pork, or try a combination. Serve these on minia-ture hamburger buns and add some sautéed onions. If you prefer, make 4 or 5 regular burgers instead of the minis.

1 lb extra-lean ground beef	2 tsp minced fresh garlic
¼ cup dry breadcrumbs	1 tsp minced fresh ginger
¼ cup chopped green onion	1 egg
3 Tbsp chopped cilantro or parsley	2 Tbsp water
4 Tbsp hoisin sauce	1 tsp sesame oil

1. Heat the barbecue to high and spray with cooking oil, or preheat the oven to 450°F.

2. Combine the beef, breadcrumbs, green onion, cilantro or parsley, 2 Tbsp of the hoisin sauce, garlic, ginger and egg in a bowl. Mix thoroughly and form into 10 mini burgers.

3. Whisk the water, remaining 2 Tbsp hoisin sauce and sesame oil together in a small bowl.

4. Brush half of the sauce over the burgers.

5. Barbecue, or place on a rack on a baking sheet and bake for 10 to 15 minutes (until no longer pink in the center). Turn the patties once, halfway through, and brush with the remaining sauce. Serve on mini hamburger buns, if desired, and garnish with sautéed onions.

NUTRITIONAL ANALYSIS PER SERVING (2 MINI-BURGERS)

Calories	264
Protein	30 g
Fat	7 g
Saturated Fat	2.5 g
Carbohydrates	15 g
Cholesterol	120 mg
Sodium	289 mg
Fiber	2.4 g

Prep Time: 10 minutes
Cook Time: 10 minutes

Make Ahead:
Prepare to grilling stage up to a day in advance, cover and refrigerate. Grill just before serving.

Serves 5

Greek Chili with Black Olives and Feta Cheese

NUTRITIONAL ANALYSIS
PER SERVING

Calories	245
Protein	16 g
Fat	8 g
Saturated Fat	2.4 g
Carbohydrates	26 g
Cholesterol	17 mg
Sodium	550 mg
Fiber	6.1 g

Prep Time: 15 minutes

Cook Time: 45 minutes

Make Ahead:
Prepare up to a day in
advance and refrigerate or
freeze for up to 2 months.
If frozen, defrost and reheat
gently over low heat.

Serves 6

Chili is a perfect comfort food. In this recipe, lean beef or lamb replaces regular ground beef, and there is only 1 teaspoon of added oil. To make the dish vegetarian, use ground soy in place of the beef; the soybeans add fiber and plant protein. If you like your chili hot, add some fresh minced jalapeño peppers. This chili is delicious on its own or served over rice, couscous or polenta. You can use whole canned tomatoes; just crush them with the back of a wooden spoon during the cooking or purée in a food processor.

1 tsp vegetable oil

1 cup chopped onion

1½ cups chopped eggplant (unpeeled)

1 cup chopped zucchini

1 cup sliced mushrooms

1 cup chopped green bell pepper

2 tsp minced fresh garlic

8 oz extra-lean ground beef or lamb

1 cup canned red kidney beans, drained
   and rinsed

1 cup canned white kidney beans,
   drained and rinsed

1 can (19 oz) crushed tomatoes

1¼ cups beef or chicken stock

⅓ cup sliced black olives

4 tsp chili powder

2 tsp brown sugar

2 tsp dried basil

1½ tsp dried oregano

⅓ cup crumbled feta cheese

⅓ cup chopped cilantro or parsley

1. Spray a large non-stick saucepan with cooking oil, add the vegetable oil and place over medium heat. Add the onion and cook, stirring frequently, for 5 minutes, or until lightly browned. Add the eggplant, zucchini, mushrooms, green pepper and garlic. Sauté for 8 minutes, or until the vegetables are softened, stirring occasionally. Add the meat and stir to break it up; cook for 2 minutes, or until it's no longer pink. Drain off the excess fat.

2. Mash ½ cup of the red kidney beans with ½ cup of the white kidney beans in a large bowl.

3. Add the mashed and whole beans, tomatoes, stock, olives, chili powder, sugar, basil and oregano to the meat mixture. Stir well and bring to a boil. Reduce the heat to low, cover and simmer for 30 minutes. Serve in individual bowls, sprinkled with feta cheese and cilantro.

Cornbread

This is the perfect accompaniment for any chili. It's best served right out of the oven. Dip it in a little olive oil for extra flavor.

1½ cups canned corn kernels, drained

1 cup cornmeal

1 cup all-purpose flour

3 tbsp granulated sugar

1 Tbsp baking powder

1½ cups yogurt

2 eggs

3 Tbsp olive oil

½ cup diced green onion

1 Tbsp minced jalapeño pepper

1. Preheat the oven to 350°F. Spray a 9-inch square baking dish with cooking oil.

2. Spray a non-stick skillet with cooking oil, add the corn and sauté until browned, approximately 5 minutes. Place in a mixing bowl.

3. Add the cornmeal, flour, sugar, baking powder, yogurt, eggs, oil, onion and jalapeño. Mix until combined. Pour into the prepared baking pan and bake for 20 minutes or until a tester comes out clean. Cut into squares and serve with chili.

NUTRITIONAL ANALYSIS PER SERVING (1 SQUARE)

Calories	167
Protein	5.3 g
Fat	3.9 g
Saturated Fat	0.6 g
Carbohydrates	28 g
Cholesterol	0.9 mg
Sodium	181 mg
Fiber	1.8 g

Prep Time: 10 minutes

Cook Time: 25 minutes

Make Ahead:
Can be baked a day ahead or frozen up to 6 weeks.

Makes 12 squares

Turkey Chili with Barley and Black-Eyed Beans

NUTRITIONAL ANALYSIS
PER SERVING

Calories	359
Protein	27 g
Fat	8 g
Saturated Fat	2.6 g
Carbohydrates	28 g
Cholesterol	67 mg
Sodium	365 mg
Fiber	9.5 g

Prep Time: 15 minutes
Cook Time: 43 minutes

Make Ahead:
Prepare a day in advance
and reheat, adding more
stock if too thick. Freeze
for up to 2 months.

Serves 6

Perfect in the cooler months, this is a complete meal in one dish, with all the nutrients you require. If you don't have ground turkey, use ground chicken, lean beef or soy meat substitute. Feel free to use any bean of your choice. If you like a smoother texture pulse it in the food processor.

2 tsp vegetable oil
1 cup chopped onion
2 tsp crushed fresh garlic
1 lb lean ground turkey
1 can (19 oz) whole tomatoes with juice
1½ cups chicken stock
¼ cup pearl barley
1 Tbsp seeded and minced jalapeño
    pepper
2 tsp dried basil
1 tsp dried oregano

2 bay leaves
1 cup black-eyed beans or black beans,
    drained and rinsed
2 Tbsp tomato paste

⅓ cup chopped green onion
⅓ cup shredded light aged cheddar
    cheese
¼ cup low-fat sour cream
¼ cup chopped fresh parsley or basil

1. Spray a large non-stick skillet with cooking oil, add the vegetable oil and place over medium heat. Add the onion and garlic and sauté until browned, about 5 to 8 minutes.

2. Add the turkey and break it up with the back of a wooden spoon; sauté until it's no longer pink, about 8 minutes. Add the tomatoes and juice, stock, barley, peppers, basil, oregano, bay leaves, beans and tomato paste to the pan. Break up the tomatoes and bring to a boil. Simmer uncovered for 30 minutes, or until the barley is tender. Remove the bay leaves.

3. Garnish each serving with green onion, cheese, sour cream and parsley.

Chili Bean Stew

This is another versatile chili where ground chicken, veal or ground soy substitute can replace the beef and any cooked beans can be used instead of kidney beans. Add some minced jalapeño for more heat. Use any grain in place of the pasta; just be aware if the cooking time varies.

1½ tsp vegetable oil

1 tsp crushed fresh garlic

¾ cup canned corn kernels, drained

1 cup chopped onion

8 oz extra-lean ground beef

1 can (19 oz) tomatoes, crushed

1¾ cups beef or chicken stock

1½ cups peeled diced potatoes

¾ cup canned red kidney beans, drained and rinsed

2 Tbsp tomato paste

2½ tsp chili powder

2 tsp dried basil

1½ tsp dried oregano

⅓ cup small shell pasta

⅓ cup chopped cilantro or parsley

1. Spray a large non-stick saucepan with cooking oil, add the vegetable oil and place over medium heat. Add the garlic, corn and onion; sauté until the onion has softened and the corn begins to brown, approximately 5 minutes.

2. Add the beef and stir to break up the chunks; cook until no longer pink, approximately 4 minutes. Drain off any fat.

3. Add the tomatoes, stock, potatoes, kidney beans, tomato paste, chili powder, basil and oregano to the pan. Stir well. Cover, reduce the heat and simmer for 30 minutes, or until the potatoes are soft. Stir occasionally.

4. Add the pasta and cook until firm to the bite, approximately 10 minutes.

5. Garnish with cilantro and serve immediately.

NUTRITIONAL ANALYSIS PER SERVING

Calories	232
Protein	15 g
Fat	6 g
Saturated fat	2 g
Carbohydrates	30 g
Cholesterol	22 mg
Sodium	480 mg
Fiber	5 g

Prep Time: 10 minutes

Cook Time: 49 minutes

Make Ahead:

Prepare up to a day in advance and refrigerate. Reheat gently, adding more stock if too thick. Freeze for up to 1 month.

Serves 6

Teriyaki Chicken Burgers

NUTRITIONAL ANALYSIS PER SERVING

Calories	276
Protein	24 g
Fat	6.7 g
Saturated Fat	1.3 g
Carbohydrates	29 g
Cholesterol	95 mg
Sodium	410 mg
Fiber	0.9 g

Prep Time: 15 minutes

Cook Time: 15 minutes

Make Ahead:
Prepare the sauce a day ahead and refrigerate. Prepare the burger mix, cover and refrigerate; cook just before serving.

Serves 5

I've always loved teriyaki sauce with fish or chicken. This preparation puts it in the burger as well as serving it on top. Substitute lean beef or turkey for the chicken, if you prefer. Serve these burgers with sautéed vegetables and rice noodles.

⅓ cup brown sugar, packed

3 Tbsp low-sodium soy sauce

1 Tbsp water

3 Tbsp rice vinegar

1 Tbsp sesame oil

1 Tbsp cornstarch

1½ tsp crushed fresh garlic

1½ tsp minced fresh ginger

1 lb ground chicken breast

1 egg

⅓ cup dry seasoned breadcrumbs

3 Tbsp finely chopped green onion

2 tsp sesame seeds, toasted

3 Tbsp chopped cilantro or parsley

1. To make the teriyaki sauce, whisk the sugar, soy sauce, water, vinegar, oil, cornstarch, garlic and ginger in a small skillet. Simmer for 3 minutes or just until thickened.

2. Place 3 Tbsp of the teriyaki sauce in a bowl and add the chicken, egg, breadcrumbs and green onion. Mix well. Form into 5 patties.

3. Spray a grill or non-stick skillet with cooking oil and heat to high. Cook the patties for about 6 minutes per side or until no longer pink in the center.

4. Serve with the remaining sauce and garnish with sesame seeds and cilantro.

Ground Soy Macaroni and Corn Chili

This is my replacement for "ski-hill" chili, and the kids love it. The soy-based beef substitute gives it a milder flavor. Serve it in a bowl, over a large bun or even in a large, hollowed-out loaf of bread for a dramatic presentation! Substitute other small shaped pasta, or another grain that cooks in a few minutes, for the macaroni. You can also omit the pasta, but reduce the stock to 1¾ cups.

¾ cup canned corn kernels, drained
1½ tsp vegetable oil
1 cup chopped onion
½ cup finely chopped carrot
1 tsp minced fresh garlic
8 oz soy-based ground beef substitute
1 can (19 oz) tomatoes, crushed
2 cups vegetable or chicken stock
1½ cups peeled diced potatoes
¾ cup canned red kidney beans, drained
  and rinsed

2 Tbsp tomato paste
1½ tsp chili powder
1½ tsp dried oregano
1½ tsp dried basil
¼ tsp salt
¼ tsp freshly ground black pepper
⅓ cup elbow macaroni
2 Tbsp grated Parmesan cheese
⅓ cup chopped cilantro or basil

1. Spray a large non-stick saucepan with cooking oil and sauté the corn over medium heat until browned, stirring constantly, about 5 minutes.

2. Add the vegetable oil and cook the onions, carrots and garlic until softened, stirring occasionally, about 5 minutes. Stir in the ground soy, tomatoes, stock, potatoes, beans, tomato paste, chili powder, oregano, basil, salt and pepper. Bring to a boil. Reduce the heat to low and simmer for 25 to 30 minutes, covered.

3. Bring the chili to a boil and add the macaroni. Cook for 5 minutes, or until the pasta is tender but firm. Ladle into individual bowls and sprinkle with the Parmesan and cilantro.

NUTRITIONAL ANALYSIS PER SERVING

Calories	165
Protein	12 g
Fat	2.3 g
Saturated Fat	0.5 g
Carbohydrates	24 g
Cholesterol	1.2 mg
Sodium	658 mg
Fiber	5.6 g

Prep Time:	15 minutes
Cook Time:	40 minutes

Make Ahead:
Prepare up to 2 days in advance, cover and refrigerate. Reheat over low heat, adding more stock if too thick.

Serves 8

Greek Feta Burgers

NUTRITIONAL ANALYSIS
PER SERVING

Calories	194
Protein	21 g
Fat	9.6 g
Saturated Fat	3.6 g
Carbohydrates	5.9 g
Cholesterol	76 mg
Sodium	210 mg
Fiber	0.8 g

Prep Time: 10 minutes

Cook Time: 15 minutes

Make Ahead:
Prepare to the grilling stage
up to a day in advance,
cover well and refrigerate.
Grill just before serving.

Serves 5

Add some mushrooms, feta cheese and oregano and you have a whole new burger. Try substituting ground chicken, turkey or veal. Forget the bun—I love to serve these over a bed of couscous. But if you're serving them on a bun, be sure to include lettuce, tomatoes and onions for an extra serving of veggies.

1 cup chopped mushrooms
½ cup chopped onion
⅓ cup light feta cheese, crumbled
1 lb extra-lean ground beef or lamb
¼ cup finely chopped fresh chives or
  green onions

3 Tbsp chopped fresh oregano
2 Tbsp barbecue sauce
3 Tbsp dry seasoned breadcrumbs
2 tsp minced fresh garlic
1 egg
3 Tbsp chopped fresh oregano or parsley

1. Spray a non-stick skillet with cooking oil; add the mushrooms and onions and cook over medium-high heat for 4 minutes or until softened and browned. Remove from the heat. Stir in the feta.

2. Combine the beef, chives, oregano, barbecue sauce, breadcrumbs, garlic and egg in a bowl. Stir in the onion mixture. Mix thoroughly. Form into 5 patties.

3. Spray a non-stick grill pan or barbecue grill with cooking oil and heat to medium-high. Grill the patties for 3 to 5 minutes per side or until no longer pink in the center. (Alternatively, place on a baking sheet in the center of a preheated 450°F oven for 10 to 15 minutes or until cooked through, turning once.) Garnish with oregano and crumbled feta cheese, if desired.

Greek Feta Burgers
Photo by Brian MacDonald

Chicken, Cheese and Tomato Enchilada

NUTRITIONAL ANALYSIS
PER SERVING

Calories	442
Protein	30 g
Fat	17 g
Saturated Fat	6.8 g
Carbohydrates	48 g
Cholesterol	84 mg
Sodium	342 mg
Fiber	4.6 g

Prep Time: 15 minutes

Cook Time: 29 minutes

Make Ahead:
Prepare enchiladas early in the day, but don't cover with sauce. Refrigerate. Add sauce and bake just before serving, adding an extra 10 minutes to the baking time.

Serves 4

I haven't often included Mexican-type foods in my books because many are loaded with fat and calories. But then I came up with this healthier version of an enchilada.

12 oz skinless boneless chicken thighs, diced
¼ cup all-purpose flour
2 tsp vegetable oil
1½ cups diced onion
2 tsp crushed fresh garlic
1 cup diced green bell pepper
1 cup medium salsa
1 tsp chili flakes, or to taste
⅓ cup chopped cilantro

1½ cups 2 percent evaporated milk
1 cup chicken stock
2 Tbsp all-purpose flour
1 cup shredded light aged cheddar cheese
1 tsp Dijon mustard
pinch freshly ground black pepper
4 large flour tortillas (preferably wholegrain)

2 Tbsp shredded aged cheddar cheese
2 Tbsp chopped cilantro

1. Preheat the oven to 425 F. Spray a 13- by 9-inch baking dish with cooking oil.

2. Place the chicken in a large bowl and sprinkle with ¼ cup of flour, making sure it's well coated. Spray a large non-stick skillet with cooking oil and place over medium heat. Sauté the chicken until seared on all sides, approximately 5 minutes. Transfer to a bowl.

3. Wipe the pan and respray. Heat the oil over medium heat and sauté the onion and garlic for 5 minutes, or until the onions begin to brown. Add the green pepper and sauté for 3 minutes. Add the salsa, chili flakes and chicken; simmer for 3 minutes. Add the ⅓ cup cilantro.

4. Place the evaporated milk, stock and flour in a medium-sized pot and whisk until smooth. Simmer over medium heat until slightly thickened, approximately 3 minutes. Add the 1 cup grated cheese, mustard and pepper; simmer for another 2 minutes. Add half the sauce to the chicken mixture.

5. Lay out the tortillas on your work surface. Divide the chicken mixture among them. Roll the tortillas up, leaving the ends open. Place in the baking dish, seam side down, so they're touching each other. Pour the remaining cheese sauce overtop and sprinkle with the 2 Tbsp cheese. Bake for 8 minutes. Serve immediately, garnished with cilantro.

Caramelized Onion Sirloin Steak Burgers Stuffed with Brie

Every major North American city has come out with its own "gourmet" burger, which can cost anywhere from $30 to $60! The price is justified by the quality of the beef, but I still think it's crazy to pay that much for a burger. I decided to develop my own version. Stuffed with brie and topped with caramelized onions, it's sensational—and it costs a lot less than the restaurant version! When purchasing barbecue sauce, look for a good quality sauce without extra flavorings. Serve with Potato Wedge Fries (see page 268).

1 tsp vegetable oil

3 cups sliced sweet onion

1 Tbsp brown sugar, packed

1 lb ground lean sirloin steak

3 Tbsp minced green onion

¼ cup dry seasoned breadcrumbs

3 Tbsp barbecue sauce

1½ tsp crushed fresh garlic

pinch salt and freshly ground black
    pepper

1 egg

1 tsp dried basil

1½ oz brie cheese, diced

2 Tbsp chopped fresh parsley

NUTRITIONAL ANALYSIS
PER SERVING

Calories	264
Protein	30 g
Fat	11 g
Saturated Fat	5 g
Carbohydrates	15 g
Cholesterol	120 mg
Sodium	289 mg
Fiber	2.4 g

Prep Time: 10 minutes

Cook Time: 23 minutes

Make Ahead:
Prepare burgers up to
the cooking stage a day in
advance and refrigerate.
Grill just before serving.

Serves 5

1. Spray a large non-stick skillet with cooking oil, add the vegetable oil and place over medium heat. Add the onion and sauté for 5 minutes, just until soft. Reduce the heat to low, add the sugar and continue cooking for 10 minutes, until browned and caramelized. Set aside.

2. To make the burgers, combine the meat, green onion, breadcrumbs, barbecue sauce, garlic, salt, pepper, egg and basil in a large bowl. Mix thoroughly and shape into 5 burgers. Form a pocket in each burger and stuff evenly with the diced brie. Make sure the beef encloses the cheese completely.

3. Preheat a barbecue or indoor grill and spray with cooking oil. Cook the burgers for about 4 minutes per side, or until no longer pink in the center. Mound the onions on top of each serving and garnish with parsley.

Veggie Burgers with Chickpeas, Carrot and Corn

NUTRITIONAL ANALYSIS
PER SERVING
(WITHOUT PITA)

Calories	320
Protein	12 g
Fat	13 g
Saturated Fat	2 g
Carbohydrates	30 g
Cholesterol	70 mg
Sodium	300 mg
Fiber	6 g

Prep Time: 15 minutes
Cook Time: 11 minutes

Serves 6

I've eaten many different veggie burgers and my complaint is that often they contain too much tofu, making them taste "too healthy" (in other words, not very flavorful), or they're fried, giving them excess oil and fat. I created this recipe for The Pickle Barrel restaurant chain and think it's the tastiest and healthiest veggie burger I've ever eaten. Try it and see if you agree!

½ cup canned corn kernels, drained

1 can (19 oz) chickpeas, drained and
    rinsed

1 cup coarsely grated carrot

⅓ cup chopped cilantro or basil

1 egg

¼ cup tahini

3 Tbsp freshly squeezed lemon juice

¼ cup breadcrumbs

¼ cup chopped green onion

1½ tsp minced fresh garlic

pinch salt and freshly ground black
    pepper

2 tsp vegetable oil

¼ cup smooth light ricotta

2 Tbsp tahini

2 Tbsp light mayonnaise

1 Tbsp olive oil

1 Tbsp low-sodium soy sauce

1 Tbsp freshly squeezed lemon juice

3 Tbsp chopped cilantro

1 tsp minced fresh garlic

Pitas, lettuce, tomatoes, onions

1. To make the burgers, spray a small non-stick skillet with cooking oil and sauté the corn for 5 minutes over medium-high heat until lightly browned. Place in a food processor.

2. Add the chickpeas, carrot, cilantro, egg, ¼ cup tahini, 3 Tbsp lemon juice, bread-crumbs, onion, 1½ tsp garlic, salt and pepper. Process just until the mixture comes together. Do not purée. Form into 4 patties.

3. Spray a large non-stick skillet with cooking oil, add the vegetable oil and place over medium heat. Sauté the patties for 4 minutes per side, until browned and warmed through.

4. To make the sauce, purée the ricotta cheese, 2 Tbsp tahini, mayonnaise, oil, soy sauce, 1 Tbsp lemon juice, cilantro and 1 tsp garlic in a food processor or blender until smooth.

5. Serve the patties with the sauce, or make burgers with pita bread, lettuce, tomatoes and onions (if desired).

Fajita Burgers with Avocado Salsa Topping

I've created many burgers, but this Tex-Mex version is one of my favorites. There is definitely no need for a bun with these delicious toppings. Serve these with baked tortilla chips or a side dish of black beans.

1 tsp vegetable oil
½ cup diced onion
¼ cup diced red bell pepper
¼ cup diced green bell pepper
1 lb extra-lean ground beef
1 egg
2 tsp crushed fresh garlic
¼ cup dry seasoned breadcrumbs
3 Tbsp medium salsa

¼ cup chopped cilantro or parsley
four ½-inch cubes (1 oz) of aged cheddar
  cheese

⅓ cup medium salsa
⅓ cup diced ripe avocado
2 Tbsp chopped cilantro or parsley

NUTRITIONAL ANALYSIS PER SERVING

Calories	282
Protein	27 g
Fat	10.6 g
Saturated Fat	2.9 g
Carbohydrates	17 g
Cholesterol	119 mg
Sodium	337 mg
Fiber	2.6 g

Prep Time: 10 minutes
Cook Time: 19 minutes

1. Spray a small non-stick skillet with cooking oil, add the vegetable oil and place over medium heat. Add the onion and sauté for 3 minutes, until lightly browned. Add the red and green pepper and sauté for 2 minutes.

2. Place the beef, egg, garlic, breadcrumbs, salsa and the ¼ cup cilantro in a large bowl. Add the onion mixture. Mix well and form into 4 patties. Insert a piece of cheese into the center of each burger and enclose it completely.

3. Spray a non-stick grill pan or barbecue with cooking oil and heat to medium. Grill the burgers for 7 minutes per side, or until no longer pink in the center.

4. While the burgers are cooking, make the topping. Mix the ⅓ cup salsa, avocado and 2 Tbsp cilantro in a small bowl.

5. Place the burgers on individual serving plates. Garnish with the salsa topping.

Make Ahead:
Prepare the burgers to the grilling stage a day in advance, wrap well and refrigerate. Grill just before serving.

Serves 4

Tuna, Feta and Dill Wrap

Wrap and roll with fresh dill, lemon juice and Dijon mustard for a delicious twist on the traditional tuna sandwich.

1 can (6 oz) flaked water-packed tuna, drained

3 Tbsp light mayonnaise

2 Tbsp low-fat sour cream

½ cup chopped red bell pepper

⅓ cup chopped Vidalia onion

⅓ cup chopped celery

¼ cup chopped black olives

¼ cup chopped fresh dill

3 Tbsp light feta cheese, crumbled

2 Tbsp freshly squeezed lemon juice

1 tsp minced fresh garlic

1 tsp Dijon mustard

pinch salt and freshly ground black pepper

4 large flour tortillas

4 pieces leafy lettuce

1. To make the filling, combine the tuna, mayonnaise, sour cream, red pepper, onion, celery, olives, dill, feta, lemon juice, garlic, mustard, salt and pepper in a medium-sized bowl. Mix until well blended.

2. Place one-quarter of the filling across the center of a tortilla, leaving a 1-inch margin at each side. Top with a piece of lettuce. Fold up the bottom of the tortilla, fold in both sides and continue to roll it up tightly. Repeat with the remaining tortillas and filling. Cut the rolls in half before serving.

NUTRITIONAL ANALYSIS
PER SERVING

Calories	170
Protein	9 g
Fat	5 g
Saturated Fat	1.3 g
Carbohydrates	22 g
Cholesterol	9 mg
Sodium	370 mg
Fiber	1.7 g

Prep Time: 20 minutes

Make Ahead:
Prepare filling up to a day in advance and refrigerate. Prepare wraps up to a couple of hours before serving time, cover well and refrigerate.

Serves 8

Roasted Vegetarian Sandwich with Brie

After tasting this sandwich you might decide to go vegetarian! The grilled vegetables, pesto and brie are a sensational combination. And, yes, you can enjoy brie when you're eating light—just watch the amounts. Each sandwich contains only ½ oz, which you'll find is enough. For the rolls, I like to use either focaccia or sourdough rolls. If using store-bought pesto, remember it is higher in fat and calories than my homemade version (see page 342); use a smaller amount or thin it with a little water.

½ large red onion, sliced

1 red bell pepper, cut in 8 wedges

1 large portobello mushroom, thickly sliced

1 zucchini, cut in 3 slices lengthwise

2 Tbsp pesto sauce

2 Tbsp low-fat sour cream

1 Tbsp olive oil

2 tsp balsamic vinegar

½ tsp minced fresh garlic

4 large rolls (each 3 ½ oz), split

2 oz brie cheese, thinly sliced

1. Preheat the oven to 425°F. Line a rimmed baking sheet with foil.

2. Place the onion, red pepper, mushroom and zucchini on the prepared baking sheet. Spray lightly with cooking oil. Roast the vegetables, turning once, for 25 to 30 minutes or until tender. Remove and allow to cool.

3. While the vegetables are roasting, combine the pesto and sour cream in a small bowl.

4. Cut the roasted vegetables into pieces that fit the shape of the bread. Place in a bowl and toss with the oil, vinegar and garlic.

5. Spread the pesto mixture over the bottom half of each roll. Top with the vegetable mixture and brie. Replace the top half of the roll and cut in half to serve.

NUTRITIONAL ANALYSIS PER SERVING

Calories	187
Protein	6 g
Fat	6 g
Saturated Fat	2.2 g
Carbohydrates	29 g
Cholesterol	9 mg
Sodium	298 mg
Fiber	2.5 g

Prep Time: 15 minutes

Cook Time: 25 minutes

Make Ahead:
Prepare vegetables a day in advance and refrigerate. Make sandwiches 2 hours before serving and cover well.

Serves 8

Roasted Vegetarian Sandwich with Brie
Photo by Per Kristiansen

Panini Clubhouse Sandwich with Grilled Chicken, Crisp Prosciutto, Avocado and Cheese

NUTRITIONAL ANALYSIS
PER SERVING

Calories	143
Protein	12 g
Fat	6.1 g
Saturated Fat	2.2 g
Cholesterol	28 mg
Carbohydrates	12 g
Sodium	333 mg
Fiber	1.6 g

Prep Time: 20 minutes

Cook Time: 14 minutes

Make Ahead:
Cook chicken and prosciutto a day in advance and refrigerate. Assemble sandwich up to 2 hours ahead, refrigerate and grill just before serving.

Serves 8

Paninis—grilled sandwiches filled with vegetables—are all the rage today. I like this take on a clubhouse sandwich. I use prosicutto instead of bacon since it has less fat and calories. One ounce of prosciutto has 50 calories and 3 grams of fat, whereas bacon has 130 calories and 10 grams of fat per ounce. Sautéing prosciutto gives it the texture of bacon.

8 oz skinless boneless chicken breast

2 Tbsp light mayonnaise

2 tsp freshly squeezed lemon juice

1 tsp Dijon mustard

½ tsp crushed fresh garlic

pinch freshly ground black pepper

4 large tortillas (preferably whole wheat)

⅔ cup grated Parmesan or Swiss cheese

⅓ cup diced, seeded plum tomatoes

⅓ cup diced sweet onion

½ diced ripe avocado

1. Spray a non-stick skillet with cooking oil and place over medium heat. Sauté the prosciutto for 5 minutes or just until dry and beginning to crisp. Remove from the pan, cool slightly and crumble. Wipe the skillet and respray.

2. Working with one at a time, pound the chicken breasts between two sheets of waxed paper to an even ¼-inch thickness. Sauté the chicken for 5 minutes, or just until cooked and no longer pink in the center, turning halfway. Cool for 5 minutes, then dice.

3. Combine the mayonnaise, lemon juice, mustard, garlic and pepper in a small bowl and mix thoroughly. Spread evenly over the entire surface of the tortillas. Scatter the chicken, prosciutto, cheese, tomato, onion and avocado overtop. Fold in the sides of each tortilla and roll it up tightly.

4. Preheat a non-stick grill pan to hot and spray with cooking oil. Sear the rolls on both sides until browned, approximately 2 minutes per side. Slice in half before serving.

Panini Clubhouse Sandwich with Grilled ▷
Chicken, Crisp Prosciutto, Avocado and Cheese
Photo by Lorella Zanetti

Shrimp Caesar Wrap with Chopped Romaine

**NUTRITIONAL ANALYSIS
PER SERVING**

Calories	157
Protein	11 g
Fat	6 g
Saturated Fat	1.5 g
Carbohydrates	17 g
Cholesterol	20 mg
Sodium	302 mg
Fiber	3.3 g

Prep Time: 15 minutes

Cook Time: 5 minutes

Make Ahead:
Prepare shrimp and
dressing a day in advance
and refrigerate. Complete
the filling and wrap just
before serving.

Serves 8

Here's another recipe that has been a huge hit in our catering company. The light Caesar dressing uses low-fat mayonnaise rather than a raw egg. Substitute chicken for the shrimp if you prefer.

10 oz raw shrimp, peeled and deveined

3 Tbsp low-fat mayonnaise

3 anchovies, minced

1 tsp crushed fresh garlic

2 Tbsp freshly squeezed lemon juice

1 Tbsp water

3 Tbsp grated Parmesan cheese

1 tsp Dijon mustard

pinch freshly ground black pepper

3 cups finely sliced romaine lettuce

large whole wheat tortillas (or flavor of
your choice)

1. In a non-stick grilling pan sprayed with vegetable oil, grill or sauté the shrimp just until cooked, about 5 minutes. Cool, then dice. Place in a bowl.

2. To make the dressing, combine the mayonnaise, anchovies, garlic, lemon juice, water, cheese, mustard and pepper in a bowl and whisk until smooth. Add the dressing and the lettuce to the shrimp and mix well.

3. Place a quarter of the shrimp mixture along the centre of a tortilla, leaving a 1-inch margin at the sides. Fold the bottom of the tortilla up and over the filling, fold in both sides and continue to roll it up tightly. Repeat with the remaining ingredients. Cut the rolls in half before serving.

Roasted Turkey and Hummus Wrap

Homemade hummus is easy to prepare and much lower in fat and calories than the store-bought version, which can be loaded with oil. Hummus is a great spread for any wrap or sandwich and goes particularly well with turkey.

1 cup canned chickpeas, drained and rinsed

¼ cup water

¼ cup tahini (sesame seed paste)

2 Tbsp freshly squeezed lemon juice

1 tsp minced fresh garlic

1½ Tbsp olive oil

4 large flour tortillas

1 plum tomato, sliced

4 slices Vidalia onion

4 pieces leafy lettuce

8 oz roasted turkey slices

¼ cup chopped cilantro or basil

1. To make the hummus, purée the chickpeas, water, tahini, lemon juice, garlic and olive oil in a food processor or blender until smooth.

2. Spread a quarter of the hummus over a tortilla, spreading it right to the edges. Place a tomato slice, an onion slice, a lettuce leaf, and one-quarter of the turkey slices overtop.

3. Sprinkle with cilantro. Fold the bottom of the tortilla up and over the filling, fold in both sides, and continue to roll it up tightly. Repeat with the remaining ingredients. Cut the rolls in half before serving.

NUTRITIONAL ANALYSIS PER SERVING

Calories	278
Protein	11.1 g
Fat	10 g
Saturated Fat	2 g
Carbohydrates	36 g
Cholesterol	15 mg
Sodium	389 mg
Fiber	3.3 g

Prep Time: 15 minutes

Make Ahead:
Prepare wraps early in the day, cover well and refrigerate.

Serves 8

Smoked Salmon, Cheese, Avocado and Caper Wrap

My version of a lox and cream cheese sandwich has fewer calories, less fat, and more interesting and tasty ingredients! The light ricotta and cream cheese combination is the key substitute for regular cream cheese.

⅓ cup smooth light ricotta

2 Tbsp light cream cheese

⅓ cup goat cheese

2 Tbsp light mayonnaise

2 tsp freshly squeezed lemon juice

1 tsp Dijon mustard

½ tsp crushed fresh garlic

pinch freshly ground black pepper

4 large tortillas (preferably whole wheat)

4 pieces leafy lettuce

4 oz smoked salmon, diced

½ cup diced red onion

½ cup diced ripe avocado

1 Tbsp capers

1. Purée the ricotta, cream cheese, goat cheese, mayonnaise, lemon juice, mustard, garlic and pepper in a small food processor, or with a hand beater, until smooth.

2. Divide the cheese mixture among the tortillas, spreading it to ¼ inch from the edges. Place the lettuce overtop.

3. Scatter the salmon, onion, avocado and capers over the lettuce. Roll the bottom of each tortilla up and over the filling, fold in the sides and roll the tortilla up tightly. Cut in half before serving.

NUTRITIONAL ANALYSIS PER SERVING

Calories	124
Protein	7 g
Fat	6.1 g
Saturated Fat	2.1 g
Carbohydrates	14 g
Cholesterol	12 mg
Sodium	324 mg
Fiber	1.8 g

Prep Time: 15 minutes

Make Ahead:
Prepare cheese mixture a day in advance, and refrigerate.

Serves 8

◀ Smoked Salmon, Cheese, Avocado and Caper Wrap
Photo by Lorella Zanetti

Rose's Low-Fat Philadelphia Cheese Steak

NUTRITIONAL ANALYSIS PER SERVING

Calories	170
Protein	12 g
Fat	8.2 g
Saturated Fat	3.4 g
Carbohydrates	9 g
Cholesterol	28 mg
Sodium	129 mg
Fiber	2 g

Prep Time: 15 minutes
Cook Time: 23 minutes

Make Ahead:
Cook vegetables up to a day in advance and refrigerate. Heat in skillet just until warm before assembling sandwich.

Serves 8

Philly steaks—grilled thin steak topped with loads of cooked vegetables and cheese—are all the rage now. Naturally, they originated in Philadelphia. Try my lighter version of this classic sandwich.

2 tsp vegetable oil
2 cups sliced onions
2 tsp crushed fresh garlic
2 tsp brown sugar
¼ tsp salt and freshly ground black pepper
1 cup sliced red bell pepper
1 cup sliced green bell pepper

8 oz grilling steak
2 Tbsp low-fat mayonnaise
3 Tbsp low-fat sour cream
2 tsp horseradish
4 small wholegrain rolls (6-inch), split
¾ cup grated provolone or Gruyère cheese

1. Preheat the oven to 425°F. Line a baking sheet with foil.

2. Spray a large non-stick skillet with cooking oil, add the vegetable oil and place over medium heat. Add the onions and sauté for 8 minutes. Add the garlic, brown sugar, salt, pepper and bell pepper. Sauté for another 5 minutes. Set aside and keep warm.

3. Spray a non-stick grill or skillet with cooking oil and place over high heat. Cook the steak just until done to your preference, approximately 5 to 8 minutes. Cool for 5 minutes before cutting into thin slices. Add to the vegetable mixture.

4. Combine the mayonnaise, sour cream and horseradish. Spread thinly over both sides of the rolls. Divide filling among the 4 rolls, sprinkle with the cheese and replace the top half of the bun. Place on the prepared baking sheet and bake for 5 minutes. Slice in half before serving.

Rose's Low-Fat Philadelphia Cheese Steak ▶
Photo by Brian MacDonald

Three-Cheese Grilled Sandwich with Tomatoes and Onions

Who would have thought that old comfort food, grilled cheese, would make such a comeback—not only as a casual sandwich at home, but also as an elegant appetizer at parties. Here's a twist on the traditional; I use it as a lunch item, on buffets and even cut into quarters as an appetizer.

¼ cup light aged cheddar cheese, thinly sliced

⅛ cup Parmesan cheese, freshly grated

¼ cup crumbled goat cheese

4 slices wholegrain bread

4 slices plum tomato

4 slices sweet onion

1. Divide the cheddar, Parmesan and goat cheese between two slices of bread. Top with the sliced tomatoes and onions. Cover with the remaining two slices of bread. Spray both sides of each sandwich with cooking oil.

2. Spray a non-stick skillet with cooking oil and place over medium heat. Cook the sandwiches for approximately 4 minutes per side, being careful not to burn them.

3. Cut each sandwich into quarters and serve 2 per person.

NUTRITIONAL ANALYSIS PER SERVING

Calories	199
Protein	11 g
Fat	11 g
Saturated Fat	6.2 g
Carbohydrates	15 g
Cholesterol	25 mg
Sodium	288 mg
Fiber	2.3 g

Prep Time:	10 minutes
Cook Time:	8 minutes

Serves 4

Three-Cheese Grilled Sandwich
with Tomatoes and Onions
Photo by Lorella Zanetti

Grilled Chicken and Roasted Red Pepper Sandwich

NUTRITIONAL ANALYSIS
PER SERVING

Calories	252
Protein	13 g
Fat	6 g
Saturated Fat	2.1 g
Carbohydrates	27 g
Cholesterol	24 mg
Sodium	235 mg
Fiber	1.7 g

Prep Time: 15 minutes

Cook Time: 12 minutes

Make Ahead:
Prepare goat cheese spread and grill chicken a day in advance; refrigerate. Sandwich can be assembled a few hours ahead and refrigerated.

Serves 8

So often chicken sandwiches are smothered with mayonnaise or butter, which adds most of the fat and calories to the sandwich. In this version, which I love to serve on a focaccia bun, the spread is tangy and light. The spread is great over fish or pork. If you can't find focaccia buns, use any other 3½-ounce roll you like—sourdough or whole-grain rolls are also delicious.

8 oz skinless boneless chicken breast

1 small red bell pepper, roasted (see page 122)

⅓ cup light cream cheese, softened

¼ cup goat cheese

2 Tbsp chopped rehydrated sun-dried tomatoes (see page 221)

2 Tbsp light mayonnaise

2 Tbsp low-fat sour cream

1½ tsp Dijon mustard

1 tsp minced fresh garlic

½ tsp dried basil

4 large rolls, each about 3½oz

sliced tomatoes and onions, lettuce leaves (optional)

1. Preheat a grill or grill pan to medium-high and spray with cooking oil. Grill the chicken for approximately 12 minutes, turning once, or until no longer pink in the center. Cut into thin slices.

2. Thinly slice the red pepper.

3. Place the cream cheese, goat cheese, sun-dried tomatoes, mayonnaise, sour cream, mustard, garlic and basil in a small food processor, and process until smooth (or use an electric mixer).

4. Cut the rolls in half horizontally. Spread the cut sides with the cream cheese mixture. Top with the chicken and red pepper strips. Garnish with tomato, onion and lettuce, if desired. Replace the tops and cut in half before serving.

Goat Cheese and Tomato Salad Wrap

This is a great vegetarian wrap that can be either a complete meal or a side dish. Non-vegetarians might want to add some grilled chicken or shrimp. Substitute any strong-tasting cheese for the goat cheese.

½ cup crumbled goat cheese

1¼ cups diced seeded plum tomatoes

1¼ cups diced English cucumber
   (skin on)

½ cup chopped green onion

2 tsp olive oil

2 tsp balsamic vinegar

1 tsp minced fresh garlic

¼ cup chopped fresh basil or parsley

4 large flour tortillas

1. Combine the goat cheese, tomatoes, cucumber, green onion, oil, vinegar, garlic and basil in a bowl, mixing well.

2. Place one-quarter of the goat cheese mixture along the center of a tortilla, leaving a 1-inch margin at the sides. Roll the bottom of the tortilla up and over the filling, fold in both the sides and continue to roll it up tightly. Repeat with the remaining tortillas and filling. Cut the rolls in half before serving.

NUTRITIONAL ANALYSIS PER SERVING

Calories	150
Protein	6 g
Fat	5 g
Saturated Fat	2.8 g
Carbohydrates	20 g
Cholesterol	6 mg
Sodium	209 mg
Fiber	1.6 g

Prep Time: 15 minutes

Make Ahead:
Prepare the filling 4 hours in advance and refrigerate. Wrap an hour before serving and cover tightly.

Serves 8

Spinach, Tomato, Chicken and Hummus Wrap

NUTRITIONAL ANALYSIS
PER SERVING

Calories	256
Protein	13 g
Fat	10.5 g
Saturated Fat	1.5 g
Carbohydrates	11 g
Cholesterol	22 mg
Sodium	280 mg
Fiber	4.5 g

Prep Time: 15 minutes

Cook Time: 8 minutes

Make Ahead:
Prepare wraps early in
the day, cover with plastic
wrap and refrigerate.

Serves 8

This is a wrap I developed for the Pickle Barrel chain of restaurants in Toronto. When the customers want a healthier wrap, this is what they order. The combination of spinach, sautéed chicken and hummus is a winner. Homemade hummus always has considerably fewer calories and less fat than the store-bought type.

8 oz skinless boneless chicken breast
1 cup thinly sliced green bell pepper
1 cup thinly sliced red bell pepper
⅓ cup thinly sliced red or sweet onion
⅓ cup low-fat feta cheese, crumbled
½ cup chopped rehydrated sun-dried
   tomatoes (see page 221)
⅓ cup diced black olives

1 Tbsp olive oil
1½ tsp dried basil
1½ tsp minced fresh garlic
⅔ cup hummus (see page 76)
4 large whole wheat tortillas
   (or flavor of your choice)
1 cup baby spinach leaves

1. Working with one at a time, pound the chicken breasts to an even ½-inch thickness between two sheets of waxed paper.

2. Spray a non-stick grill pan with cooking oil and sauté the chicken for approximately 8 minutes, or until no longer pink in the center. Slice into thin strips.

3. Stir the green and red pepper, onion, feta, tomatoes, olives, oil, basil and garlic together in a large bowl.

4. Spread the hummus over the entire surface of the tortillas. Place the vegetable mixture over the hummus. Scatter the spinach leaves overtop and add the chicken. Roll the bottom of each tortilla up and over the filling, fold in both sides, and continue to roll up tightly. Cut each roll in half before serving.

Spinach, Tomato, Chicken and
Hummus Wrap
Photo by Brian MacDonald

Tex-Mex Beef Panini

NUTRITIONAL ANALYSIS
PER SERVING

Calories	134
Protein	9.3 g
Fat	5.3 g
Saturated Fat	2.1 g
Carbohydrates	15 g
Cholesterol	16 mg
Sodium	146 mg
Fiber	1.8 g

Prep Time: 10 minutes

Cook Time: 15 minutes

Make Ahead:
Prepare filling a day
in advance and
refrigerate. Fill and grill
just before serving.

Serves 8

This Southwest-style filling is great when finished like a panini. You can also use left-over beef, cooked chicken or pork for this grilled sandwich.

6 oz grilling steak

2 tsp vegetable oil

1½ cups diced onion

2 tsp crushed fresh garlic

1 cup diced green bell pepper

1 tsp minced, seeded jalapeño pepper or
    ½ tsp hot chili paste

¼ cup chopped cilantro or parsley

4 large flour tortillas (preferably whole
    wheat)

⅓ cup grated light aged cheddar cheese

2 Tbsp low-fat sour cream

2 Tbsp medium salsa

1. Heat a non-stick grill pan to high heat and spray with cooking oil. Sear the steak on both sides and continue cooking on medium-high heat until cooked to your liking. Remove from the pan and let rest for 10 minutes.

2. Spray a large non-stick skillet with cooking oil, add the vegetable oil and place over medium heat. Sauté the onion and garlic until lightly browned, about 5 minutes. Add the green pepper and jalapeño and sauté for 3 minutes. Remove from the heat and add the cilantro.

3. Dice the steak and stir into the onion mixture. Divide the mixture among the tortillas and scatter the cheese overtop. Drizzle with the sour cream and salsa, dividing it evenly among the tortillas. Roll the bottom of each tortilla up and over the filling, fold in the sides and roll them up tightly.

4. Heat a non-stick grill pan to high and spray with cooking oil. Sear the tortillas until browned on both sides, approximately 2 minutes per side. Cut in half before serving.

Falafel with Creamy Tahini Lemon Dressing

Middle Eastern cuisine is known for its falafels—chickpea-based deep-fried balls served with tahini sauce. My version is baked, with a light and creamy tahini sauce. You can make double the falafels by making them smaller. Serve them in mini pitas as an appetizer. You'll have a few tablespoons of leftover dressing; store it in the refrigerator and use it as a salad dressing or sauce over chicken or fish.

FALAFELS

1 can (19 oz) chickpeas,
    drained and rinsed
¼ cup chopped green onion
¼ cup chopped fresh cilantro or parsley
¼ cup dry breadcrumbs
2 Tbsp tahini
1 Tbsp freshly squeezed lemon juice
1½ tsp minced fresh garlic
¼ tsp baking powder
¼ tsp ground cumin
1 egg
pinch freshly ground black pepper

DRESSING

⅓ cup vegetable stock
⅓ cup smooth light ricotta
2 Tbsp tahini
2 Tbsp low-fat mayonnaise
2 Tbsp olive oil
1 Tbsp freshly squeezed lemon juice
1 Tbsp low-sodium soy sauce
1 tsp minced fresh garlic
¼ cup chopped fresh cilantro or parsley

4 large pita breads, sliced in half
tomato slices and lettuce leaves

1. Preheat the oven to 400°F. Spray a baking sheet with cooking oil.

2. Combine all the falafel ingredients in a food processor. Pulse on and off until well-mixed. Form into 16 balls (about 2 Tbsp each). Flatten slightly. Place on the prepared baking sheet.

3. Bake in the center of the oven, turning once, for 15 to 20 minutes or until golden.

4. To make the dressing, combine the stock, ricotta, tahini, mayonnaise, oil, lemon juice, soy sauce and garlic in a food processor. Process until smooth. Stir in the cilantro.

5. Place two falafels in the pocket of each pita half. Drizzle about 2 Tbsp of dressing over each. Tuck tomato slices and lettuce inside each pita.

NUTRITIONAL ANALYSIS PER SERVING

Calories	242
Protein	8 g
Fat	8 g
Saturated Fat	1.3 g
Carbohydrates	33 g
Cholesterol	29 mg
Sodium	433 mg
Fiber	4.1 g

Prep Time:	20 minutes
Cook Time:	20 minutes

Make Ahead:
Prepare sauce a day in advance and refrigerate. Bake falafels a day in advance, refrigerate and reheat in preheated 300°F oven for 10 minutes.

Serves 8

Creamy Dijon Chicken Salad in a Pita

NUTRITIONAL ANALYSIS
PER SERVING

Calories	240
Protein	17 g
Fat	8 g
Saturated Fat	2.6 g
Carbohydrates	25 g
Cholesterol	37 mg
Sodium	290 mg
Fiber	2 g

Prep Time: 15 minutes

Cook Time: 12 minutes

Make Ahead:
Prepare salad a day in
advance. Fill pita breads
just before serving.

Serves 4

I tend to avoid chicken salad in restaurants because it's loaded with mayonnaise, which gives this innocent-seeming salad an abundance of calories and fat. This sandwich incorporates lots of diced vegetables and a light dressing that gives plenty of flavor without the fat.

6 oz skinless boneless chicken breast

1 cup diced plum tomatoes
¾ cup diced green bell pepper
⅓ cup chopped green onion
3 Tbsp chopped black olives
⅓ cup crumbled light feta cheese
¼ cup low-fat sour cream

2 Tbsp light mayonnaise
1 Tbsp freshly squeezed lemon juice
2 tsp dried tarragon or basil
1 tsp Dijon mustard
1 tsp minced fresh garlic
pinch freshly ground black pepper
2 large pita breads
lettuce

1. Preheat the grill or grill pan to medium-high and spray with cooking oil. Grill the chicken, turning once, until cooked through and no longer pink in the center, about 12 minutes. Remove from the grill, cool and dice.

2. Stir the chicken, tomatoes, green pepper, green onion, olives and feta together in a bowl.

3. Combine the sour cream, mayonnaise, lemon juice, tarragon, mustard, garlic and black pepper in another bowl; mix well. Pour the dressing over the chicken mixture and toss to coat.

4. Cut the pita breads in half and line the pockets with lettuce leaves. Divide the filling among the pitas (about ¾ cup per half). Serve immediately.

CHAPTER TWELVE

Dressings and Sauces

NUTRITIONAL ANALYSIS
PER SERVING (1 TBSP)

Calories	41
Protein	2 g
Fat	2 g
Saturated Fat	0.3 g
Carbohydrates	2 g
Cholesterol	9 mg
Sodium	112 mg
Fiber	0 g

Prep Time: 5 minutes

Make Ahead:
Prepare up to 5 days ahead
and refrigerate.

Makes ½ cup

Light Creamy Dill Dressing

Use this in a seafood salad or serve it as a tartar sauce with grilled fish.

½ cup low-fat yogurt

2 Tbsp light mayonnaise

3 Tbsp chopped fresh parsley

¼ cup chopped fresh dill

1 tsp Dijon mustard

¾ tsp crushed fresh garlic

salt and freshly ground black pepper to
taste

1. Combine all the ingredients in a bowl and stir until well mixed.

2. Serve at room temperature or chill.

NUTRITIONAL ANALYSIS
PER SERVING (2 TBSP)

Calories	11
Protein	0.5 g
Fat	1 g
Saturated fat	0 g
Carbohydrates	1 g
Cholesterol	1 mg
Sodium	21 mg
Fiber	0 g

Prep Time: 5 minutes

Make Ahead:
Refrigerate for up to 1 day.

Makes ¾ cup

Creamy Blue Cheese Dressing

I love this with a salad that has fruit or nuts in it. It also makes a fabulous sauce with seared tuna or flank steak. There are mild blue cheeses available; use the one your palate prefers.

2 oz blue cheese

⅓ cup low-fat sour cream

¼ tsp crushed fresh garlic

2 Tbsp low-fat yogurt

1. Combine all the ingredients in the bowl of a small food processor and process until smooth. (Or, if a chunky consistency is desired, crumble the cheese and mix by hand.)

2. Serve at room temperature or chill.

Creamy Russian Dressing

This is my version of Thousand Island dressing. It's wonderful with any salad greens and I use it as a sandwich spread and a dip for vegetables.

½ cup light mayonnaise

½ cup low-fat sour cream

⅓ cup sweet chili sauce

3 Tbsp minced green bell pepper

3 Tbsp minced red bell pepper

3 Tbsp minced red onion

1. Stir all the ingredients together in a bowl, mixing well.

NUTRITIONAL ANALYSIS
PER SERVING (1 TBSP)

Calories	24
Protein	0 g
Fat	1 g
Saturated Fat	0.1 g
Carbohydrates	3 g
Cholesterol	0.2 mg
Sodium	91 mg
Fiber	0 g

Prep Time: 5 minutes

Make Ahead:
Refrigerate for up to 3 days.
Stir well before serving.

Makes 1½ cups

Lemon Dill Vinaigrette

This tart vinaigrette is perfect for dressing soft greens, such as Boston or leafy lettuce. It also makes a tasty sauce for grilled chicken or fish.

3 Tbsp balsamic vinegar

2 Tbsp freshly squeezed lemon juice

1 Tbsp water

1 large green onion, minced

¾ tsp crushed fresh garlic

2 Tbsp chopped fresh dill

3 Tbsp olive oil

1. Combine all the ingredients in a bowl. Whisk in the oil until well combined.

2. Use immediately or refrigerate. Serve at room temperature.

NUTRITIONAL ANALYSIS
PER SERVING (1 TBSP)

Calories	48
Protein	0 g
Fat	5 g
Saturated Fat	0 g
Carbohydrates	1 g
Cholesterol	0 mg
Sodium	2 mg
Fiber	0 g

Prep Time: 5 minutes

Make Ahead:
Refrigerate for up
to 3 weeks.

Makes ½ cup

NUTRITIONAL ANALYSIS
PER SERVING (1 TBSP)

Calories	40
Protein	0.2 g
Fat	3 g
Saturated Fat	0 g
Carbohydrates	0.5 g
Cholesterol	0 mg
Sodium	100 mg
Fiber	0 g

Prep Time: 5 minutes

Make Ahead:
Refrigerate for up
to 2 weeks.

Makes ⅓ cup

Oriental Sesame Dressing

Try this over a fresh spinach salad or steamed vegetables. I also use it with grilled chicken or fish.

4 tsp rice vinegar
1 Tbsp low-sodium soy sauce
1 Tbsp freshly squeezed lemon juice
1 tsp sesame seeds, toasted
½ tsp Dijon mustard
4 tsp vegetable oil
1½ tsp sesame oil

1. Combine the vinegar, soy sauce, lemon juice, sesame seeds and mustard in a small bowl. Whisk in the vegetable and sesame oils until well combined.

2. Use immediately or refrigerate.

NUTRITIONAL ANALYSIS
PER SERVING (1 TBSP)

Calories	14
Protein	0.3 g
Fat	0.3 g
Saturated fat	0 g
Carbohydrates	1 g
Cholesterol	1 mg
Sodium	50 mg
Fiber	0 g

Prep Time: 5 minutes

Make Ahead:
Refrigerate for
up to 3 days.

Makes ⅓ cup

Ginger Soy Dressing

A light, creamy, Asian-style dressing that's perfect for spinach, bib lettuce, green vegetables and as a sauce for fish or chicken.

1½ tsp low-sodium soy sauce
2 Tbsp low-fat sour cream
¾ tsp crushed garlic

1 tsp minced fresh ginger
1 Tbsp rice vinegar

1. Combine all the ingredients in a small bowl and mix well.

2. Use immediately or refrigerate.

Hoisin Marinade

Use this to marinate beef, poultry, lamb or fish, or add it to stir-fried vegetables. When stir-frying vegetables, add the sauce after the vegetables are slightly sautéed and cook for 2 more minutes.

2 Tbsp low-sodium soy sauce

2 Tbsp hoisin sauce

2 Tbsp rice vinegar

1 Tbsp brown sugar

1 Tbsp vegetable oil

½ tsp minced fresh ginger

½ tsp crushed fresh garlic

1. Combine all the ingredients in a bowl and mix well.

NUTRITIONAL ANALYSIS PER SERVING (1 TBSP)

Calories	33
Protein	0.6 g
Fat	2 g
Saturated Fat	0 g
Carbohydrates	4 g
Cholesterol	0 mg
Sodium	220 mg
Fiber	0 g

Prep Time: 5 minutes

Make Ahead:
Refrigerate for up to 4 days.

Makes ½ cup

Teriyaki Marinade

This is a great marinade for fish, poultry, beef, pork or firm tofu. Marinate for a minimum of 30 minutes or overnight (marinate fish for no more than 30 minutes). Use a non-reactive container when marinating.

3 Tbsp rice wine vinegar

2 Tbsp low-sodium soy sauce

2 Tbsp water

2 Tbsp brown sugar

1 Tbsp vegetable oil

1 tsp minced fresh ginger

1 tsp sesame oil

½ tsp crushed fresh garlic

1. Combine all the ingredients in a small bowl. Mix well.

NUTRITIONAL ANALYSIS PER SERVING (1 TBSP)

Calories	37
Protein	0.3 g
Fat	2 g
Saturated Fat	0 g
Carbohydrates	4 g
Cholesterol	0 mg
Sodium	150 mg
Fiber	0 g

Prep Time: 5 minutes

Make Ahead:
Refrigerate for up to a week.

Makes ½ cup

Apple Cider Vinaigrette

NUTRITIONAL ANALYSIS
PER SERVING (1 TBSP)

Calories	39
Protein	0 g
Fat	3.3 g
Saturated Fat	0.4 g
Carbohydrates	2.5 g
Cholesterol	0 g
Sodium	10 g
Fiber	0 g

Prep Time: 5 minutes

Make Ahead:
Refrigerate for up to 3 days.

Makes ⅔ cup

This fruity light vinaigrette is great with any mixture of lettuces, as well as cooked asparagus or broccoli. It's also a nice light sauce to serve with chicken, pork or fish. The fruit juice concentrate intensifies the flavor.

3 Tbsp olive oil

5 Tbsp apple cider vinegar

3 Tbsp apple juice concentrate

1 Tbsp brown sugar

1 tsp fresh garlic

1½ tsp Dijon mustard

1. Combine all the ingredients in a small bowl and mix until well combined.

Basil Pesto Sauce

NUTRITIONAL ANALYSIS
PER SERVING (1 TBSP)

Calories	32
Protein	1 g
Fat	2.8 g
Saturated Fat	0.4 g
Carbohydrates	0.3 g
Cholesterol	2.9 mg
Sodium	30 mg
Fiber	1.9 g

Prep Time: 10 minutes

Make Ahead:
Refrigerate for up
to 3 days or freeze for
up to 4 months.

Makes ¾ cup

This is a staple in my kitchen. I make batches of it when basil is in season and freeze it so I always have some on hand. I use it as a spread over pizzas, sandwiches and wraps, a topping for grilled fish or chicken and a sauce for any grain. For different flavors, use a combination of basil, parsley and cilantro. Keep in mind that store-bought pesto can be double in calories, fat and sodium!

1 cup packed fresh basil leaves

2 Tbsp grated Parmesan cheese

1 Tbsp toasted pine nuts

2 Tbsp light cream cheese

1 tsp minced fresh garlic

3 Tbsp chicken stock or water

2 Tbsp olive oil

1. Place all the ingredients in the bowl of a small food processor and purée until smooth.

Quick Basic Tomato Sauce

This is a great sauce to have in the refrigerator or freezer for pasta or other grains, homemade pizzas or any dish requiring tomato sauce. You can make it more interesting by adding dried herbs, your choice of vegetables, or ground beef, chicken or soy. To make a thicker sauce, add 2 tablespoons of tomato paste.

2 tsp olive oil	2 tsp dried basil
⅔ cup finely chopped onion	1 tsp dried oregano
2 tsp crushed fresh garlic	2 bay leaves
1 can (28 oz) plum tomatoes, crushed	2 tsp brown sugar

1. Heat the oil in a large non-stick saucepan over medium heat. Sauté the onion and garlic for 3 minutes, stirring often.

2. Add the tomatoes, basil, oregano, bay leaves and brown sugar. Reduce the heat to low and cook for 15 to 20 minutes, stirring occasionally, until it has reduced slightly.

NUTRITIONAL ANALYSIS
PER SERVING (½ CUP)

Calories	60
Protein	2 g
Fat	2 g
Saturated Fat	0 g
Carbohydrates	10 g
Cholesterol	0 mg
Sodium	360 mg
Fiber	1 g

Prep Time	5 minutes
Cook Time:	15 minutes

Make Ahead:
Refrigerate for up to 2 days, or freeze for up to 6 weeks. After defrosting, add 2 Tbsp tomato paste to thicken. To reheat, place over low heat for 15 minutes.

Makes 2½ cups

Sun-Dried Tomato Sauce

Calories	98
Protein	1 g
Fat	4 g
Saturated Fat	0 g
Carbohydrates	4 g
Cholesterol	0 mg
Sodium	280 mg
Fiber	1 g

Prep Time: 15 minutes

Make Ahead:
Refrigerate for up to a week
or freeze for 4 weeks.

Makes 2 cups

I love this sauce with chicken or fish and it's a great way to dress up pasta or rice (add water if it's too thick). I also use it as a spread on sandwiches, rather than mayonnaise or butter. Buy dry sun-dried tomatoes, not the ones soaked in oil. You can purchase pine nuts in bulk and preserve their freshness by freezing them, or substitute any nuts you like.

2 cups dry sun-dried tomatoes

1½ tsp crushed fresh garlic

¾ cup water or chicken stock

½ cup chopped fresh parsley

2 Tbsp olive oil

2 Tbsp pine nuts, toasted (see page 75)

2 Tbsp grated Parmesan cheese

1. Place the tomatoes in a bowl and add enough boiling water to cover them. Let sit for 15 minutes, until soft enough to cut. Chop into smaller pieces.

2. Combine the rehydrated tomatoes with the remaining ingredients in the bowl of a food processor. Process until well blended.

Mushroom Sauce

This sauce is especially good over meat, poultry or fish dishes. I love to use oyster mushrooms for this, but choose any type you like.

2 tsp vegetable oil

1½ cups sliced mushrooms

2 Tbsp all-purpose flour

½ cup chicken or beef stock

½ cup 2 percent evaporated milk

½ tsp Dijon mustard

1 Tbsp sherry (optional)

1. Heat the oil in a small non-stick saucepan over high heat. Add the mushrooms and sauté for approximately 5 minutes or until the liquid evaporates and the mushrooms are dry. Add the flour and stir until well combined.

2. Add the stock and milk. Cook over low heat, stirring constantly, until thickened, 4 to 5 minutes. Stir in the mustard and sherry (if using). If the sauce is too thick, add more milk.

NUTRITIONAL ANALYSIS
PER SERVING (1 TBSP)

Calories	43
Protein	2 g
Fat	2 g
Saturated Fat	0.2 g
Carbohydrates	3 g
Cholesterol	1 mg
Sodium	101 mg
Fiber	0.3 g

Prep Time:	5 minutes
Cook Time:	10 minutes

Make Ahead:

Refrigerate for up to a day; reheat in a saucepan over low heat. Add milk if mixture is too thick.

Makes 1½ cups

Calories	72
Protein	4.4 g
Fat	4.1 g
Saturated Fat	1.1 g
Carbohydrates	1 g
Cholesterol	13 mg
Sodium	155 mg
Fiber	0 g

Prep Time: 5 minutes

Cook Time: 4 minutes

Make Ahead:
Prepare up to 2 days in
advance and refrigerate.
Reheat in a saucepan over
low heat until warmed
through, adding a couple
of tablespoons of milk
to loosen it.

Makes 2 cups

Cheese Sauce

You can use this basic cheese sauce for pasta, vegetables or even chicken. Vary it by using different cheeses.

1 cup 2 percent milk

1 cup chicken or vegetable stock

2 Tbsp all-purpose flour

1 tsp Dijon mustard

1 cup grated aged cheddar cheese

¼ cup grated Parmesan cheese

1. Combine the milk, stock and flour in a small saucepan and mix well. Whisking constantly, bring the mixture to a boil, then simmer for 3 minutes, or until the sauce begins to thicken. Add the mustard, cheddar and Parmesan cheese and simmer for 1 minute, or until the cheese melts.

Chocolate Sauce

This is my basic low-fat chocolate sauce, which I love over almost any dessert. It goes well with other chocolate- and fruit-based desserts, as well as with cheesecakes, soufflés, jelly rolls, coffee cakes … just about any sweet!

⅓ cup granulated sugar

3 Tbsp unsweetened cocoa powder

2 Tbsp semi-sweet chocolate chips

¼ cup corn syrup

¼ cup water

2 Tbsp 2 percent evaporated milk

1. Whisk the sugar, cocoa, chocolate chips, corn syrup and water together in a small saucepan. Bring the mixture to a boil. Reduce the heat and simmer uncovered for 5 minutes, or until it is slightly thickened, stirring occasionally. Add the evaporated milk and simmer for 1 minute.

2. Pour the sauce into a bowl and cover. Reheat if it gets too thick.

NUTRITIONAL ANALYSIS PER SERVING (1 TBSP)

Calories	58
Protein	0.3 g
Fat	0.2 g
Saturated Fat	0.1 g
Carbohydrates	12 g
Cholesterol	0 g
Sodium	15 g
Fiber	0.5 g

Prep Time: 5 minutes
Cook Time: 6 minutes

Make Ahead:
Cover well and refrigerate for up to 3 days. Reheat in a skillet over low heat for 1 minute before serving.

Makes about ¾ cup

CHAPTER THIRTEEN

Desserts

Rocky Mountain Miniature Chocolate Cheesecakes

Individual cheesecakes are so elegant, especially these, which are almost mousse-like in texture. Serve them with Chocolate Sauce (see page 347). Light cream cheese is 25 percent reduced in fat, but it's still high in fat and calories, so I use it sparingly to highlight a dessert. If you only have large marshmallows, use scissors to cut them into small pieces.

1¾ cups smooth light ricotta

½ cup light cream cheese, softened

½ cup low-fat sour cream

1 egg

¾ cup granulated sugar

3 Tbsp unsweetened cocoa powder

1½ Tbsp all-purpose flour

⅓ cup miniature marshmallows

3 Tbsp semi-sweet chocolate chips

1. Preheat the oven to 350°F. Line a 12-cup muffin tin with paper liners.

2. Combine the ricotta, cream cheese, sour cream, egg, sugar, cocoa and flour in a food processor. Purée until smooth. Divide the mixture among the prepared muffin cups.

3. Set the muffin tin in a larger pan. Pour enough hot water into the pan to come halfway up the sides of the muffin cups.

4. Bake in the center of the oven for 20 minutes. Remove and sprinkle the marshmallows and chocolate chips evenly over the cheesecakes. Return to the oven and bake for 5 minutes longer, or until the marshmallows and chocolate chips begin to melt.

5. Remove the muffin tin from the water bath and cool on a rack. Chill well before removing the paper liners and serving.

NUTRITIONAL ANALYSIS PER SERVING	
Calories	161
Protein	6.2 g
Fat	6.2 g
Saturated Fat	3.8 g
Carbohydrates	20 g
Cholesterol	36 mg
Fiber	0.6 g
Prep Time:	10 minutes
Cook Time:	25 minutes

Make Ahead:
Refrigerate for a day, or freeze for up to 2 weeks.

Serves 12

Triple Chocolate Brownies

I created this recipe for the Mövenpick restaurant chain in Toronto, which sold more than 1,500 of these brownies per month—not only because they're delicious, but also because they're lighter than other brownies. They're now featured in my catering company and still rank as the number-one dessert. The cocoa, oil and yogurt that replace the traditional butter and chocolate are the way to keep the calorie and fat count low.

⅔ cup granulated sugar

¼ cup vegetable oil

1 egg

1 tsp pure vanilla extract

⅓ cup unsweetened cocoa powder

⅓ cup all-purpose flour

1 tsp baking powder

¼ cup low-fat yogurt or sour cream

¼ cup semi-sweet chocolate chips

⅓ cup light cream cheese

⅔ cup icing sugar

1½ tsp unsweetened cocoa powder

1½ tsp water

dusting of icing sugar

1. Preheat the oven to 350°F. Spray an 8-inch square pan with cooking oil.

2. For the brownies, combine the sugar, oil, egg and vanilla in a bowl and mix well. Add the cocoa, mixing it in well. Add the flour, baking powder, yogurt and chocolate chips, mixing just until combined and smooth. Don't overmix.

3. Pour the batter into the prepared pan. Bake in the center of the oven for 15 to 20 minutes, just until set. Do not overbake. Cool on a rack for 15 minutes before icing.

4. To make the icing, place cream cheese, icing sugar, 1½ tsp cocoa powder and water in a blender or food processor and process until smooth. Spread over the top of the brownies.

5. Cut into squares and garnish with a dusting of icing sugar, or drizzle melted dark and white chocolate overtop.

NUTRITIONAL ANALYSIS PER SERVING

Calories	140
Protein	2.3 g
Fat	7 g
Saturated Fat	1.5 g
Carbohydrates	20 g
Cholesterol	19 mg
Fiber	1.2 g

Prep Time: 10 minutes

Cook Time: 20 minutes

Make Ahead:
Bake and store for a day, well wrapped, or freeze for up to 2 weeks.

Serves 12

Triple Chocolate Brownies
Photo by Lorella Zanetti

Banana Chocolate Chip Pound Cake with Streusel Topping

NUTRITIONAL ANALYSIS PER SERVING (½ SLICE)

Calories	194
Protein	3 g
Fat	6.4 g
Saturated Fat	1.8 g
Carbohydrates	31 g
Cholesterol	18 mg
Fiber	1 g

Prep Time: 15 minutes

Cook Time: 40 minutes

Make Ahead:
Refrigerate, well wrapped, for up to 2 days, or freeze for up to 2 weeks.

Serves 16

This banana cake beats all the others. It's moist from the banana and yogurt, it has a delicious crunchy topping and a few chocolate chips are thrown into the mix. Grape Nuts, a low-fat breakfast cereal made from toasted wheat and barley, gives a delicious nutty texture and taste to baked goods without adding a lot of fat or calories. Use the ripest banana you can find. In fact, keep overripe bananas in the freezer so they're handy for baking—just defrost and mash them.

¾ cup granulated sugar

1 large ripe banana, mashed (½ cup)

¼ cup vegetable oil

2 eggs

2 tsp pure vanilla extract

1 cup low-fat yogurt

1⅔ cups all-purpose flour

1½ tsp baking powder

½ tsp baking soda

⅓ cup semi-sweet chocolate chips

⅓ cup Grape Nuts cereal

¼ cup packed brown sugar

1 Tbsp all-purpose flour

1½ tsp vegetable oil

1 tsp water

1. Preheat the oven to 350°F. Spray a 9- by 5-inch loaf pan with cooking oil.

2. For the cake, combine the granulated sugar, banana, oil, eggs, vanilla and yogurt in a large bowl. Beat with a whisk or an electric mixer. Combine the flour, baking powder, baking soda and chocolate chips in another bowl. Use a wooden spoon to stir the dry ingredients into the banana mixture, mixing just until everything is combined. Pour the mixture into the prepared pan.

3. For the topping, mix cereal, brown sugar, 1 Tbsp of flour, vegetable oil and water until well combined. Sprinkle evenly over the top of the cake batter.

4. Place the pan in the center of the oven and bake for 40 to 45 minutes or until a tester inserted in the center comes out dry. Cool to room temperature on a rack before turning out and slicing.

Double Chocolate Chip Banana Cake

The surprise ingredient in this chocolate cake is zucchini. Along with the banana and pineapple, it makes the cake moist and delicious without a lot of fat. Carrots also work well; if you substitute, use the same amount. The cocoa and sprinkling of chocolate chips give it a dense chocolate flavor. Try the cake without the icing— it's delicious either way.

1 cup packed brown sugar
½ cup granulated sugar
⅓ cup vegetable oil
1 ripe medium banana, mashed (⅓ cup)
1 tsp pure vanilla extract
2 eggs
2 cups peeled grated zucchini or carrots
½ cup canned crushed pineapple,
   drained
2 cups all-purpose flour
⅓ cup unsweetened cocoa powder

1½ tsp baking powder
1½ tsp baking soda
⅓ cup semi-sweet chocolate chips
¼ cup low-fat sour cream

⅓ cup light cream cheese, softened
1 cup icing sugar
1 Tbsp unsweetened cocoa powder
1 Tbsp low-fat milk

**NUTRITIONAL ANALYSIS
PER SERVING**

Calories	270
Protein	3.7 g
Fat	7.5 g
Saturated Fat	2.2 g
Carbohydrates	63 g
Cholesterol	30 mg
Fiber	2.2 g

Prep Time: 20 minutes

Cook Time: 45 minutes

Make Ahead:
Store at room temperature
for up to 3 days,
well wrapped, or freeze
for up to 2 weeks.

Serves 16

1. Preheat the oven to 350°F. Spray a 12-cup Bundt pan with cooking oil.

2. For the cake, combine the brown sugar, granulated sugar, oil, banana, vanilla and eggs in a food processor. Process until smooth. Add the zucchini and pineapple and process until just combined.

3. Combine the flour, cocoa, baking powder and baking soda in a large bowl, mixing well.

4. Stir the wet ingredients into the dry ingredients until they are just mixed. Stir in the chocolate chips and sour cream. Spoon the mixture into the prepared pan.

5. Bake in the center of the oven for 40 to 45 minutes, or until a tester inserted in the center comes out clean. Place the pan on a rack to cool. Invert carefully onto a serving plate.

6. For the icing, combine the cream cheese, icing sugar, cocoa and milk, using an electric mixer or food processor. Spread the mixture over the cooled cake.

Marble Mocha Cheesecake

Coffee and chocolate go so well with this creamy cheese batter. You can double this recipe: bake it in a 10-inch pan and add another 10 minutes to the baking time, baking until the center is still loose.

1½ cups chocolate wafer crumbs
2 Tbsp water
2 Tbsp sugar
1 Tbsp vegetable oil

1⅔ cups smooth light ricotta
⅓ cup softened light cream cheese
¾ cup granulated sugar
1 egg

⅓ cup light sour cream or 2 percent yogurt
1½ Tbsp all-purpose flour
1 tsp pure vanilla extract
2 tsp instant coffee granules
2 tsp hot water

3 Tbsp semi-soft chocolate chips
1 tsp vegetable oil

NUTRITIONAL ANALYSIS
PER SERVING

Calories	210
Protein	8 g
Fat	7 g
Saturated Fat	4 g
Carbohydrates	29 g
Cholesterol	34 mg
Fiber	1 g

Prep time: 15 minutes
Cook Time: 40 minutes

Make Ahead:
Refrigerate for up to 3 days;
freeze for up to 2 weeks.

Serves 12

1. Spray an 8-inch springform pan with cooking oil. Preheat the oven to 350°F.

2. For the crust, combine the crumbs, sugar, water and oil. Mix thoroughly. Press into the bottom and up the sides of the prepared springform pan.

3. For the filling, beat the ricotta, cream cheese, sugar, egg, sour cream, flour and vanilla in a large bowl or food processor until well blended. Dissolve the coffee granules in the hot water. Add to the batter and mix until incorporated. Pour the batter over the crust and smooth the top.

4. Place the chocolate chips and oil in a small bowl and microwave on medium high for 30 seconds or just until soft. Drizzle the melted chocolate over the top of the batter. Draw a knife or spatula through the batter several times to create a marbled effect.

5. Bake for 35 to 40 minutes. The center will be slightly loose when you jiggle the cake.

6. Cool on a rack. Refrigerate for at least 2 hours before removing the sides of the pan and serving.

◄ Marble Mocha Cheesecake
Photo by Mark Shapiro

Chocolate Sour Cream Cheesecake Squares

NUTRITIONAL ANALYSIS
PER SERVING

Calories	138
Protein	3.2 g
Fat	4.2 g
Saturated Fat	1.5 g
Carbohydrates	21 g
Cholesterol	18 mg
Fiber	0.6 g

Prep Time: 10 minutes

Cook Time: 25 minutes

Make Ahead:
Refrigerate, well
wrapped, for a day, or
freeze for up to 2 weeks.

Serves 16

Chocolate cheesecake in any way, shape or form is not to be refused. These luscious squares have a brownie-type crust that's simply mouth-watering. They freeze beautifully and my children love to eat them frozen—they say it tastes like a creamy frozen chocolate bar! To get chocolate chunks, use a sharp knife to shave off pieces from a solid block of chocolate.

CRUST

½ cup granulated sugar

3 Tbsp unsweetened cocoa powder

2 Tbsp vegetable oil

1 egg

½ tsp pure vanilla extract

⅔ cup all-purpose flour

FILLING

⅔ cup granulated sugar

2 Tbsp unsweetened cocoa powder

1 Tbsp all-purpose flour

⅔ cup smooth light ricotta

¼ cup light cream cheese, softened

2 Tbsp low-fat sour cream

1 large egg

½ tsp pure vanilla extract

TOPPING

1 oz white or semi-sweet chocolate chunks or 2 Tbsp chocolate chips

1. Preheat the oven to 350°F. Spray an 8-inch square baking dish with cooking oil.

2. For the crust, combine the sugar, cocoa, oil, egg, and vanilla in a bowl. Stir in the flour, mixing just until combined. Pat the mixture into the bottom of the prepared dish.

3. For the filling, combine the sugar, cocoa, flour, ricotta, cream cheese, sour cream, egg and vanilla in a food processor. Purée until the mixture is smooth.

Cocoa and Chocolate

For my chocolate desserts, I depend upon cocoa and highlight the dessert with a small amount of chocolate chips. Cocoa only has 3 g of fat per ounce, whereas chocolate has 9 g per ounce.

4. Spread it over the crust.

5. Bake in the center of the oven for 20 to 25 minutes. The center will still be slightly loose in the middle when the pan is jiggled.

6. Sprinkle with the chocolate, cool to room temperature on a rack and refrigerate until chilled.

Chocolate Sour Cream Cheesecake Squares ▶
Photo by Per Kristiansen

Baklava Pecan Phyllo Squares

NUTRITIONAL ANALYSIS
PER SERVING

Calories	155
Protein	1.6 g
Fat	4.1 g
Saturated Fat	0.4 g
Carbohydrates	28 g
Cholesterol	0 g
Fiber	1.3 g

Prep Time: 25 minutes

Cook Time: 25 minutes

Make Ahead:
Prepare up to 2 days
in advance and store at
room temperature.

Serves 12

Baklava, popular in Greece and Turkey, is a sweet dessert that usually consists of many layers of butter-drenched phyllo pastry, spices and nuts, drenched with a lemon-honey syrup. You can imagine how high it is in calories and fat! One tablespoon of butter contains 100 calories and 11 g of fat. This version uses no fat except for vegetable oil spray—it's the filling that makes it so divine. The Grape Nuts cereal provides the texture of chopped nuts without the excess calories or fat.

⅓ cup granulated sugar
¼ cup water
3 Tbsp honey
1½ Tbsp freshly squeezed lemon juice

½ cup chopped toasted pecans
  (see page 75)
⅓ cup packed brown sugar
½ tsp ground cinnamon

½ cup Grape Nuts cereal
½ cup raisins

4 sheets phyllo pastry (see page 71)

1. Preheat the oven to 350°F. Spray an 8-inch square baking dish with cooking oil.

2. For the syrup, combine the granulated sugar, water, honey and lemon juice in a saucepan. Cook over medium heat for 5 minutes, until slightly thickened.

3. Stir the cereal, raisins, pecans, brown sugar and cinnamon together in a bowl. Drizzle with 3 Tbsp of the syrup. Mix well.

4. Place 2 sheets of phyllo pastry on a work surface, one on top of the other, and cut into 4 equal pieces. Place one quarter in the prepared dish and spray with vegetable oil. Layer another quarter on top and spray. Repeat with the remaining quarters. Scatter the nut mixture overtop.

5. Lay out the remaining phyllo sheets, cut into 4 equal pieces and continue as above, placing the phyllo over the nut mixture and spraying after each addition. Spray the top.

6. With a sharp knife, cut into 12 squares, being careful not to tear the phyllo.

7. Bake for 20 to 25 minutes or until the phyllo is golden. Reheat the remaining honey mixture if necessary and pour it over the hot baklava. Cool in the pan for at least 15 minutes before serving.

Lemon Tiramisu

Thanks to ricotta and light cream cheese, there is little fat in this traditional dessert with a twist. Be sure to beat the egg whites and sugar until all the granules are dissolved, and process the cheeses until the batter is no longer grainy. Use only fresh lemon juice. For a great presentation, double the recipe and place in a clear glass bowl with berries between the layers.

1 ¾ cups smooth light ricotta
¾ cup light cream cheese, softened
½ cup granulated sugar
1 Tbsp finely grated lemon rind
⅓ cup freshly squeezed lemon juice
1 egg yolk

3 egg whites
¼ tsp cream of tartar
⅓ cup granulated sugar
½ cup boiling water
3 Tbsp freshly squeezed lemon juice

3 Tbsp granulated sugar
20 ladyfinger cookies (3 inches long)

NUTRITIONAL ANALYSIS PER SERVING

Calories	204
Protein	7.8 g
Fat	6.3 g
Saturated Fat	3.4 g
Carbohydrates	29 g
Cholesterol	88 mg
Fiber	0.2 g

Prep Time: 25 minutes

Make Ahead:
Prepare and refrigerate a day in advance to allow the flavors to combine.

Serves 12

1. Spray a 9-inch square cake pan or decorative serving dish with cooking oil.

2. Combine the ricotta, cream cheese, ½ cup sugar, lemon rind, ⅓ cup lemon juice and egg yolk in a food processor. Purée the mixture until completely smooth. Transfer to a large bowl.

3. In another bowl, beat the egg whites with the cream of tartar until foamy. Gradually add the ⅓ cup sugar, beating until stiff peaks form. Stir one-quarter of the egg whites into the ricotta mixture. Gently fold in the remaining egg whites just until blended.

4. Whisk the water, the 3 Tbsp lemon juice and the 3 Tbsp sugar until the sugar dissolves.

5. Dip each ladyfinger in the lemon mixture just long enough to moisten it. Place 10 dipped ladyfingers in the bottom of the serving dish. Pour half the ricotta-lemon mixture over the ladyfingers. Repeat the layers. Chill for at least 2 hours before serving.

Sour Cream Brownie Cheesecake

This cake is sinfully delicious. For a mocha-flavored brownie, dissolve 1 teaspoon powdered coffee in 1 tablespoon of hot water, or use a tablespoon of strong brewed coffee; add it to the wet ingredients when making the batter.

⅔ cup granulated sugar

¼ cup vegetable oil

1 egg

1 tsp pure vanilla extract

⅓ cup all-purpose flour

⅓ cup unsweetened cocoa powder

1 tsp baking powder

¼ cup low-fat sour cream

1 cup smooth light ricotta

½ cup granulated sugar

⅓ cup light cream cheese

¼ cup low-fat sour cream

1 egg

2 Tbsp all-purpose flour

1 tsp pure vanilla extract

2 Tbsp semi-sweet chocolate chips

1 cup low-fat sour cream

2 Tbsp granulated sugar

1 tsp pure vanilla extract

1 Tbsp semi-sweet chocolate chips

NUTRITIONAL ANALYSIS PER SERVING

Calories	225
Protein	7 g
Fat	8 g
Saturated Fat	3 g
Carbohydrates	31 g
Cholesterol	47 mg
Fiber	1 g

Prep Time: 15 minutes

Cook Time: 50 minutes

Make Ahead:
Refrigerate for a day, or freeze for up to 2 weeks.

Serves 12

1. Preheat the oven to 350°F. Spray an 9-inch springform pan with cooking oil.

2. For the brownie layer, beat the sugar, oil, egg and vanilla together in a bowl. Combine the flour, cocoa and baking powder in another bowl, mixing well. Add the wet mixture to the dry mixture, stirring until just combined. Stir in the sour cream. Pour the mixture into the prepared pan.

3. For the cheesecake layer, combine the ricotta, sugar, cream cheese, sour cream, egg, flour and vanilla in a food processor. Process until smooth. Stir in the chocolate chips. Pour the mixture on top of the brownie layer.

4. Bake the cheesecake in the center of the oven for 40 minutes. The brownie layer may rise slightly around the edges.

5. For the topping, stir the sour cream, sugar and vanilla together in a small bowl. When the cake has baked for 40 minutes, pour the topping mixture carefully over the top, smoothing it with the back of a spoon. Sprinkle the chocolate chips overtop. Bake for 10 more minutes. Cool in the pan on a rack. Chill before slicing and serving.

◀ Triple Chocolate Brownies (without icing) (page 351), Carrot Cake with Cream Cheese Frosting (page 373), Date Pecan Oatmeal Squares (page 363)
Photo by Brian MacDonald

Date Cake with Coconut Topping

**NUTRITIONAL ANALYSIS
PER SERVING**

Calories	217
Protein	3 g
Fat	5 g
Saturated Fat	2 g
Carbohydrates	41 g
Cholesterol	27 mg
Fiber	2 g

Prep Time: 10 minutes

Cook Time: 50 minutes

Make Ahead:
Store covered at room temperature for 2 days or freeze for up to 2 weeks.

Serves 16

Dates are a good way to lower the fat in desserts—they have a buttery taste when puréed and provide the moisture that fat would supply. Dates are a good source of protein and iron, too. To chop dates easily, use kitchen shears—or cook whole pitted dates and use a food processor to mash them after they're cooked. Chopped, pitted prunes can be substituted for the dates.

12 oz pitted dried dates, chopped
    (2 ½ cups)
1 ¾ cups water
¼ cup vegetable oil
1 cup granulated sugar
2 eggs
1 ½ cups all-purpose flour
1 ½ tsp baking powder
1 tsp baking soda

⅓ cup unsweetened coconut
¼ cup packed brown sugar
¼ cup 2 percent evaporated milk
2 Tbsp vegetable oil

1. Preheat the oven to 350°F. Spray a 9-inch square cake pan with cooking oil.

2. For the cake, place the dates and water in a saucepan and bring them to a boil. Reduce the heat to low, cover and cook, stirring often, until the dates are soft and most of the liquid has been absorbed, about 10 minutes. Set the pan aside to cool for 10 minutes.

3. Mix the oil and granulated sugar in a large bowl or food processor. Beat in the eggs. Add the cooled date mixture and mix well.

4. Combine the flour, baking powder and baking soda in a bowl, mixing well. Stir the flour mixture into the date mixture until everything is just blended. Pour into the prepared pan.

5. Bake in the center of the oven for 35 to 40 minutes, or until a tester inserted in the center comes out dry. Cool in the pan on a rack.

6. For the topping, combine the coconut, brown sugar, milk and oil in a small saucepan. Cook over medium heat, stirring, for 2 minutes, or until the sugar dissolves. Pour the topping over the cooled cake and cut into squares.

Date Pecan Oatmeal Squares

Date squares, often known as matrimonial squares, have been a classic for decades, but the oatmeal crust often contains a cup or more of butter or vegetable shortening. My version only uses ⅓ cup of oil, yet it's incredibly delicious and rich tasting. Dates are an excellent source of energy and carbohydrates, as well as protein and iron. Eat them in moderation, because their nutrients and calories are concentrated. I buy my pitted dates at a bulk food store and keep them in the freezer. To chop dried fruits, I use scissors, which is easier than a knife.

1½ cups chopped pitted dates (8 oz)

¼ cup granulated sugar

1 cup orange juice

1 tsp grated orange zest

1¼ cups quick-cooking oats

1 cup all-purpose flour

¾ cup packed brown sugar

¼ cup chopped toasted pecans
  (see page 75)

1 tsp ground cinnamon

⅓ cup vegetable oil

¼ cup water

1. Preheat the oven to 350°F. Spray an 8-inch square baking dish with cooking oil.

2. Combine the dates, granulated sugar and orange juice in a saucepan and bring the mixture to a boil. Reduce the heat to medium and simmer for 15 minutes, or until the dates are soft and the liquid is absorbed. Mash the mixture and let it cool.

3. Stir the orange zest, oats, flour, brown sugar, pecans, cinnamon, oil and water in a bowl until combined. Pat half of the mixture onto the bottom of the prepared dish. Spread the date mixture overtop. Sprinkle the remaining oat mixture on top of the dates.

4. Bake in the center of the oven for 25 minutes, or until the squares are golden.

5. Cool to room temperature on a rack before slicing and serving.

NUTRITIONAL ANALYSIS PER SERVING

Calories	280
Protein	3.2 g
Fat	8.5 g
Saturated Fat	0.6 g
Carbohydrates	48 g
Cholesterol	0 g
Fiber	2.8 g

Prep Time: 10 minutes

Cook Time: 40 minutes

Make Ahead:
Store at room temperature for up to 2 days, or freeze for up to 2 weeks.

Serves 12

Chocolate Fudge Cheesecake

Calories	259
Protein	6.2 g
Fat	10 g
Saturated Fat	5.0 g
Carbohydrates	36 g
Cholesterol	34 g
Fiber	1.2 g

Prep Time: 10 minutes

Cook Time: 40 minutes

Make Ahead:
Refrigerate for 2 days
or freeze for up to 2 weeks.

Serves 12

You'll never eat a cheesecake that's so dense and rich tasting, yet so low in fat and calories. The combination of semi-sweet chocolate and cocoa powder gives this cheesecake its velvety chocolate flavor. Garnish with fresh berries if desired.

2 cups chocolate wafer crumbs

2 Tbsp water

1 Tbsp vegetable oil

⅓ cup semi-sweet chocolate chips

2 Tbsp water

1½ cups smooth light ricotta

¾ cup light cream cheese

1 cup granulated sugar

¼ cup unsweetened cocoa powder

1 large egg

½ cup low-fat sour cream

2 Tbsp all-purpose flour

1¼ cups low-fat sour cream

2 Tbsp sugar

1. Preheat the oven to 350°F. Spray a 9-inch springform pan with cooking oil.

2. For the crust, combine the wafer crumbs, 2 Tbsp water and oil in a small bowl and mix well. Pat onto the bottom and slightly up the sides of the springform pan.

3. For the filling, combine the chocolate chips and 2 Tbsp water in a small microwaveable bowl and microwave for 40 seconds. Stir until smooth.

4. Combine the chocolate mixture with the ricotta and cream cheese, 1 cup sugar, cocoa, egg and ½ cup sour cream in the bowl of a food processor and purée until smooth. Pour over the crust. Bake for 30 minutes. The center should still be slightly loose.

5. For the topping, mix the 1 ¼ cups sour cream and 2 Tbsp sugar. Carefully spoon over the cake. Bake for another 10 minutes. Cool on a rack, then chill completely before removing the sides of the pan and serving. Top with chocolate wafer crumbs

Chocolate Fudge Cheesecake
Photo by Mark Shapiro

New York-Style Miniature Cheesecakes

NUTRITIONAL ANALYSIS
PER SERVING
(1 CHEESECAKE)

Calories	130
Protein	6.2 g
Fat	4.7 g
Saturated Fat	2.9 g
Carbohydrates	17 g
Cholesterol	35 mg
Fiber	0.1 g

Prep Time: 10 minutes

Cook Time: 20 minutes

Make Ahead:
Refrigerate for 1 day or
freeze for up to 2 weeks.

Makes 12 cheesecakes

These petite cheesecakes are perfect for one serving and leave none to go to waste. They can also be ready sooner than a regular-sized cheesecake, since they chill much faster. Baking the cheesecakes in a water bath—a pan filled with water—keeps them moist and prevents them from sinking in the middle. Serve with fresh berries or a fruit-based dessert sauce and a dusting of icing sugar. I like to garnish with a drizzle of melted fruit sorbet, such as mango or raspberry.

1¾ cups smooth light ricotta

½ cup low-fat cream cheese, softened

½ cup low-fat sour cream

1 egg

1 tsp pure vanilla extract

2 Tbsp freshly squeezed lemon juice

1 tsp grated lemon zest

2 Tbsp all-purpose flour

⅔ cup granulated sugar

1. Preheat the oven to 350°F. Line a 12-cup muffin tin with paper muffin liners.

2. Combine the ricotta, cream cheese, sour cream, egg, vanilla, lemon juice, zest, flour and sugar in a food processor and process until smooth and creamy. Divide the mixture among the prepared muffin cups.

3. Set the muffin tin in a larger pan or on a baking sheet with sides. Pour enough hot water into the pan to come one-third to one-half up the sides of the muffin cups.

4. Bake in the center of the oven for 20 minutes.

5. Remove the muffin tin from the water bath and cool to room temperature on a rack. Chill for 1 hour.

6. To serve, remove the paper liners and place on individual serving plates. Garnish with berries and a sprinkle of icing sugar.

New York-Style Miniature Cheesecakes ▶
Photo by Brian MacDonald

Lemon Poppy Seed Loaf

This is a delicious and versatile loaf that can be served at breakfast or brunch or for dessert at dinner. If you prefer muffins, just spray 12 muffin cups with vegetable oil, pour in the batter and bake in a 375°F oven for 15 to 20 minutes. If you like a strong lemon taste, add an extra teaspoon of grated lemon rind.

¾ cup granulated sugar

⅓ cup vegetable oil

1 egg

2 tsp grated lemon rind

3 Tbsp freshly squeezed lemon juice

⅓ cup 2 percent milk

1¼ cups all-purpose flour

1 Tbsp poppy seeds

1 tsp baking powder

½ tsp baking soda

⅓ cup 2 percent yogurt or light sour cream

¼ cup icing sugar

2 Tbsp freshly squeezed lemon juice

1. Preheat the oven to 350°F. Spray a 9- × 5- inch loaf pan with cooking oil.

2. For the cake, combine the granulated sugar, oil, egg, lemon rind and 3 Tbsp juice in a large bowl or a food processor; mix well. Add the milk, mixing thoroughly.

3. Combine the flour, poppy seeds, baking powder and baking soda. Add to the wet mixture alternately with the yogurt, mixing just until incorporated. Do not overmix.

4. Pour into the prepared pan and bake for 35 to 40 minutes, or until a tester inserted in the center of the cake comes out dry. Set the pan on a rack to cool for 10 minutes. The center of the cake may sink slightly when it cools.

5. For the glaze, combine the icing sugar and 2 Tbsp lemon juice. Prick holes in the top of the loaf with a fork or wooden skewer and pour the glaze over the loaf.

NUTRITIONAL ANALYSIS PER SERVING (½ SLICE)

Calories	126
Protein	1.2 g
Fat	3.7 g
Saturated Fat	0.2 g
Carbohydrates	18 g
Cholesterol	13 mg
Fiber	0.6 g

Prep Time: 10 minutes

Cook Time: 40 minutes

Make Ahead:
Bake a day ahead and keep well wrapped, or freeze for up to 4 weeks.

Serves 16

Lemon Poppy Seed Loaf
Photo by Mark Shapiro

Pecan Cream Cheese Pie

NUTRITIONAL ANALYSIS PER SERVING

Calories	290
Protein	5.1 g
Fat	10 g
Saturated Fat	2.9 g
Carbohydrates	46 g
Cholesterol	48 mg
Fiber	0.7 g

Prep Time: 15 minutes

Cook Time: 40 minutes

Make Ahead:
Refrigerate for a day.

Serves 12

This combination of cheesecake and pecans is too good for words. Pecans are a good source of protein and a healthy polyunsaturated fat, but nuts are high in calories and fat, so eat them in moderation. Be sure to process the cheesecake batter well to make it as smooth as possible. Don't be concerned if the crust seems to stick to the pan when cutting—just use a sharp knife.

1½ cups vanilla wafer crumbs
2 Tbsp granulated sugar
2 Tbsp water
1 Tbsp vegetable oil

¾ cup smooth light ricotta
⅓ cup granulated sugar
⅓ cup light cream cheese
¼ cup low-fat sour cream
1 egg

1 Tbsp all-purpose flour
1 tsp pure vanilla extract

⅔ cup packed brown sugar
½ cup chopped pecans
2 eggs
½ cup corn syrup
1 Tbsp molasses

1. Preheat the oven to 375°F. Spray a 9-inch pie plate with cooking oil.

2. For the crust, mix the crumbs, sugar, water and oil together until the mixture holds together. Press it onto the bottom and up the sides of the pie plate. Bake for 8 minutes.

3. For the cheesecake filling, purée the ricotta, sugar, cream cheese, sour cream, egg, flour and vanilla in a food processor until the mixture is smooth. Pour it into the pie crust.

4. For the pecan filling, whisk the brown sugar, pecans, eggs, corn syrup and molasses together. Pour carefully over the cheesecake layer so the layers don't mix.

5. Bake in the center of the oven for 30 to 35 minutes, or until the filling is almost set. It may rise up around the edges or even through the middle of the pecan filling.

6. Cool on a rack. Serve chilled or at room temperature.

Orange Pecan Biscotti

To get the most intense orange flavor, I use orange juice concentrate, rather than orange juice. Keep a can in the freezer at all times, just for baking and cooking. Nuts are a great source of protein and contain a fair amount of iron, phosphorus and thiamine. They are high in calories and fat, but it's the good type of fat (unsaturated). Eat them in moderation.

1¼ cups granulated sugar

2 eggs

¼ cup vegetable oil

5 Tbsp orange juice concentrate

2 tsp finely grated orange rind

1½ tsp pure vanilla extract

2 cups all-purpose flour

1½ tsp baking powder

1 tsp ground cinnamon (optional)

pinch salt

½ cup chopped toasted pecans
  (see page 75)

1. Preheat the oven to 350°F. Spray a baking sheet with cooking oil.

2. Combine the sugar, eggs, oil, juice concentrate, orange rind and vanilla in a large bowl and beat well with a whisk or electric beater.

3. Combine the flour, baking powder, cinnamon (if using), salt, and pecans in a bowl. Add to the wet ingredients and mix by hand just until everything is combined. Divide the dough in half. Shape each half into a 12- by 4-inch log. Place well apart on the prepared baking sheet.

4. Bake for 20 minutes in the center of the oven. Remove the sheet from the oven and let the logs cool on the pan for 5 minutes.

5. Transfer the logs to a cutting board. Slice them on the diagonal into ½-inch-thick cookies. Place the cookies flat on the baking sheet. Return to the oven and bake on the center rack for 15 minutes, or until they are crisp and lightly browned. Remove to a rack and cool for 10 minutes before serving.

NUTRITIONAL ANALYSIS PER SERVING (1 COOKIE)

Calories	93
Protein	1.6 g
Fat	3.2 g
Saturated Fat	0.4 g
Carbohydrates	14 g
Cholesterol	14 mg
Fiber	0.4 g

Prep Time:	10 minutes
Cook Time:	35 minutes

Make Ahead:
Store at room temperature for up to 2 days.

Makes 30 cookies

Carrot Cake with Cream Cheese Frosting

People often think carrot cake is healthier than other desserts, but beware of recipes that sound healthy! Most carrot cakes are full of oil, butter, eggs and regular sour cream. This version greatly reduces the fat by using pineapple, extra carrots, low-fat yogurt and ripe banana to create the moist texture typical of carrot cake. You can replace the raisins with chopped, pitted dates, apricots or prunes. If you use a food processor to mix the batter, take care not to overprocess it. A garnish of shredded carrots or orange zest is a nice touch.

⅓ cup vegetable oil

1 cup granulated sugar

2 eggs

1 tsp pure vanilla extract

1 large ripe banana, mashed

2 cups grated carrots (about 6 oz)

⅔ cup raisins

½ cup canned crushed pineapple, drained

½ cup low-fat yogurt

2 cups all-purpose flour

1½ tsp baking powder

1½ tsp baking soda

1½ tsp ground cinnamon

¼ tsp ground nutmeg

⅓ cup light cream cheese, softened

⅔ cup icing sugar

1 Tbsp low-fat milk or water

NUTRITIONAL ANALYSIS PER SERVING	
Calories	223
Protein	4 g
Fat	5 g
Saturated Fat	1 g
Cholesterol	30 mg
Carbohydrates	41 g
Fiber	1 g

Prep Time:	15 minutes
Cook Time:	40 minutes

Make Ahead:
Keep for up to 3 days, well wrapped, or freeze for up to 2 weeks.

Serves 16

1. Preheat the oven to 350°F. Spray a 9-inch Bundt pan with cooking oil.

2. For the cake, beat the oil and granulated sugar in a large bowl until smooth. Add the eggs and vanilla, beating the mixture well (it may look curdled). Add the banana, carrots, raisins, pineapple and yogurt. Stir until everything is well combined.

3. Combine the flour, baking powder, baking soda, cinnamon and nutmeg in a separate bowl, mixing well. Add to the carrot mixture and stir just until everything `is combined.

4. Pour the mixture into the prepared pan.

5. Place the pan in the center of the oven and bake for 40 to 45 minutes, or until a tester inserted in the center comes out clean. Cool in the pan on a rack. When it's no longer hot, invert the cake onto a serving plate.

6. For the icing, beat the cream cheese, icing sugar and milk in a bowl or food processor until smooth. Drizzle over the top of the cake.

◀ Carrot Cake with Cream Cheese Frosting
Photo by Mark Shapiro

Espresso Biscotti with Toasted Pecans

NUTRITIONAL ANALYSIS
PER SERVING (1 COOKIE)

Calories	74
Protein	1.2 g
Fat	2.8 g
Saturated Fat	0.3 g
Carbohydrates	11 g
Cholesterol	11 mg
Fiber	0.3 g

Prep Time: 10 minutes

Cook Time: 40 minutes

Make Ahead:
Store for 2 days in an
air-tight container or
freeze for up to 3 weeks.

Makes 30 cookies

When I want something sweet but not too rich tasting, biscotti hits the spot. The espresso and pecans are a perfect flavor match. Instant espresso can often be found in the coffee section, or you can use regular instant coffee granules.

2 Tbsp instant espresso granules
    dissolved in 1 Tbsp hot water
¾ cup granulated sugar
½ cup brown sugar
¼ cup vegetable oil
2 eggs

1 tsp pure vanilla extract
2 ¼ cups all-purpose flour
2 tsp baking powder
½ cup toasted chopped pecans
    (see page 75)

1. Preheat the oven to 350°F. Line a large cookie sheet with foil and spray with cooking oil.

2. Combine the dissolved espresso, granulated and brown sugars, oil, eggs and vanilla in a medium bowl, stirring until smooth. Add the flour, baking powder and pecans. Mix only until the flour is combined. Divide the batter in half and form into two 12- by 3-inch logs.

3. Place on the prepared baking sheet, spacing them well apart.

4. Bake in the center of the oven for 20 minutes. Remove and cool for 5 minutes. Using a serrated knife, cut the logs into ½-inch slices and place them flat on the baking sheet. Return to the oven and bake for another 15 to 20 minutes or until crisp. Cool on a rack.

Chocolate Chip Crumb Cake

If I had to choose my number-one dessert of all time, it would be this crumb cake. I created it for *Enlightened Home Cooking* in 1996 and I still whip it up all the time. My children can bake it blindfolded! I adapted it from a recipe from the Silver Palate bakery in New York City, using cocoa and low-fat ricotta and yogurt to reduce the amount of fat and calories. Even though chocolate is higher in fat and cholesterol than cocoa, ½ cup spread over 16 slices is acceptable. Here's proof you don't have to eliminate chocolate when you eat light! You can use 9-inch springform pan instead of a Bundt pan—just check the cake at 30 to 40 minutes to see if it needs to cook a few minutes longer. For a pretty presentation, sprinkle lightly with icing sugar.

8 oz smooth light ricotta

⅓ cup vegetable oil

1¼ cups granulated sugar

2 eggs

2 tsp pure vanilla extract

1½ cups all-purpose flour

2 tsp baking powder

½ tsp baking soda

¾ cup low-fat yogurt

½ cup semi-sweet chocolate chips

½ cup packed brown sugar

4 tsp unsweetened cocoa powder

½ tsp ground cinnamon

1. Preheat the oven to 350°F. Spray a 9-inch Bundt pan with cooking oil.

2. Beat the ricotta, oil and granulated sugar in a large bowl or food processor. Add the eggs and vanilla, mixing well.

3. Combine the flour, baking powder and baking soda in a separate bowl. Add the flour mixture to the cheese mixture in batches, alternating with the yogurt. Mix just until everything is incorporated. Stir in the chocolate chips. Pour half the batter into the prepared pan.

4. Combine the brown sugar, cocoa and cinnamon in a small bowl. Sprinkle half the sugar mixture over the batter in the pan. Add the remaining batter and top with the remaining sugar mixture.

5. Bake in the center of the oven for 35 to 40 minutes, or until a tester inserted in the center comes out dry.

6. Cool the cake in the pan on a rack. When it's completely cool, invert it carefully onto a serving plate.

NUTRITIONAL ANALYSIS PER SERVING

Calories	226
Protein	5 g
Fat	7 g
Saturated Fat	4 g
Carbohydrates	36 g
Cholesterol	42 mg
Fiber	2 g

Prep Time: 15 minutes

Cook Time: 35 minutes

Make Ahead:
Prepare a day in advance or freeze for up to 2 weeks

Serves 16

Coconut Layer Cake with Italian Meringue Icing

NUTRITIONAL ANALYSIS PER SERVING

Calories	270
Protein	3.7 g
Fat	7.5 g
Saturated Fat	2.2 g
Carbohydrates	63 g
Cholesterol	30 mg
Fiber	2.2 g

Prep Time: 20 minutes

Cook Time: 15 minutes

Make Ahead:
Store cake layers at room temperature for up to 3 days, well wrapped, or freeze for up to 2 weeks.

Serves 14

I used to avoid coconut desserts entirely but now that light coconut milk is available, I'm always looking for ways to use it. To toast the coconut, brown it in a skillet over high heat for approximately 2 to 3 minutes.

1¼ cups granulated sugar
¾ cup light coconut milk
⅓ cup vegetable oil
2 eggs
1½ tsp pure vanilla extract
1¼ cups all-purpose flour
1½ tsp baking powder
¼ tsp salt
2 Tbsp coconut, toasted

2 egg whites
¼ tsp cream of tartar

3 large egg whites
¾ cup granulated sugar
¼ cup water
¼ tsp cream of tartar
3 Tbsp coconut, toasted

1. Preheat the oven to 350°F. Spray two 9-inch round cake pans with cooking oil.

2. For the cake, beat 1 cup of the sugar, the coconut milk, oil, eggs and vanilla in a large bowl, using a whisk or electric mixer.

3. Combine the flour, baking powder, salt and coconut in another bowl, mixing well. Stir the dry ingredients into the coconut milk mixture by hand, mixing just until combined.

4. Beat the 2 egg whites with the cream of tartar in a clean bowl until foamy. Gradually add the remaining ¼ cup sugar, beating until stiff peaks form. Stir one-quarter of the egg whites into the cake batter. Gently fold in the remaining egg whites. Divide the mixture between the prepared pans.

5. Bake in the center of the oven for approximately 15 minutes or until a tester inserted into the center comes out clean. Cool in the pans on a rack.

6. For the icing, combine the 3 egg whites, sugar, water and cream of tartar in the top of a double boiler over simmering water (or use a heatproof glass or metal bowl over a saucepan). Beat the mixture with an electric mixer for 6 to 8 minutes or until it thickens and soft peaks form. Remove it from the heat. Beat for 1 minute or until stiff peaks form. Stir in 2 Tbsp of the toasted coconut.

7. When the cakes are completely cooled, spread one-quarter of the icing over 1 cake layer. Place the second layer on top of the first and ice the top and sides with the remainder. Sprinkle with the remaining 1 Tbsp toasted coconut.

Coconut Layer Cake with ▶
Italian Meringue Icing
Photo by Per Kristiansen

Index